ISLAMIC VALUES
IN THE UNITED STATES

Islamic Values
in the United States

A COMPARATIVE STUDY

Yvonne Yazbeck Haddad
Adair T. Lummis

New York   Oxford
OXFORD UNIVERSITY PRESS
1987

Oxford University Press

Oxford   New York   Toronto
Delhi   Bombay   Calcutta   Madras   Karachi
Petaling Jaya   Singapore   Hong Kong   Tokyo
Nairobi   Dar es Salaam   Cape Town
Melbourne   Auckland

and associated companies in
Beirut   Berlin   Ibadan   Nicosia

Library of Congress Cataloging-in-Publication Data

Haddad, Yvonne, Yazbeck.
Islamic values in the United States.

Bibliography: p.
Includes index.
1. Muslims—United States.   2. Muslims—United
States—Religious life and customs.   3. Islam—
United States.   I. Lummis, Adair T.   II. Title.
E184.M88H33   1987   973'.0882971   86-12568
ISBN 0-19-504112-7
ISBN 0-19-504113-5 (pbk.)

2 4 6 8 10 9 7 5 3
Printed in the United States of America

Acknowledgments

This book is the result of a two-year study of Muslim immigrants, their children, and their grandchildren in the United States. It was undertaken as a joint project by the Duncan Black Macdonald Center for the Study of Islam and Christian-Muslim Relations and the Center for Religious Research, both of Hartford Seminary. It was funded by a grant from the National Endowment for the Humanities. The viewpoints expressed are those of the authors and do not necessarily reflect those of the National Endowment for the Humanities.

The authors wish to express special thanks to Willem Bijlefeld, Jackson Carroll, and David Roozen for their support on various aspects of the study; to Nabeel Abraham and Jane I. Smith who were consultants to the project and provided invaluable expertise and insight; to Mohammad Okdie, Najwa Denny Dweik, Salahuddin Malik, and Tima Smejkel, who gathered the information, conducted interviews, and provided input and comment; and finally to Mary Jane Ross, Judy Figueroa, Barbara Haines, Teri Nelson, Sheryl Wiggins, and Elizabeth D'Amico who handled the actual production of the report.

Contents

CHAPTER 1 Introduction   3
   Significance of the Project
   Study Design
   Description of Sites
      Midwest
      East Coast
      Upstate New York
   Description of the Sample
   Fundamentals of the Muslim Faith
   Islamic Values

CHAPTER 2 Islamic Institutions in the United States   24
   Muslim Responses to Issues of Islamic Observance
   The Mosque: Its Form, Constituency, and Function
      Structure and Establishment of the Mosque
      Constituency
      Sources of Conflict
      Functions
      Liaison with American Culture
      Financial Aspects
   The Imam
      The Imam in the American Context
      The Imam as Professional
      Cross-cultural Conflicts
      The Importance of Arabic

CHAPTER 3 Living in America: Social Integration   67
   Desirability of Location for Muslim Settlement
      Midwest
      East Coast
      Upstate New York

Integrating into the Community and Workplace
Integration of Muslim Children
Care of the Elderly
Celebrating and Coping with American Holidays
Pets

CHAPTER 4 Islamic Laws, Muslim Praxis, and American
               Culture   98
Economics, Welfare, and Occupations
   Usury, Loans, and Interest
   Welfare
   Appropriate Occupations for Muslims
   Occupations for Women
Inheritance and Wills
Dietary Restrictions, Alcohol Consumption, and Participation
in American Culture
   Dietary Restrictions
   Alcohol Consumption
   Participation in Other Forms of American Culture

CHAPTER 5 Gender and Sex: Roles of Muslim Women
               and Men   122
The Position of Women in Muslim Society
Women's Clothing
Relations Between the Sexes
   Shaking Hands
   Dating
   Birth Control
   Abortion
Marriage
Divorce and Child Custody

CHAPTER 6 Muslims in America: Apprehensions,
               Associations, Aspirations, and Achievements   155

Notes   173
Bibliography   175
Index   193

ISLAMIC VALUES
IN THE UNITED STATES

CHAPTER 1

Introduction

The religion of Islam is now an American phenomenon. Once thought of primarily as the way of life of the Arabs and a faith alien to the Judeo-Christian heritage in this country, it has moved into a position of sufficient size and strength that it must be counted today as one of the prominent, and rapidly growing, religious movements of America. There are now 598 mosques/Islamic centers operating in the United States (see Table 1.1), and although a wide discrepancy continues to exist in the estimates of the number of persons who count themselves among the Islamic community in this country,[1] the consensus of several scholars is somewhere in the range of two or three million.[2] The high rate of birth, the growing number of converts, and the continuing flow of immigration of some twenty-five thousand to thirty-five thousand Muslims a year make it possible to predict that by the first decade of the twenty-first century Islam will be the second largest religious community in the United States (after Christianity).[3]

In the most general terms, the Muslims of North America can be divided into two distinct groups: immigrant Muslims and indigenous Muslims. In the first category are those who have come, or whose parents or grandparents have come, from other areas of the world to this country including the increasingly large numbers of students on college and university campuses. Originally mainly Lebanese, they now represent Islamic communities from more than sixty nations, especially Pakistan, Iran, Afghanistan, Turkey, and Eastern Europe.[4] The second category, that of so-called indigenous Muslims, is composed mainly of members of the African-American community of the United States, and now includes a growing number of "Anglo" converts (estimated up to seventy-five thousand). The present study treats the first of these groups, the immigrant Muslims, considering five communities in detail.

3

TABLE 1.1 Islamic Mosques/Centers in the United States

State	Muslim Student Association/University Campuses	Mosques/Centers Associations	Masjids of the American Muslim Mission	Total
Alabama	1	2	10	13
Arkansas	1	1	1	3
Arizona	2	5	2	9
California	10	32	17	59
Colorado	3	3	2	8
Connecticut		5	5	10
Delaware		1	1	2
DC		8	1	9
Florida	4	10	7	21
Georgia	2	5	12	19
Hawaii	1			1
Idaho	1			1
Illinois	4	20	9	33
Indiana	5	8	7	20
Iowa	2	3	1	6
Kansas	2	3	3	8
Kentucky		2	2	4
Louisiana		3	4	7
Maine	1			1
Maryland	1	4	3	8
Massachusetts	5	12	4	21
Michigan	3	17	9	29
Minnesota	1	1	2	4
Mississippi	1	1	4	6
Missouri	2	3	2	7
Nebraska	1		2	3
Nevada	1		1	2
New Hampshire		1		1
New Jersey		22	9	31
New Mexico	2	2	1	5
New York	7	61	14	82
North Carolina	3	7	8	18
North Dakota	2			2
Ohio	3	14	11	28
Oklahoma	1	3	3	7
Oregon	3	1	2	6
Pennsylvania	7	17	5	29
Rhode Island		2	1	3
South Carolina		1	7	8
Tennessee	2	1	4	7
Texas	7	8	11	26
Utah	1			1
Virginia	1	6	5	12
Washington	1	3	2	6
West Virginia	1	1	1	3
Wisconsin	3	3	2	8
TOTAL	98	302	198	598

Compiled from published lists by the American Muslim Mission, Council of Masajid, Federation of Islamic Associations, and the Muslim Student Association, as well as the newsletters of independent associations.

Early mosques/centers in America were established by individuals and groups to meet the social and religious needs of the community. They were local in focus and interest. A loose federation of these mosques was formed by second-generation Muslims (mostly of Lebanese origin) to help pool resources and provide contact with other communities. This organization is now known as the Federation of Islamic Associations. Its headquarters is located in Detroit, Michigan. Since the 1960s other Islamic organizations with similar purposes have come into existence with the help of foreign support. These organizations are playing an increasingly significant role in the activities of various mosques and centers. They include the Muslim World League, with headquarters in Mecca and a U.S. office at the United Nations that has formed the Council of Masajid (membership includes more than seventy mosques), which provides funding for mosque construction and the distribution of Qur'ans and other educational information. Another active group is the newly organized Islamic Society of North America, the umbrella organization for Muslim Communities in America and the Muslim Student Association (MSA), with several hundred chapters on various American university campuses. The MSA is the most active and best organized of the groups, with a publishing firm and a large book distribution network specializing in the dissemination of what some have called "fundamentalist" literature.[5]

The past decade has seen significant changes in the makeup and direction of all the Islamic groups in this country. The immigrant Muslims are experiencing new pressures, both domestic and foreign, which have led to alterations in the constituency and direction of their community. Initially early immigrants gathered in small groups more in the nature of social and ethnic clubs than religious organizations. They were quite well integrated into the American culture, adopting patterns that in many ways paralleled those of mainline Protestant denominations. In recent years persons involved in mosque/Islamic center activities have moved steadily in the direction of wanting more leadership and instruction in the religion of Islam, working toward building new mosques and selecting trained persons to act as imams or religious leaders of their congregations. Recent immigrants are much more likely to be university graduates than were immigrants earlier in this century. (The Islamic community of North America is now the most educated per capita of all Muslims in the world.) A substantial number of the more recent settlers tend to have been trained in a specific interpretation of Islam. This is advocated and supported by the Islamic Society of North America, which is dedicated to providing guidance for Muslims in how to live an Islamic life in a secular context while striving to bring about an Islamic state. Recent events in Iran appear to have had a profound impact on these communities, providing what is perceived as proof that strict adherence to the teachings of Islam will provide victory and relevance for Muslim countries.

Significance of the Project

A study of Islamic centers in America is justified because of the increasing importance played by Islamic groups in American society today, and it is necessary because no other study has attempted either to consider the role of the mosque/center in helping Muslims to integrate into American life and culture or to analyze the value system that is perpetuated through these institutions. The emigration of Muslims from abroad and the establishment of Islamic communities in this country are little-explored areas of American history. Studies to date—which are relatively few in number—have generally suffered from several notable shortcomings. Providing little significant data, most are case studies of specific communities or ethnic studies reflecting the various interests of their authors.[6] Little of the work to date indicates an adequate understanding of the character of the newest immigrants as devout Muslims, most of them highly Westernized but still critiquing or rejecting the Western way of life as inadequate and inferior to Islam. Missing in these studies has been any significant attempt to analyze the intergenerational, interethnic, and international pressures that characterize mosque politics and the educational programs of these institutions. Most studies are now dated, lacking any consideration of the most recent developments in the Islamic community such as the influence of the Muslim World League and the Islamic Society of North America.

Of particular interest to us in designing our set of questions were the following issues: (1) the extent to which Muslims differ in their espousal and practice of various Islamic laws and prohibitions according to age, sex, time in the United States, national background, education, type of occupation, and other factors; (2) the extent to which Muslim children born to immigrant parents adapt to life in the American school system, and the extent to which they retain, adopt, or drop Muslim life-styles and Islamic values as they mature, marry, and integrate into the American work-force; (3) the role of women in the Islamic communities, and evolving patterns of family interaction; and

(4) the pressures faced by Muslims living in a non-Muslim (secular) culture and the ways in which they have adapted to that culture.

The available literature to date has failed to take into account the significance of the Arab-Israeli conflict and the Iranian and Lebanese situations, as well as the ramifications of political and military upheavals in the Islamic world for the social and political outlook of Muslims in the United States. Attempts to address these issues in the present study generally were met with a firm insistence on the part of those interviewed that political concerns should not be emphasized. Thus, this remains an important but very difficult goal to achieve, one which future researchers in the field must be both aware of and sensitive to.

We hope that the present in-depth study of selected Islamic centers will provide reliable information for students of religious history and American society about the role that Islam as religion, culture, and ideology plays in enculturating Muslim communities in the United States. The following analysis is based on a thorough study of five Islamic communities in this country, considering in each instance the constituency of the community, its social, religious, educational, and political institutions, and its influence on the socialization of its members. The attempt was made to understand individual mosques/centers in terms of their internal environments—the ethnic backgrounds of their members, attitudes and responses of leadership and constituents, and current practices—and in terms of their relationship to the surrounding culture and its ethnic, social, and political institutions. Included in our investigations were such concerns as the kinds of religious education provided through mosques in the Sunday schools and youth organizations, the role of women in the Islamic communities, the variety of Islamic worldviews propagated by the mosques, and the tensions that have come into the older established mosque structures in the large cities as a result of the influx of new fundamentalist immigrants in the last decade.

The present study centered on communities on the East Coast, in upstate New York, and in the Midwest. Future studies might take into consideration Muslims located in such areas as Chicago, New York City, and Los Angeles to begin to address broad questions about the relationship of local environment to particular attitudes of Muslims and varieties of Islamic practice. Is there a difference, for example, between areas of low Muslim population density and those of high density? Or are there differences based on the degree to which new immigrants are received by the resident populations of respective areas? What are the relative roles of leadership in the Islamic community in sharpening or softening differences between Muslims and the host culture?

Further work needs to be done in a number of other specific areas, considered to some extent in the present study but beyond its scope as detailed investigation. We had hoped to gather and analyze the literature used in education and preaching that is produced and distributed by these centers in order to discover the current interpretation of Islam, but we found that little if any such literature is available in the centers we visited. When it is available, such literaure should be reviewed, particularly in regard to the ways in which it addresses itself to the situation of Islam in the United States. Increased attention needs to be given to such issues as the following: (1) the ways in which living under American civil law conflicts with shari'a family law and, in particular, how this affects the self-image of women; (2) the growing influence of centralized Islamic institutions on "unmosqued" Muslims and the types of methods used to elicit their participation in Islamic causes; (3) the missionary outreach (da'wa) movement of Islam in this country and the reasons why some Americans, black and white, choose to convert to Islam (particular attention should be given to the role and influence of converts, a substantial number of whom are alienated from or antagonistic to Western culture, in confirming a negative image of American society); (4) the relationships among the several umbrella organizations such as the Muslim World League, the Islamic Society of North America, and the Federation of Islamic Associations, and the influence of each of these on the variety of groups that constitute the Islamic community; (5) the analysis of the "unmosqued" among second- and third-generation Muslims in this country (currently estimated at about 80 to 90 percent of the total U.S. Muslim population); and (6) the contribution of Muslim individuals and organizations to American society.

Study Design

This two-year project was begun in January 1983, with in-depth interviews of mosque leaders by Muslim interviewers using guides supplied by the researchers. Eight mosques were studied (with special concentration on five) in the three aforementioned geographical areas: the Midwest, upstate New York, and the East Coast. In the first stage of the research we concentrated on exploring the personal backgrounds of members, their religious attitudes and mosque participation, their life-styles, and their perceptions of how they are treated by non-Muslim Americans. Close to eighty interviews were taped and transcribed; this process was completed in the fall of 1983. These interviews were mainly with persons in leadership capacities in the various mosques, including imams, members of mosque boards, Sunday school teachers, and past office holders. Through this process we were able to pretest and get feedback on the appropriateness of the questions, thereby eliminating those considered unacceptable and adding others that the interviewers felt would be important. We also gained insight into what the mosque leadership thought were the essential values of Islam that they are trying to maintain in the American context.

The second stage of the research began in late fall of that year. Questionnaires designed as a result of information obtained from the first phase of the research were distributed by the field researchers; these short-answer questionnaires were set up for computer analysis. The interviewers were asked to attempt a stratified random sampling of seventy-five completed questionnaires in each mosque area, sixty from regular mosque attenders and fifteen from nonattending Muslims or those we termed "Eid Muslims" (those who attend the mosque once or twice a year on special celebration days). Gathering of these data was completed in April 1984, with a total of 347 questionnaires received. The present study is a report of the findings from both stages of the research.

The primary focus of these investigations has been on Muslims who attend the mosque or Islamic center with some degree of regularity and who depend on the institution itself as an instrument for maintaining and disseminating the faith. This is not, however, to suggest that unmosqued Muslims—who are in a very large majority in the United States—do not identify with Islam. For those immigrants who have been born into the faith and are raised in an awareness of that communal affiliation, despite the fact that they may have little to do with the mosque, Islam functions as a kind of binding ethnic association. Community identity is thus primarily a matter of confessional allegiance, even though one may not be a practicing Muslim or even a believer in the traditional sense.

A number of problems arose as we moved through the early phase of this study, in some cases necessitating modification of the original plans. Some mosques were reluctant to cooperate, and others simply refused, out of fear of misuse or distortion of the information. Many immigrants are suspicious of researchers because they come from countries where the only people asking questions are government agents or spies. One of the major difficulties we encountered in collecting our research was that of establishing sufficient trust that our questions could be answered openly and honestly. Assurance of anonymity was helpful, but the bitter experience that some in the Muslim community have had in the American context made many of those interviewed suspicious of our motives and watchful of our methods. Such problems might be at least partially alleviated if future studies were carried out either by or under the supervision of Muslim scholars. This would help encourage an atmosphere of more complete trust and also provide better access to certain areas, which would broaden the base of information. One must raise the question of whether our results might have been different if we had not been investigating at a time in which current political circumstances have fostered a strong negative image of Muslims among much of the American population. Because of this situation, many of those we interviewed were hesitant to respond, fearing that such an investigation might have been sponsored by government agencies. Others went to some length to present Islam as a religion very much like Christianity and Judaism to counter its image as a foreign (and different) phenomenon.

Initially we had difficulty locating qualified Muslim field researchers. In the case of three mosques a variety of factors combined to make the interview process all but impossible, necessitating the substitution of other mosques. In one of the original sites the Muslim researcher hired was not a member of the mosque. This fact, in addition to his being Shi'ite rather than Sunni, apparently alarmed the imam, who feared the spread of information about the activities of the local congregation to persons outside the community or even a possible takeover of the mosque by an outside group. When the imam repeatedly prevented the researcher from interviewing members of the mosque, the project became unworkable, and the mosque had to be abandoned as a site for research.

In another instance the field researcher was neither a Muslim nor a member of the mosque, although not a stranger to its activities. When the mosque came under the influence of an evangelical Muslim group (Jamaati Tableegh), the formerly congenial situation changed noticeably. Furthermore, an Austrian convert from Christianity happened to be visiting the mosque, conducting a seminar warning members of the dangers of cooperating with Christians, whom he said harbored a hatred for Islam. When he was shown a copy of the interview guide intended for use in our study he interpreted the project as another Christian attempt to undermine Islam, and warned the leaders of the mosque against participating in it. This site also had to be dropped. Such experiences indicate that research must be legitimated by leaders of the respective mosques if it is to be thorough and effective, and that this legitimacy most likely will be obtained if the field researchers at each mosque are members in good standing, or at least are known to its members.

Description of Sites

In the end, five major sites were selected for in-depth study, with supplementary information gathered from another three. Assurance to participants that their responses would be kept anonymous prevents specific identification of these sites. General descriptions of their constituencies in terms of the three geographical areas covered, however, will give the reader a sense of the range of the survey.

Midwest

This is the area of the largest Arab immigrant community in the United States, and it contains several sizable mosques (represented by three cities in our study). The majority of Muslims in this area are of Lebanese origin and tend to be both liberal and quite Americanized, although recent circumstances have altered the homogeneous nature of the community. The influx of Muslim immigrants from other countries, including professional Pakistanis, illiterate Yemenis, and Palestinians and Shi'ites from Southern Lebanon, has placed a variety of pressures on the existing social and religious institutions in the community. This has been aggravated by the assumption of religious leadership by foreign-born, foreign-trained imams who are appalled at what they see as the "Americanization" of Islam. Some of them are now pressing for a more conservative interpretation of Islam, urging members to reject those elements of American culture (such as female attendance of prayer services, the consumption of alcohol, or the holding of social events that include dancing in the mosque basement) that do not accord with the shari'a (Islamic law) or with traditional Islamic observance. In some instances problems have arisen as mosques attempt to serve and integrate new arrivals from abroad as well as the student population of the area. Particular efforts are being made in one area of the Midwest to integrate a sizable group of Southeast Asian Muslim refugees into their community.

In one of the cities surveyed in the Midwest, the Muslim minority is of significant size. Its presence as part of the American melting pot is recognized by public officials who have made facilities available for social services especially designed for the group. Some of the public schools provide bilingual education, and children are given time off to celebrate the Muslim Eids (holidays). One section with a very high density of Muslim residents has become a kind of residential enclave with stores catering to the different ethnic tastes in music, spices, pastries, restaurants, entertainment, and reading materials.

East Coast

Begun originally by a group of Lebanese immigrants, the community has grown to include members from a range of Muslim countries. They tend to be geographically dispersed around the area and normally socialize with non-Muslim Americans as well as with Muslims. The presence of large educational, medical, and academic institutions in the area means that a variety of students have, to a greater or lesser extent, become affiliated with the community. Similar to the situation in the Midwest, the presence of foreign-educated imams in the East has led to certain tensions between a conservative leadership and a more liberal body of mosque members. The conservative element, with little apparent success, has encouraged women to wear Islamic dress and the community in general to adopt a life-style that distinguishes it from the surrounding population. International politics and the conflict between third-generation Lebanese Muslims and those who are more recently arrived, especially revivalists, help maintain tensions in the community.

The influx of new immigrants in this area has not left any visible impact on the city in which the mosque is built. This is because they are educated professionals, able to acquire housing in different towns and suburbs. Furthermore, the vast majority are not relatives of earlier immigrants. They may represent the initial link for future chain migration. Their presence has altered the nature of the Islamic center because they outnumber the core group. Their impact is felt mostly on Sundays when they gather for prayer and for the instruction of their children in the Sunday school. Very little social interaction appears to occur among the various ethnic groups, or among new immigrants and the original group. This group can be described as a dispersed community.

Upstate New York

Muslims in this area represent three predominant ethnic groups—Pakistani, Yemeni, and Turkish. For the most part the Yemenis and Turks have little education, whereas the Pakistanis are mostly university graduates. The Pakistanis are professional, upper middle class, and committed to efficient institutional functioning. At the same time they are often more self-consciously Muslim in a traditional sense than Arabs tend to be. The Pakistani mosque community includes some Indians, Egyptians, and other Arabs such as Yemenis. The small group of Turkish immigrants, mainly employed in tailoring in the urban areas, has established a separate community and mosque and has little contact with the predominantly Pakistani Muslims except for some joint religious celebrations.

Most of the Muslims in this area are recent immigrants who have come to the United States within the last ten to fifteen years. They came initially as graduate students in area universities; upon completing their studies they have been able to join the professional and scientific establishment. They are now middle aged with young children, anxious to perpetuate Islamic values in the younger generation. Although they are unlikely to live near one another or work in the same organization, they maintain fairly close relationships with other Muslim families. Because doing this involves more effort and travel time than socializing with their neighbors, this type of immigrant Muslim community in the United States may be called a commuter enclave.

Descriptions of the Sample

Muslim immigrants, like any new arrivals to this country, reflect the political, ideological, and territorial differences of the countries from which they emigrated, as well as the variety of social, political, and psychological forces that have impacted on their corporate lives in the United States. Immigrants have brought to America their distinctive identity, as fashioned and comprehended by their generation. This, in turn, has been honed over the years, reflecting an increasing understanding of their American identity, with the limitations it places on them as well as the possibilities it provides.

Migrations of Muslims to the United States occurred in several waves. The first, from about 1875 to 1912, consisted mostly of uneducated and unskilled young Arab men from the rural areas of what now constitutes Syria, Jordan, Palestine, and Lebanon, then under Ottoman rule. Because of worsening economic circumstances in the Middle East, these Arab Muslims were hoping to achieve the financial success reported from Lebanese Christian emigrants. While some who did acquire wealth returned to the Middle East, many remained and began to form Muslim communities. Suffering from lack of education or facility in English, many had to work in factories or mines or as small merchants. Settling mainly in industrial centers, they had difficulty integrating into American society and thus tended to form their social bonds almost exclusively with fellow Muslims and compatriots.

The second wave, from 1918 to 1922, following the First World War, included a smattering of urban people, but the majority were relatives, friends, and acquaintances of the earlier immigrants. They had experienced the liberation of Greater Syria from Ottoman domination only to find that rule supplanted by the British and French colonial powers. The third wave, from 1930 to 1938, was conditioned by American immigration laws confining immigration primarily to relatives of those already in the country.

The fourth wave, from 1947 to 1960, included immigrants not only from the Middle East but from India, Pakistan, Eastern Europe, the Soviet Union, and other parts of the Islamic world. A growing number were the children of the ruling elites in various countries, mostly urban in background, educated, and Westernized prior to their arrival in the United States. They came to America as refugees or in quest of a better life, higher education, or advanced technical training and specialized work opportunities, as well as for ideological fulfillment.

The fifth wave has been from 1967 to the present. Along with economic reasons, political factors have weighed heavily in the decision of many Muslims to come to this country. The Arab world during this period has suffered several defeats at the hands of the Israelis, a fact that has left an indelible mark on the identity of Arabs and their commitment to various ideologies. Unlike earlier immigrants, many of the arrivals from Pakistan and the Arab world since the middle of the century have been educated professionals eager to enjoy the economic and political advantages of the United States. More recently groups of semiskilled workers have come from such countries as Pakistan, Yemen, and Lebanon, as well as a substantial number of Muslims from Iran after the revolution. On the whole, the recent immigrants have had an easier time finding substantial employment than those who came earlier in the century.

For the present study, 347 Muslims were surveyed. Of these, nearly two thirds (64 percent) are themselves immigrants, and half of the remainder (16 percent) are children of immigrant parents. Almost all of the first-, second-, and third-generation Muslims are of Lebanese ancestry, making the Lebanese, as a full third of our sample (34 percent), the largest single immigrant group. This is not surprising in view of the fact that the Lebanese were the first to settle in the United States in substantial numbers. The next largest immigrant group in the sample is the Pakistanis, comprising a little over one fourth (28 percent) of those surveyed. Immigrants of other nationalities, such as those born in Egypt, Jordan, Turkistan-Turkey, Kuwait, Yemen, Saudi Arabia, Iran, and Iraq, are also included in the immigrant sample, but none of these countries are represented by more than eighteen people (less than 9 percent of the total) and most countries are represented by far fewer.

Many of these Muslims came to the United States fairly recently, three quarters arriving after 1968 and most of these (42 percent) after 1977. They vary greatly in age at time of arrival. Some 30 percent settled in this country at age eighteen or younger. Another 35 percent came from age nineteen to twenty-five, often specifically to attend college or graduate school, and another third (33 percent) settled here between the ages of twenty-six and thirty-nine. Only 2 percent of this sample emigrated to the United States at age forty or older. This age distribution, as well as comments made in interviews, suggests that the majority of Muslim immigrants we surveyed came to this country independently, as fairly young adults (or with their parents who were fairly young at the time), to achieve educational and economic benefits they thought to be more easily attainable here than in their home countries.

To some fair extent it seems that these immigrants, their children, and their grandchildren have been successful in achieving relative prosperity and social standing. Although a range of income is represented in the sample, more than three fourths (78 percent) have total yearly family incomes of fifteen thousand dollars or higher and about half (49 percent) have incomes of thirty-five thousand dollars or higher. About half (51 percent) have at least a four-year college degree, and one fourth have graduate degrees. They are in a variety of occupations. About two fifths are presently unemployed, mainly because they are students (21 percent), housewives (18 percent), or retirees (4 percent). Of the remainder, about one fourth (26 percent) are professionals, half of whom (13 percent) are doctors, lawyers, or college and university professors. A few (8 percent) are in business as executives, middle management employees, or store owners, and slightly more than one fifth (22 percent) are civil service workers, sales people, clerks, secretaries, and skilled workers. A majority seems to be relatively content with life in this country; only 18 percent say it is unlikely that they will live here after they and their spouse retire.

Also important in determining a sense of Islamic consciousness for Muslims in the United States is the presence of large ex-patriot communities in major urban areas. Although members of these communities are not immigrants or voting citizens, they do participate in various ethnic organizations influencing their self-definition. These include large numbers of students from all over the Islamic world, businessmen, diplomats, and tourists.

Fundamentals of the Muslim Faith

Beyond the variety of practices and customs that may distinguish one Islamic culture from another and one individual Muslim from another, a basic commonality is provided by the overall structure of Islam that binds the adherents together. Belief that the Qur'an is the final revelation of God to humanity and adherence to its specific injunctions is the cornerstone of that common identity. In addition to the Qur'an, the collections of traditions (*hadith*), which are believed to be sayings from and about the Prophet Muhammad as remembered and written down by his followers, are an integral part of Islamic teaching. Together, the Qur'an and the *hadith* provide a common bond for all Muslims and are the basis for the Islamic law or shari'a, which sets out a complete way of life.

Five specific acts of worship, popularly called the "five pillars of Islam," provide a structure for the life of every Muslim, although the extent to which these responsibilities are observed naturally varies from one individual to another. Each Muslim is expected to affirm the oneness of God and the prophethood of Muhammad by saying the *shahadah* or testimony of those realities. To attribute divinity or absolute authority to anything other than God is considered the most reprehensible sin. The Muslim is also required to pray five times daily by responding to the call to prayer at the designated times. In addition, a common prayer service is traditionally held at Friday noon with a sermon (*khutba*), delivered by the imam of the mosque, emphasizing the communal aspect of worship. During the month of Ramadan all Muslims are called on to observe the fast during the daylight hours, classically understood as that period when there is enough light to distinguish between a white and black thread. The fourth responsibility, worship of God through paying the alms tax (*zakat*), again stresses communal account-ability; monies collected in this manner go for the support of those less able to provide for themselves and their families. Finally, every Muslim is required to go at least once in a lifetime, if financial resources and health permit, to the holy city of Mecca for the rites of pilgrimage (*hajj*), an experience that all Muslims affirm is a signal one in recognizing the unity of the worldwide community of Islam.

These five responsibilities, then, form the basic structure of the prac-tice of Islam, those acts by which one proclaims devotion to God and membership in the Muslim community. Another dimension of Islam as a religion is the expression of faith in those articles that make up the Muslim worldview. Faith (*iman*) is defined in the Qur'an as ac-knowledgment of God, his Messengers, his Books, his Angels, and the Last Day. It is in the first area—belief in God's oneness and omnipo-tence and eternality—that faith and practice are identical, as the first of the pillars noted above is in fact testimony to faith in God.

Muslims believe that God revealed his Lordship of the world, hu-manity, and the flow of history to a select number of prophets and messengers, beginning with Adam and ending with the Prophet Muhammad. The Qur'an records the work of these prophets and the fact that succeeding revelations were necessary because the message in every instance was either unheeded or distorted. In the case of the Torah, the Psalms, and the Gospel, God had given particular revela-tions to communities and nations, which eventually became so cor-rupted that the texts now recognized by Jews and Christians are much changed from the original. The Qur'an, as the last of the Books of God, was sent by God as a final revelation, one designed not for a particular community but for all people in all times. It came first to the Prophet Muhammad, who is the last and final prophet, through the medium of the angel Gabriel.

Other angels play prominent roles in the unfolding of God's plan for humanity. Angels are spiritual beings of light, whose task is to worship and obey God and carry out his will in the world. The angel Israfil is responsible for signaling with his horn the immanence of the Last Day, that time at which all human beings will be called to account for the quality of their lives in terms of thought, deed, and intent. After the judgment the righteous will dwell eternally in the Garden in the pre-sence of God, while those who have strayed from God's way will find their reward in the agonizing punishment of the Fire.

It is obvious that Muslims vary widely in their theological under-standing as well as in the degree of adherence to Islamic law. Many factors come to play in determining the extent to which one observes the various injunctions of the shari'a; the very fact of location in a non-Muslim culture itself presents for Muslims in America a variety of problems that we shall consider later. The issue is not simply that of being a minority religion in a country whose inhabitants are primarily members of another faith; Muslims in many areas of the world experi-ence that status. America presents a unique situation insofar as it is publicly committed to the separation of religion and state yet guaran-tees the right to worship to members of all religious groups and sects within its borders.

From the earliest days of the establishment of the Islamic community in Arabia there has been a tension among the faithful between those who believe that strict adherence to praxis is essential for one to be a true Muslim and those who hold to a more flexible interpretation. This kind of tension, generally creative in the continual process of attending to responsibilities of the faith, is common to members of all religious groups as they attempt to determine what constitutes a moral life. In the American context it is possible to distinguish among three general types of Muslims, a characterization that could also apply to members of mainline Christian denominations. There are those who are liberal, generally secularized, and governed more by collective consensus than by any judicatory or ecclesiastical organization. For Muslims of this category, the only umbrella organization has been the Federation of Islamic Associations, which is totally independent of the mosques and centers that brought it into being. Then there are members of the "born-again evangelical" independent groups, with strong emphasis on personal piety and righteous living, which attempt to bring both back-sliders and new members into the faith. Finally, there are those who are highly organized, with international connections and specific iden-tification of what constitutes right practice. They are committed to an Islamic vision, striving to realize an Islamic order and an Islamic status where religious laws are implemented and where a just government rules equitably.

Muslims with a more rigorous interpretation of Islam generally em-phasize practice as necessary for Islamic solidarity and communal iden-tity as essential for the preservation of the social order. Throughout history groups of Muslims have championed strict adherence to the law, especially at periods of peak social change when confrontations with new ideas and cultural practices have seemingly threatened a breakdown of the social order. For many today, such a threat seems present in the American context. Others prefer a more privatized concept of religion, in which the relationship is focused less on community as such than on the relationship between the individual and God.

Those for whom Islam is not only a faith commitment but a total way of life feel a clear responsibility to draw others into community. Muslims, according to the Qur'an, are enjoined to command what is good and forbid what is evil. Hence it is seen as the duty of every Muslim to summon others to proper ritual as well as appropriate moral behavior. For these stricter Muslims, the five daily prayers frame all of human existence, providing not only the time to remember God but the structure through which God directly impinges on all of life's daily routine. They feel that adherence to practice ensures that the individual is not unduly distracted by the temptations of worldly affairs and is constantly aware of and open to God and to his fellow Muslims.

The American context presents particular problems for Mulsims who do attempt to follow the specifics of the Islamic law as rigorously as possible. Many of those who adhere strictly to Islam affirm, however, that if one is rightly intended anything is possible and a good Muslim should not be discouraged by adverse circumstances. Nonetheless, the difficulties are apparent. Observance of the prayers at those times when one is in the workplace has, at times, resulted in embarrassment and inconvenience. The Muslim is expected to perform thorough ablutions before prayer, a requirement that normally is difficult to fulfill in the office environment. He or she should pray in a room that is clean and free of adornment such as pictures on the wall. Many employers provide neither the facilities nor the time for such activities. Actually leaving work to attend the Friday noon prayer at the mosque or Islamic center may be perceived to be even more difficult.

Fasting during the month of Ramadan presents its own particular difficulties. Because the Islamic calendar is lunar, Ramadan falls at different times in different years. When it comes in the summer, with its long daylight hours, it is particularly hard for Muslims to observe the prohibition against eating or drinking any liquid. For the Muslim to observe this rigorous regulation while working with colleagues who are not under similar restrictions adds to the burden.

Other problems arise for Muslims in the American context relating to Islamic injunctions beyond the "five pillars." For example, Muslim law forbids the charging of interest in financial transactions on the understanding that it is a form of usury. Although a great deal of attention has been given to efforts to reinterpret this law by drawing a distinction between usury and interest per se, enormous difficulties remain for Muslims using the American banking system who attempt to adhere strictly to the shari'a. Dietary restrictions present other difficulties. In addition to the prohibition of alcohol, eating pork and pork by-products or the meat of animals who have not been slaughtered in a specific manner is not allowed. Increasing vigilance on the part of the Muslim community has led to the discovery that many packaged products such as cheese, and some pastries, contain pork products unidentified on the labels. To obtain the properly slaughtered meat, many Muslims go to Jewish delicatessens or shops; others have begun businesses specifically catering to meet the demand for *halal* (acceptable) meat and food products.

In many cases the distinctions between Muslims who continue strictly to observe Islamic laws and practices despite the problems and those who do not is precisely the distinction between Muslims who wish to affirm their individual and communal identity in the American context and those who prefer to "melt" and become part of the larger culture.

Islamic Values

Throughout this century Muslim thinkers have been redefining what they consider to be "pristine Islam." In that effort, they have attempted to crystalize the faith into its simple and basic constituents. They have removed the accretions of centuries of commentary and dogmatic formulation and stressed what they understand to be the essential rational nature of man. In the growing body of literature produced by twentieth-century Muslim thinkers, man is seen as a responsible agent of God placed on earth to care for it. This is based on an interpretation of S. 2:30 of the Qur'an in which God designates the first man, Adam, to be his vicegerent on earth.

Man is thus understood to be accountable for his own behavior, an interpretation consciously formed to counter the centuries-old assumption that humans are completely at the mercy of the divine will and can exercise no freedom of action. This is not to say that humankind in this understanding is independent of the ultimate authority of God, but rather that humans have the responsibility to choose and implement a moral and righteous life in obedience to God's commandments.

What the reformers are attempting to do, therefore, is to free Islam from the kind of rigid formalism that so long characterized its predominant interpretation, as well as from mystical (Sufi) practices prevalent in the nineteenth century. Reformers feel that the strong belief in predestination combined with what is now seen as dependence on semimagical formulations common in many of the Sufi orders often led to indolence as a result of feelings of individual powerlessness. Absolute trust in God, according to that interpretation, became synonymous with dependency and lack of initiative; piety deteriorated into inertia and renunciation of the world.

Eager both to have the Muslim countries competitive in terms of education and economics and to distinguish the value structure of Islam from that identified with the West, reformers placed a strong emphasis on what can be called a Muslim work ethic, stressing that it is the responsibility of the Muslim to build the Islamic community and thus enhance the world. In the fast pace of modern life, compromises were effected by believers convinced that Islam, in order to make its impact in the public domain, does not have to restrict believers to commitment to a devotional life but should urge them to build an equitable modern system that can be a showpiece for the relevance of Islam in the contemporary world. From this point of view it becomes necessary to deemphasize the intricate details of proper action; the motto "religion is for ease and not difficulty" thus became popular.

This perception of the world has been challenged, especially recently, by those who emphasize that proper Islamic life must be bound by strict adherence to the tenets of Islam. Although they, too, reject the older notion that man has no free choice in determining his destiny, this group is committed to the understanding that it is only within the established structure of Islamic laws that the true Islamic community can be created.

Advocates of both of these perspectives are represented in the United States, and the confrontation in views occasionally manifests itself in some of the kinds of tensions described in the interaction between new immigrants and older established communities. Other constituencies are also present in the American scene, including a group of "evangelical" missionary Muslims called Jamaati Tableegh, who constituted the leadership in more than twenty-five centers while at times maintaining affiliation with the Islamic Society of North America, which advocates a modern, normative interpretation of Islam. There are also several groups of Sufis. In some cases immigrants affiliated with Sufi orders brought over their own brand of Sufism and continue to practice it in the American context. In other cases groups sprang up as part of the recent interest spawned in this country in

Asian religions, appealing especially to the disenchanted youth of the 1960s and 1970s.

The research for this study has been focused on liberal and moderate Muslim communities, primarily because we were unable to obtain access to other centers. Thus, the findings and conclusions offered here do not generally reflect the more "fundamentalist" or normative affirmations of Islam as a particular system of values. Although we had access to the literature provided by normative Islam, it was not possible to include representatives of this group in the selection of participants from whom we got responses.

The questions used for the study were developed in consultation with the leadership of the various mosques in the areas indicated above. The questions that were framed focused on aspects that the various leaders thought were most important for highlighting basic Islamic values. A number of immigrants had never gone to a mosque before being in the United States and had believed that adherence to particular Islamic teachings is not a crucial issue. Many have actually found their consciousness about religious identity enhanced in the American context as people question them about the basic tenets of their religion. They are also intrigued by media reports and are perplexed as to why Western society and the press seem to fear Islam and Muslims. Many students report that they have become committed to their faith after a search for roots in the American context.

Many of the early immigrants and their children are aware that Islam requires five daily prayers, but they also know that exceptions are allowed in extenuating circumstances. They opt for a more flexible interpretation. Others, particularly the practicing Muslims among those more recently arrived from Pakistan, feel that the performance of the specific acts of worship is crucial and that adherence to the formalism of a daily schedule begun and ended with prayer in obedience to God is the only way to keep Islam alive. To abandon its teachings is to set up human structures in competition with God's way.

Several years ago a Muslim leader condemned the notion that there should be localized forms of Islam, calling into question the existence of such an entity as "American Islam." Our experience in considering the three areas surveyed for this study, and in talking personally with numbers of Muslims at these sites, provides persuasive evidence that indeed there is an American Islam, and that it comes in more than one form.

Muslims in America have the unusual luxury of being able to devise their own Islamic institutions. Here modern Muslims, whether liberal or conservative, generally feel some freedom of choice as to the practices they will follow and those they will ignore. They are of such independence that if an imam does not agree with them they can fire him. They therefore decide what it means to be Muslim as well as American, and in what order priorities should be set. In a sense America has become a kind of laboratory for creative Islamic institutions. Whether some of these will be able to provide new models for change in already established systems in other countries remains to be seen. But here, away from the watchful eyes of Islamic government, American Muslims enjoy and exercise the freedom to practice Islam in the way they believe it should be practiced. In the following chapters we will examine how some of their choices and decisions are manifested.

CHAPTER 2

Islamic Institutions in the United States

Muslims today exhibit a range of responses in their understanding of what constitutes the essentials of Islam and Islamic law and what is required to be a good and responsible Muslim. Those living in the United States face not only the kinds of interpretive questions that are being raised across the Islamic world but are in the unique situation of having to reconcile their understanding of Islam and the way it should be practiced with the special circumstances of being Muslim in an essentially alien culture. They must, therefore, determine both what it means ideally to observe Islam in a proper way and the degree to which they as individuals feel this observance is possible, or even desirable, in the American context. The complexity of this issue is revealed as much in the excerpts from individual interviews provided in this and succeeding chapters as in the tabulated responses to the questions posed. We begin with a consideration of the kinds of answers given to the question of how strictly respondents think Islam should be observed; we then turn to some of the ways in which varieties of interpretation are expressed in opinions about the functions and operation of the mosque and the particular role of the imam in the American milieu.

Muslim Responses to the Issues of Islamic Observance

Nearly half of the Muslims interviewed for this study indicated that they feel Islam should be strictly observed, while somewhat fewer said they think "moderate" observance is appropriate (see Tables 2.1A–G). It is not quite accurate to say that those who favor a strict observance are unwilling to look for some compromise with modernity. Generally, those whom some may call "revivalist Muslims" also affirm that scripture should be interpreted to fit current times. Rather than

TABLE 2.1A   Religious Perspectives: Overall Responses

Questions	Percentage of Responses (total number of responses in parentheses)
1. Which of the following statements comes *closest* to your view:	
Everything in life is determined by God	33
God allows man to have some free choice in life	38
God gives man total free choice	29
	100 (333)
2. How strictly should Islam be observed?	
Strictly	46
Moderately	36
Adjusted if necessary	18
	100 (342)
3. Generally, how religious do you consider yourself?	
Very religious	15
Quite religious	47
Somewhat religious	33
Not very religious	5
	100 (343)
4. In the last four years, would you say you have	
Become more religious	45
Remained about the same	43
Become less religious	12
	100 (342)

sanction prevalent practices, however, as the more liberal Muslims tend to do, they often censure "alien" practices as innovation because they are perceived as deviations from the truth.

Imams of the mosques or Islamic centers surveyed represented a range of responses to questions about the degree to which the injunctions of the Qur'an and Islamic law should be followed by Muslims in America today. Most oppose what could be called a symbolic rather than a literal interpretation, yet clearly recognize the difficulties presented to the Muslim in the American context. While one imam is known through lectures, essays, and sermons to have urged members of his congregation who are bar owners to divest themselves of their businesses because association with alcohol is forbidden in Islam, another American-born imam offered an interpretation highly unusual

TABLE 2.1B   Religious Perspectives: Correlations

	1 Determined By God	2 Islam strictly Observed	3 Self Religious	4 Self Become More Religious
1. Everything in life is determined by God	—	.16[b]	.11[a]	n.s.[d]
2. Islam should be observed strictly		—	.27[c]	.21[c]
3. Consider self very/quite religious			—	.23[c]
4. In the last four years have become more religious				—
5. Seldom attend mosque	n.s.	−.28[c]	−.28[c]	−.20[c]
6. Born in the United States	n.s.	n.s.	−.19[c]	n.s.
7. Low formal education	.20[c]	n.s.	n.s.	n.s.

[a]$p \leq 0.5$
[b]$p \leq .01$
[c]$p \leq .001$
[d]n.s. = not significant (for all subsequent tables)

TABLE 2.1C   Religious Perspectives: Items on Religious Perspectives by Place of Birth

	United States	Lebanon	Other Muslim Countries	India, Pakistan
1. Percent saying "everything in life is determined by God"	30	29	29	47
2. Percent saying "Islam should be observed *strictly*"	40	40	45	68
3. Percent saying they consider self somewhat to not religious	52	33	26	33
4. Percent saying in last four years, have become *more religious*	45	45	44	46
5. Percent saying they attend mosque once a week or more	50	41	58	53

TABLE 2.1D   Religious Perspectives: Self-Perceptions of Lebanese and Pakistani Immigrants

Self-perceptions	Born in Lebanon	Born in Pakistan
Very religious	69 (of 13)	75 (of 8)
Quite religious	50 (of 36)	69 (of 35)
Somewhat religious—Not religious	12 (of 25)	63 (of 19)

TABLE 2.1E   Religious Perspectives: Frequency of Mosque Attendance and
Related Items

Questions	Percentage of Responses (total number)
1. About how often on the average did you attend a prayer service or Islamic class at any mosque/Islamic center during the past year?	
Never	10
Just on the *Eids* (and maybe one or two other times)	20
About once every other month	6
Once a month usually	4
About twice a month usually	9
Once a week usually	39
Twice a week or more	12
	100 (343)
2. How important do you think mosques are in keeping Muslims in the Islamic faith?	
Very important	71
Quite important	16
Somewhat important	8
Of little or no importance	2
I have no idea	3
	100 (344)
3. If you had to move to another state for family or business reasons, how important would it be for you to live in an area somewhere near a mosque?	
Very important	46
Quite important	25
Somewhat important	21
Of little or no importance	8
	100 (339)
4. One can be a good Muslim without attending mosque.	
Agree	57
Have mixed feelings	23
Disagree	20
	100 (342)

in the Muslim community. Commenting that Islam sets behavioral
standards and guidelines but does not insist that a Muslim follow these
if in so doing he or she would suffer needlessly or would assume a
position that is ridiculous in American society, he added the following:

> In Islam, necessities will legitimize the prohibitions . . . but if I were not
> an educated man and had to be a bartender, I should not leave my
> children to starve to death because it is prohibited to be a bar-
> tender. . . . The Prophet cursed the one who is selling the wine and

TABLE 2.1F   Religious Perspectives: Beliefs about How Strictly Islam Should Be Observed (Determined by Frequency of Mosque Attendance Controlling for Country of Birth)[a]

Place of Birth	Tau C Correlations
United States	−.21 (significant to .003)
Lebanon	−.25 (significant to .008)
Other Muslim countries	−.40 (significant to .0001)
Pakistan	−.03 n.s.

[a]Correlations indicate that the more frequently Muslims attend the mosque, the more likely they are to believe Islam should be observed strictly, *except for the Pakistanis*. The Pakistanis are likely to believe Islam should be observed (the full distribution shows) whether they attend a mosque often or rarely.

drinking the wine and sitting where the wine is distributed. But, how can I apply that Hadith while I am on a TWA aircraft and all the people on the plane are drinking? Should I throw myself out of the window because I am sitting with the drinkers?

A more conservative attitude was expressed by another imam who believes that if Muslims do not follow Islamic laws in the United States, no matter how difficult it may be to do so, their religion and personal morality will begin to disintegrate:

The reason we have fallen into these problems is that we are not following the principles of Islam. If we were, we would not be facing these problems. These problems would be eliminated in a Muslim society. The Islamic theology really applies to all contemporary issues very appropriately and perfectly because Islam is for all times and all things.

This kind of perspective is characteristic of conservative Muslims who believe Muslims in America should strictly observe Islamic law and work toward this end through specific programs of evangelization. This perception, much like those of the early centuries of Islam, occasionally leads them to accuse those of a more liberal persuasion of being "non-Muslims."

Some differences in the interpretation of how strictly to follow Islamic law and tradition are explained by the regional identities of the immigrants. To an extent this can be identified as a difference in stress on ritual. In particular, there seem to be distinct differences between Pakistanis and Arabs, which may be accounted for in several ways. In the first place, the nation of Pakistan was formed about the same time that Arab nations gained their independence from the colonial powers.

TABLE 2.1G Religious Perspectives: Distribution of Religious Behaviors Prescribed by the Qur'an

Behavior	In the Last Six Months, Have Done This (%)				Percent Saying They Do This Often by Country of Birth			
	Often	Sometimes	Rarely	Never	United States	Lebanon	Other Muslim Countries	Pakistan
Fasted during Ramadan	50	22	14	14	33	47	59	73
Read the Qur'an	31	34	22	13	16	36	33	48
Invited a Muslim to join you in prayer	15	30	24	31	12	12	18	19
Prayed five times a day	24	21	21	33	14	31	26	34
Went to a Friday prayer at a mosque/Islamic center	29	16	26	29	21	27	36	37
Percent saying living near a mosque would be *very important* if had to move					41	40	52	53

While Arab nationalism incorporated members of all religious traditions as citizens of the state, in Pakistan Islam was the raison d'etre of the nation as an entity. Thus, Pakistani Muslims tend to identify Islam more with ideological statements and ritual traditions than do Arabs. Second, in the Indian subcontinent the majority of Muslims converted centuries ago from Hinduism and their experience as Muslims has been definitely influenced by the confrontation with that religion. This has led to an emphasis on Islamic ritual. Finally, although Islam is a total historical and cultural experience for Arabic-speaking Muslims, Pakistanis, for whom Arabic is not a native language, tend to stress ritual as their link with the sacred language of Islam.

These regional differences showed up in our study in several ways. We found, for example, that Muslims from Pakistan often feel that an injunction forbidding a man to touch a woman who is not a relative means that he should not even shake hands with her. Most of the other Muslims we interviewed, however, interpret this injunction to apply only to sexual advances. Other variations are explained by the differing lengths of time immigrants have been in this country. Some members of mosques, for example, expressed irritation at being reprimanded by more conservative or fundamentalist Muslims for not following Islamic guidelines in dress, eating habits, or other daily activities. The following statement was made by a sixty-year-old man who was born in this country of immigrant parents:

> Muslims in America will suffer from the image portrayed by fanatics in the name of Islam. . . . I don't really resent the fanaticism in the Islamic faith, as expressed by religious leaders in the Middle East where the society is Islamic and where there is no problem confronted by the young, the old, or male or the female . . . everyone knows his place. What I resent is this fanaticism being imposed on us in America. I would want these people who are fundamentalists all over the world to recognize and realize that we are preserving Islam against all odds here in this society. It is difficult to preserve Islam where every corner has a bar and the women and the men all do those things that fundamentalists don't appreciate. . . . But if these fundamentalist fanatics want to preserve Islam as they see it, wear Islamic garb, I recommend that they stay in their country. If they are so unhappy in their fundamentalist beliefs to see what we do, and they are going to come here and belittle and malign the way we dress, the way we eat, the way we sleep, the way we talk— then my recommendation to these brothers and sisters is to return to that beautiful country from whence you came, and live there under Islamic law and wearing Islamic garb. But leave me here—because I like these shores!

Among those who indicated that they feel Islam should be strictly observed (nearly half the Muslims interviewed), it is possible to identify some differences in terms of nationality. Country of origin is to some verifiable extent a factor in determining the degree to which one is "conservative" or "liberal" in this matter. Pakistanis in our sample, for instance, tend to be far more likely than others to favor a strict observance (see Table 2.1C). Furthermore, they seem less likely to modify this opinion in response to factors in the American context that cause others to be more flexible. The longer that Lebanese Muslims live in America, the more likely they are to believe that Islam should be interpreted "moderately" or even that it may be "adjusted if necessary," whereas Pakistanis seemingly retain their insistence on strict observance no matter how long their residence in the United States.

The degree to which one tends toward relative strictness or flexibility in relation to observances and interpretation of Islamic regulations also seems to bear some relationship to one's opinion about human free will in determining choices and actions. In this, the contemporary Islamic community in America reflects many of the kinds of theological responses that have characterized Muslims historically. In the early centuries of Islam the predominant theological position was that God is the determiner of all human actions and that things happen only insofar as God wills them to happen. Much contemporary Islamic interpretation, though not suggesting any diminution of the understanding of God's omnipotence and omniscience, reflects a rethinking of issues of human free will and an understanding of the Qur'an as fully justifying human responsibility in carrying out God's plan for humankind.

A range of responses to this issue was exhibited by the respondents to our survey. Exactly a third confirmed the classical Islamic position that everything in life is determined by God (see Table 2.1A). Slightly more than a third felt that even assuming the presence of an all-powerful God, it is possible to believe that God allows humans some free choice in life, whereas a significantly smaller portion is persuaded that God gives humans total free choice. To a slight degree those who take the first position are also those who believe that Islam should be observed strictly.

Our sample showed that generally those who assume a more deterministic position in regard to God's authority over humans are the less educated; those with higher education (college or graduate degrees) are more likely to believe that God allows humankind at least some free choice. The relationship between degree of education and theological interpretation holds regardless of country of birth, with the exception of the Pakistanis. Although some Arab thinkers in the twentieth century have tended to limit the essentials of faith to the Qur'anic definition of belief in God, the Prophets, the Books (revealed by God to humankind), the angels, and the Day of Judgment (S. 4:136), Pakistanis generally add another element to that definition. This is the belief in God's decree of predestination (*qadar*), whether to the good or the evil, an elaboration formulated in several of the Islamic creeds of the first three centuries. More highly educated on the average than any other national group in our survey, the Pakistanis nonetheless tend to believe that God is the determiner of everything in life. Aside from this group, those in the Muslim community with higher education, especially those who have received such education in the United States, generally understand that God allows humans a significant measure of free will in determining their lives and their destinies.

Another issue to which there was a wide range of response in our survey has to do with self-defined religiosity. With a small portion registering themselves as very religious, and an even smaller group saying that they are not very religious, most ranged from "quite" (about three fifths of the total) to "somewhat" religious (see Table 2.1A). One of the questions we posed to our respondents was whether or not they felt they had become more religious over the past four years. Slightly less than half said that they had become more religious in that period, while only a small number indicated that they had become less so. This increase in self-perception of being religious among half the respondents may be partly due to the Islamic revival in the Middle Eastern countries, but these data do not permit such an interpretation to be made with any certainty (see Table 2.1C).

On the whole, those who identify themselves as very religious also feel that their level of religiosity has risen in the last four years and tend to advocate strict adherence to Islam. They are also a bit more likely to believe that man does not have complete free choice. Muslims born in the United States are less likely than immigrants to consider themselves very religious. In line with these observations about nationality, while the Lebanese are more likely to believe that Islam should be observed strictly if they are very religious and less likely if they are not, self-defined religiosity for the Pakistanis seems to have no bearing on the common response that Islam should be strictly observed (see Table 2.1D).

For many Muslims, attendance at the mosque is an important aspect of religiosity as well as a major element in the cohesiveness of the Islamic community. The sample of Muslims surveyed in this study indicated a wide variation in frequency of mosque attendance (see Table 2.1E). About half indicated they go at least once a week on a regular basis, while slightly less than a third said they attend only for the major holidays (Eids) if at all. There are two such holidays or festivals in the course of the Islamic year. The first is the Eid al-Adha, or festival of the sacrifice. For this occasion Muslims in traditional Islamic societies buy sacrificial animals of which part is eaten and the rest given to the needy. The second festival is the Eid al-Fitr, marking the end to the month of Ramadan when the difficult period of fasting is over. The Eid al-Fitr in particular is a time of great celebration and enjoyment.

Those Muslims who attend the mosque only for these high holidays we call "Eid" Muslims. Although by definition our sample includes mainly those who are mosque attenders (interviewers were asked to select sixty of their seventy-five interviews per site from those so identified), undoubtedly a much higher proportion of Muslims in each of the three major mosque areas surveyed do not attend a mosque regularly.

Attendance at mosque services on a regular basis may not be a direct indicator of the degree of one's religious commitment, although there is evidence that among Hanbalites and revivalist Muslims it is considered increasingly important. Studies in Canada have indicated that relatively low regular mosque attendance is less a rejection of Islam than a conviction on the part of many immigrant Muslims that their religion is a personal matter and does not require the institutional locus of the mosque to make it viable.[1]

More than half of the Muslims surveyed in the present study indicated that it is possible to be a good Muslim without attending a mosque. "In Islam," said one, "the organized religious aspect perhaps does not take the same kind of importance as in some of the other religions. It is still very much a one-to-one relationship between the person and God, though the mosque is definitely the better forum." A fifth of those interviewed did, however, feel that mosque attendance is essential, perhaps recognizing the increased pressure to maintain an Islamic identity in an environment that does not naturally support it. Muslims who attend the mosque regularly, not surprisingly, are much more likely to consider themselves religious than those who do not attend, as well as to feel that Islam should be strictly observed and to acknowledge their own increased religiosity over the past four years. Once again, the only significant exception to the correlations noted here is that of the Pakistanis, who believe that Islam should be observed strictly regardless of how often they attend a mosque.

Regular attendance at the mosque and the conviction that Islam should be strictly observed are clearly related to adherence to the prescribed acts of worship such as fasting during the month of Ramadan and praying five times daily. In our sample, Muslims born in Pakistan are more likely to observe the fast than those born in other countries, although they are not more likely than others to pray five times a day. Only about one third of American-born Muslims reported that they often observe the fast, compared with nearly three quarters of the Pakistanis. Although mosque attendance does not seem to be as important in solidifying group identity for Pakistanis as for other groups of Muslims, this group is a bit more likely than American-born and Lebanese Muslims to say they would value proximity to a mosque if they had to change location in the United States.

The Mosque: Its Form, Constituency, and Function

The mosque traditionally has played an extremely important role in Islamic society. It is not only a house of worship; it has been the center of Islamic learning, a locus of political activity, a haven from the press of everyday life, and a place where Muslims join together to share in the community of Islam as well as a retreat where it is possible to rest in individual silence. This heritage of the significance of the mosque in the Islamic world as a whole, combined with the importance of maintaining a locus for Muslim identification in the American culture, undoubtedly helps determine the response of the great majority of those interviewed in this study affirming the importance of the mosque in helping Muslims maintain the faith.

Structure and Establishment of the Mosque

An impressive white building in a midwestern city, noteworthy for its large domed roof flanked on either side by a long, thin tower or minaret, proclaims by its traditional Islamic architecture that the structure is a mosque. Inside there is a large hall, well carpeted but without seats, where worshipers sit, stand, or kneel for prayer services, sermons, and instruction. Off this hall are several other sizable rooms as well as smaller spaces for men and women to perform ablutions and to put on proper attire. The larger rooms are used for offices, for the instruction of children or adults, or for cooking and recreational purposes. This building is also used as an Islamic center where members can congregate for communal activities.

Not all mosques and Islamic centers fit the above description, any more than one model fits all churches or synagogues. Some Muslims use the term mosque for a building that is used exclusively for worship whereas for still others it is used only when the structure includes a distinctive Islamic architectural feature such as a minaret or a dome. Without the latter the building most likely will be referred to as an Islamic center. In some cases the term mosque does not designate a building at all but is used as an inclusive term for a group of people coming together for worship, scripture reading, and fellowship. Often meetings are held first in people's homes. When the group expands, it may move to a larger space where services and events can be held for a larger number of persons. Eventually the group may rent all or part of a building. If the community expands sufficiently and has adequate resources, it may decide to invest in its own building to use as a mosque. Sometimes this means buying an already existing facility, and sometimes members design and build their own mosque.

Mosques visited for the present study represented all of these stages of development. In the case of one mosque, six immigrant Arab families had settled in a town on the East Coast of the United States shortly after the turn of the century. They began to get together weekly for prayer, moving from house to house. Their numbers increased as new immigrants arrived, other Arab families moved into the area, and their own progeny increased. As their numbers increased, the group realized they needed a more formal (and sizable) facility than individual living rooms to accommodate themselves and attract new Muslim families. They formed a legal association and bought land in the name of that association. It took another twenty years, however, before they could raise the capital to build on the site. The pressure to build mounted as parents feared that without a place for regular meeting and instruction their children would lose touch with the fundamentals of the Islamic faith as well as the Arab language and culture.

Finally a building was constructed, solid but without excess ornamentation. It did serve the purpose of providing a central place where members of the community could come to worship, take classes, and socialize. New waves of immigration of Muslims to the area, combined with the drawing power of a building designated as a mosque, brought a sizable increase in mosque revenues. These new monies were put back into the mosque; the structure was enlarged and a dome was added to the main building. Attendance at mosque events continued to escalate, and further capital permitted the addition of a new structure adjacent to the original one with a large social hall and several classrooms.

This mosque presently serves as a center of religious, educational, and social activity for more than one thousand Muslims within a seventy-five mile radius. Despite the continued growth in the number of immigrant Muslims in the area, weekly attendance has leveled off. The increase of Muslims in the outlying areas has led to the formation of smaller community mosques separate from the larger "mother" mosque. Attendance at the large mosque is confined mainly to those who live in close proximity to it, except for the times of Eid celebration. As one currently elected leader of this mother mosque explains:

> Since the establishment of our mosque twenty years ago, we now have about ten Islamic centers in the region, which you might say are "children" of our Islamic center here. When people first come to our building they wonder at how a small group could build a place like this. When they find out that in their area there are fifteen or twenty Muslim families living, they decide to build their own Islamic center there. Something like this has happened in several towns. So it seems that as people who come to our mosque get to know each other, and they know that they live in a certain urban area, they decide that if we could do it here they can do it also. Another thing is that a year ago a Muslim was afraid to identify himself as a Muslim because he might have been a member of only one or two Muslim families in the city or town where he lived. But now, with so many Muslims coming and moving into the suburbs, more and more are making themselves known. I expect that in the near future we will have twenty-five to thirty Islamic centers in this region.

Another mosque started and developed in another eastern city in a different manner. About fifteen years ago a few immigrant families from Pakistan came to know one another in the city where they had moved to take good professional and corporate positions, and they began to meet for prayers in one another's homes. Because jobs and salaries for highly educated people were very attractive in this area, there was an influx of more Pakistanis seeking professional opportunities. They became acquainted with one another through work and through social contacts. Sharing both a national origin and a religion of which they were proud, they made special efforts to associate with others of their nationality and faith for prayers and for the instruction of their children. As with the first group described, they began to plan for their own structure when new immigrants and their own offspring enlarged their community. Although their generally high incomes and stable financial circumstances provided a solid base of income and good potential for obtaining sizable loans, they strictly held to the Islamic injunction against usury and refused to borrow money on which they would have to pay interest. Eight years ago they began to rent spaces in a variety of places, first for a couple of days a week in a school, then in a university. For the last several years they have rented space in an industrial building of their own. Soon they will be able to give up renting; through donations and fund-raising events they have collected more than three hundred thousand dollars to begin construction of a mosque. The money already in hand will allow them to do the major exterior and interior work. Exterior decoration, such as a planned thirty-thousand-dollar dome, and most of the interior decoration will not be done until the money for it is raised.

Although the new building will soon be available for use as a mosque and social center by the estimated five thousand or so Muslims in the city and surrounding area, probably only about a fourth of that number will show up on a regular basis. This is partly because many Muslims, like members of other religious traditions, simply do not attend worship services regularly. It is also because there are two other mosques in the vicinity, both of which have been in existence for about a decade. These two mosques, however, are unlikely to attract the Pakistani Muslims from their new mosque, because one is mainly for Turkish immigrants and the other for indigenous African-American Muslims. Though the imams and presidents of all three mosques plan to continue to communicate and cooperate on joint programs and festivities on religious holidays, their relative autonomy illustrates the fact that mosques (like churches and synagogues) serve the special social and religious needs of members who share a common language and culture, as well as provide them with a special sense of ownership of "their" mosque. Our study has shown that the growth in the size of the Muslim community is providing opportunities for further distinctions between various centers. It is clear in several areas that new mosques and centers are being organized to serve the middle class and professional groups.

Constituency

Some of the larger mosques and Islamic centers in the United States clearly wish to grow in size and influence by appealing to a broad-based constituency of Muslims with a variety of national backgrounds.

These appear to have the understood intention of being centers for all the Muslims in their vicinities. Other small mosques, however, do not wish to expand if such enlargement means they will sacrifice their identity as centers for particular groups of Muslims. As illustrated in the preceding examples, these mosques as loci of ethnic/national identity play a role in the lives of their members not dissimilar to that played by some ethnic churches in this country. In addition to being places of worship, they function as social centers and organizing units providing cohesion to national groups and the comfort of a common cultural and linguistic identity. It is also true that in some cases the mosque may be the only avenue available for positions of leadership in society, giving added significance to the maintenance of a distinctive minority status.

Experiments in combining mosques of different national or ethnic identities have raised serious questions about the feasibility of such efforts. Some Muslims, unhappy at having their mosques taken over by immigrants from other Muslim countries, have established as a basic institutional goal the desire to have a center especially for Muslims of their own nationality. Typically such an intention is supported by legal documentation and constitutional regulation. Groups who are disaffected from a mosque for reasons of national difference, because they are unhappy with the parent organization, or for any of a number of other reasons, may elect to establish a second mosque somewhere in the vicinity of the first. Such proximity does not seem to lead to competition for members insofar as individual mosques serve different needs by providing the services and supportive environment that members seek. These range from a demand that the preaching of sermons or instruction be given in specific regional languages to the insistence that certain customs, such as proper attire identified with a specific country, be adhered to.

In certain areas of the United States, particularly some midwestern cities with sizable Muslim populations, the situation is somewhat different. There we find several large mosques and Islamic centers over ten years old that serve varied constituencies. In addition, new mosques are being built with some rapidity, as well as educational centers designed to train Muslims in Qur'anic and Arabic studies. These are often less ethnic than those described earlier, cater rather to particular professional or racial classes. The prevalence of mosques not far from each other creates a situation in which Muslims can "mosque-shop," selecting the institution that seems most congenial to them for any of a variety of reasons. Because mosques house a number of different activities they can, in these circumstances, compete with each other in everything from quality of educational and social events scheduled on Sundays to convenience of the hours of prayer services. In one of the cities considered in this study, there are so many mosques and educational centers that some Muslims regularly attend several; more than one fifth of those surveyed in the area attend at least two. Interviews with some of these two- and three-mosque attenders indicated that attendance at each is determined by some particular element or activity such as the quality of the imam's sermons, the adult education program, or the nature of the social events offered.

Sources of Conflict

In addition to those factors that might differentiate one mosque from another, in some cases by conscious self-definition along national or other lines, certain things sometimes prove devisive within already established congregations. Internal mosque conflict can arise when the addition of new members results in grouping around certain issues such as how Islam should be interpreted in the American context, what a mosque should do or be, or particular theological positions. If such groups of new members assume leadership positions and their ideas differ from those of the longer established members of the mosque, antagonism quite naturally can result.

In two of the mosques we studied in this survey, serious conflicts arose when new groups with different national identities from those already established came with strong opinions about the interpretation of Islam. In one case the result was a takeover by the new group and a loss of control by the founders of the mosque and their descendants. Some founders simply lost interest in the mosque as it had evolved under the influence of the new immigrant group and went elsewhere. This situation is described by a woman in her late thirties who came to this country as an adolescent.

> In the early seventies the mosque was a place where you did your prayers and also had a lot of social gatherings. I enjoyed it very much because there were youth clubs and all sorts of things. . . . But later on, people started coming from different countries and the attitude in the mosque started changing, getting more strict. The [new] people started bringing their own customs into the mosque. A lot of these customs didn't really have much to do with Islam. But people have practiced them for many years. They thought this was the way it should be done, and they started forcing it on the people who were members of the

mosque. Because of that . . . you could see the younger generation . . . like the grandchildren or great-grandchildren of the founders leaving the mosque.

Others were anxious to preserve the mosque as an institution that serves their needs. The conflict between recent immigrants and first- and second-generation Muslims born in the United States grew to such dimensions that it resulted in a court case, which the founding national group eventually lost. The following events led to this situation.

A group of immigrants from one country started attending the mosque, which had been established through the efforts of another group of immigrants from a different country. Soon the new group began to outnumber the old at the mosque services, finally assuming power in running the mosque. The new group then initiated a number of changes as well as new rules for the use of the mosque. Particularly disturbing to the founding group were the decisions that there could no longer be social activities in the mosque building and that, if they attended the mosque at all, women had to wear traditional dress and pray in a room apart from the men.

Prior to that, as one member put it, they had "showers, and weddings, and bingo, and things that the youth might like—such as dances and Halloween parties—and the women worshiped with the men and shared leadership responsibilities at the mosque." One member of the founding group, attempting to be fair in his representation, offered this description of what happened:

> The mosque building was used for a dual purpose for prayers and social functions. When the upper level was completed it became the legitimate, official mosque and the downstairs was the kitchen, the social hall, and all those things. . . . Not too long ago, many people were displaced from their ancestral home and came here . . . a great influx of people from a remote society, an Islamic society, straight by air with no transitional period they came and landed here. So now we have a culture that has its own standards, imposing the standards of newly arrived immigrants, on the established people who were born here and who immigrated here long before them. . . . It caused friction, God bless them. They are all good intentioned people, not to malign anyone, but it caused friction between human beings.
>
> They became critical of us. They said we were dancing in the mosque. We said, "Yes, the people have the traditional village dance." But they said, "No, that is illegal. It is against Islamic law. You cannot use the mosque except for prayer." We tried to explain to our brothers that they have no authority over us (but think they have), though we tried to be

generous and kind. We explained to them that in this society the Muslim people, until they become very wealthy, cannot afford to have social halls and mosques with separate furnaces and separate land areas and separate parking facilities. Sometimes these poorer people will have to incorporate the social hall with the mosque to facilitate and expedite the instruction of Islam and the worship of God. . . .

Well, this didn't go over very good. They began to make a gradual encroachment into the mosque until they became dominant. They were offered the mosque to pray in five times a day . . . and then they wanted control of the mosque and to set their own standards. . . . We have to be fair and say that the mosque is open for prayer everyday, and for any Muslim who wants to go and pray there. That is very good.

But the part that seems not right according to ethics is that they should take something built by our people primarily who sacrificed to build it, and they should take it without a by-your-leave. . . . They didn't mean any harm, they thought all mosques were like in the old country—government controlled, government built, and government supported. In the old country, nobody owns a mosque. Our people on the other hand didn't understand that they could lose it—they thought it was like a private house.

These new people outnumbered us. They made changes. They didn't want to go to a mosque and hear English spoken—only Arabic. So now that is the case. They don't want women in the mosque or children. If the children come to the mosque, they would tell them, "You cannot be in the mosque. You must leave, it is haram." If a woman walked across the floor, they would say, "You have left the floor impure for prayer," because maybe she is having her period. So, there are few women and children who now attend.

The question of women praying in a room separate from men, which was so upsetting to the founders of this mosque, was addressed in our questionnaire. Nearly half of those surveyed not only did not think it was important to have such a separate facility but clearly did not want it at all. Other responses were mixed (see Table 2.2A); persons born in the United States were less likely to think it necessary than those from overseas, but neither sex nor age seems to have been related to responses on the issue. Overall those we talked to expressed their feeling that the most important thing is to provide a context in which Muslims can come together to pray and worship, no matter what the facility, as well as to provide Islamic education for the children.

The issue of language is particularly important to many Muslims. Those who favor a return to a more conservative style in the mosque want to hear Arabic used exclusively in the prayer services instead of

TABLE 2.2A   Mosque Functions and Programs: Responses to Selected Items*

Questions	Importance (%)			
	Very	Quite	Somewhat	Not Important
1. Having a Friday prayer service	81	10	6	3
2. Having a Sunday prayer service	59	21	12	8
3. Having a mosque open seven days a week for several hours each day	52	24	19	5
4. Having Sunday school for children (primary age)	87	9	3	1
5. Having a special educational and recreational program for teenagers	67	20	9	3
6. Sponsoring social events, coffee hours, suppers, etc.	39	33	22	6
7. Having a separate prayer room for women	20	13	19	48

*Responses to other items can be found in distribution of responses on the total survey, at the end of this report.

English. Naturally this means that a large number of those attending will have difficulty understanding, which some in our survey identified as a major problem for American-born Muslims. According to one Muslim who was referring to the takeover of the mosque by the immigrant group discussed above, the adoption of Arabic as the primary language of the mosque was the major factor in the voluntary withdrawal of the founding national group, their children, and their grandchildren.

Ninety-nine percent of those worshiping there now know and speak Arabic . . . so there is no need for English to be spoken in that mosque for a successful religious service. But the Muslim community born here, who have little or no knowledge of Arabic, suffers and continues to suffer because of this reversion. Because the parents themselves don't understand and can't speak Arabic, they cannot insist their children do. You cannot say to your child, "You have to go to learn Arabic, and go to the mosque and hear the imam speak in Arabic." The child will not stand for that. So for those Muslims born here, the mosques must increase the instruction of Islam through the medium of English, or they are going to have always rejection and lack of interest.

As a result of the situation, the founders and their children have purchased a new building that they are using as a center to provide for their social as well as their religious needs. Although there seems to be general agreement within the group that Sunday school classes will have to be in English in order to provide relevant grounding in the faith for their American-born children, there is no consensus as yet on whether Arabic or English or a combination of both will be used in the sermons.

These examples illustrate the disparity in needs of the various groups of Muslims in this country. In particular, the language issue points to a major difficulty in attempting to integrate American-born and new immigrant Muslims into one community. For uneducated Muslims from rural areas of the Arab world, the mosque is needed to provide identity and comfort in a new and alien world. What may appear to longer established groups who are more at home in this culture as ultraconservatism or an arbitrary return to outdated customs can be, for the uneducated immigrant, a much needed stability and a means of preserving that which is most deeply cherished.

Although differences are sometimes theological, and other times simply cultural, occasionally problems arise because of actual sectarian divisions. Muslim leaders in this country try in many cases to foster communities in which Shi'i and Sunni Muslims can worship and study together. Occasionally, however, such attempts break down. When they do, anger and bitterness can run high, as illustrated in this description of one partisan community:

> It is basically a Shi'i mosque, so many of the lectures and discussions are really from that viewpoint. A——, a popular teacher of young adults and adults in this mosque, was not focusing on tenets of the Shi'i school. He was not focusing on the Sunni school of thought either. He was just focusing on Islam . . . period, and not giving impartiality to either side. But this was perceived as being worse than if he were teaching the Sunni school of thought exclusively, because the teaching was neither one. When he was confronted by the leadership of the mosque and told they did not want him to teach the Sunni school of thought he refused. The whole situation just deteriorated after that to the point where he was asked to leave and has not been invited back since.

Social class differences can also lead to problems within a given mosque. The process whereby a congregation is formed is, to some extent, self-selecting, however, and normally ends up with a group that is fairly homogeneous in socioeconomic terms. This is especially true in areas where the existence of several mosques makes genuine choice possible. Thus, in cities with large Muslim populations from a variety of countries, factors of national identity, socioeconomic status, theological orientation, and the like will come into play as the different groups attempt to identify with mosques most congruent to their primary point of reference, whether that be occupational/educational/economic status, theological focus, or national origin.

Functions

Most Muslims in our interview sample believe that the family is the single most important element in keeping Muslims identified with the faith. Close to half the respondents (see Table 2.2B) identify the mother as the most significant familial figure in religious socialization, who with the support of the father and the mosque or Islamic center is the one directly responsible for the religious instruction of the children. Two thirds of those questioned agreed (and very few disagreed) with the statement that "the Muslim family is much more important than the mosque/Islamic center in keeping its young people within the Islamic faith."

Nonetheless, it is also clear that the mosque is considered extremely important in and of itself in helping keep Muslim individuals and families within the fold. Muslims seem to feel that, although the family may be the most important institution in raising children to be Muslims, the mosque provides not only instruction and a place for the children to

TABLE 2.2B   Mosque Functions and Programs: Comparison of Familial Socialization in Islam and Mosque Religious Socialization

Questions	Percentage of Responses (Total Number of Respondents)
1. Who has the most responsibility for the religious instruction of the children?	
Mother	42
Mother and father	16
Mother, father, and mosque/Islamic center	10
Father	18
Mosque/Islamic center	14
	100 (339)
2. The Muslim family is much more important than the mosque/Islamic center in keeping its young people with the Islamic faith:	
Agree	66
Mixed Feelings	26
Disagree	8
	100 (341)

meet but also a place for individuals to find support in Islamic identity, especially in the American context. Interviews suggest that many adults find the mosque reminds them they are Muslims and helps them maintain their faith, as in this statement from a thirty-one-year-old first-generation woman:

> The mosque reinforces; it is a supplement to the family. The most important, of course, is your family life and whether or not you see examples and see the religion practiced. But the mosque can be a supplement and maybe also a substitute . . . if Muslims have not practiced the religion at home much.

A thirty-two-year-old male immigrant from Jordan made the following statement:

> The mosque plays a definite role here in keeping people within the faith. People are thinking about the religion more if a mosque is near. Even if they don't go, they still know the mosque is there; it helps. If it wasn't there, some people wouldn't even think of praying.

Not all of those interviewed found the mosque unqualifiedly valuable in maintaining the faith. Said one thirty-five-year-old woman born in America of Lebanese parents:

> I don't think the mosque has an important role for keeping people in the Muslim faith. I think it is up to each individual and his immediate environment . . . in the way he was brought up. I think that everyone is so busy with his or her education, or profession or own life, that the amount of time that you spend at the mosque is minute compared to the amount of time you spend doing other things. So I don't think the mosque could shape a person's faith, but it might reinforce it especially for those youngsters who attend the religious school there.

In fact, the majority of our sample did praise the mosque, not only for its prayer services and sermons for adults and its educational classes for children, but because it serves as a locus for socialization and interaction. Particularly important for all members of the Islamic community—those who attend the mosque regularly and those who do not—are the celebrations for the Eids or religious festivals. These holidays provide an opportunity for Muslims of all persuasions to mingle with one another and to reaffirm their own sense of what it means to be Muslim.

Though it physically attracts the largest numbers of Muslims, this largely social function of the mosque is less important, in the views of almost all those responding to our survey, than fulfilling the specific religious responsibilities. Thus, they see one of the main functions of the mosque to be providing the context for prayer on Fridays, whether or not they personally attend such services. It is interesting to note that, although more Muslims attend services on Sunday than on Friday, fewer (only slightly over half) indicated they feel it is very important for the mosque to have a Sunday prayer service. Frequent mosque goers are slightly more likely to want the mosque to offer Sunday services too. (It should be noted that Sunday services are an innovation in Islam and not a traditional part of its structure.) A little more than half the respondents think it is very important to have the mosque open several hours every day (see Table 2.2B); practical concerns such as safety mitigated this for many.

Older persons in this group are a bit more likely than younger ones to stress the importance of the Friday service at the mosque, and men more likely than women to emphasize its value. One of the notable differences between the practice of Islam in the United States and that in Muslim cultures is the fact that women in this country attend the mosque. Although a woman in the Middle East or Pakistan, for example, rarely attends mosque services, in the American setting women naturally go to services and appear to be extremely active in the range of events that take place in mosques here (see Table 2.2C).

Mosque attendance is related to some degree to the age factor. Like their counterparts in the Christian and Jewish communities, young Muslims in their late teens and young married adults are less likely to

TABLE 2.2C   Mosque Functions and Programs: Correlations of Items in Table 2.2A with Other Characteristics

	Characteristics	Friday Service	Sunday Service	Open Seven Days	Sunday School for Children	Program for Teenagers	Sponsoring Social Events
1.	Date of birth	.15[a]	n.s.[d]	n.s.	n.s.	.18[a]	.11[b]
2.	Frequency of mosque attendance	−.23[c]	−.16[a]	−.16[a]	−.14[b]	n.s.	n.s.
3.	Male gender	+.26[c]	n.s.	n.s.	n.s.	n.s.	n.s.
4.	Important mosque sponsor social events	n.s.	.27[c]	n.s.	.17[b]	.34[c]	—

[a]$p \leq .05$
[b]$p \leq .01$
[c]$p \leq .001$
[d]n.s. = not significant (for all subsequent tables)

attend religious services than parents of school-age children and older persons. One notable exception is that group of Muslim students from overseas who have come to the United States for university or graduate work and to whom forms of revivalist Islam particularly appeal. For these students attendance at the mosque is part of an ideological commitment to Islam as a way of life which manifests itself in a concern for the da'wa, or missionary outreach. They see it as their task to attend first to the conversion of backsliding Muslims and then to that of non-Muslims. Mosque participation is high among recent college graduate alumni of the Muslim Student Association (MSA), who have identified it as a central place in which to nurture an Islamic identity in the United States. Many young parents whose children are old enough to receive an Islamic education find it important to involve themselves in mosque activities with new vigor. The following comment is from a Muslim woman in her early thirties:

> I have been coming to the mosque periodically since I have been in this area. But I have just recently started coming regularly to this mosque, basically because my son is older now (will be starting public school) and I am worried about him as a Muslim in a Christian society. I would like to show him our picture through associating ourselves with other Muslim families.

This concern for providing religious instruction for children was a common theme among respondents. Some first-generation Muslim young adults interviewed indicated that, although they had been pressured into going to Sunday school when they were children, the experience had nonetheless been very important to them. One teenage Muslim girl born in this country indicated her own desire for religious instruction even though her parents did not insist on it: "I grew up in this country knowing more about Christianity and Judaism than I did about my own religion. People could tell me I prayed to three gods and I wouldn't know the difference. What happened was for my own identity's sake; I had to find out about my religion." Muslim parents often increase their own attendance at the mosque at the same time they insist on their children's participation in Sunday instruction. Feelings run strong that it is crucial to introduce children to the fundamentals of the Islamic faith. "They have to identify with the Muslim faith," said one woman, "otherwise we are going to lose them." An older woman remarked sadly, "If we had [had] the mosque years ago when I got married, and I was starting to raise a family, we would not have lost some of our children [from the faith]."

The study of Arabic often accompanies instruction in the Qur'an. Although most adults surveyed felt that this language study is important, and over half even said "very important," they recognized that there are severe limitations as to quantity and quality possible in a brief exposure each week. General instruction with stories from the Qur'an and about the Prophet Muhammad is common and provides not only training in Islam but an opportunity for Muslim children to socialize with one another. Normally instruction is limited to one or two hours a week.

A very large majority of Muslims feel that providing some programming at the mosque for teenagers is important, although not as important as instruction for younger children. This may well reflect an attitude that imparting of value systems is achieved in childhood rather than in adolescence. (An Arab proverb says that "learning in childhood is like carving in stone.") Nonetheless, it is also clear that programming for teens is no easy task, a problem faced by churches and synagogues as well as mosques. Quite a few of those interviewed said that they do not feel their own mosque does enough for older teenagers and young adults, a particular problem for many Muslims who wish to protect their young people from the free dating system of the American population.

Part of the difficulty in providing adequate religious instruction for Muslim children and youth lies in the paucity of well-trained teachers and the lack of adequate instructional material and facilities. As the imam of a fairly large mosque commented:

> The mosque initially plays a very important role in the education of young persons or even older adults whose knowledge of Islam, about its history, is limited. But then there comes a point where the student has the basics, and wants to know more. The mosque does not have the facilities available to them, it does not have a large collection of books on Islam, does not have the teachers, and does not have frequent lecture programs.

This observation by a girl in her late teens illustrates another problem faced by—but not unique to—the Muslim community in trying to provide programming for its teens:

> I am right at the age where nobody else at the mosque is at—too young for adults or too old for the kids. There tends to be no kids my age. The social activities are the potluck dinners—and for me that would be a babysitting venture or helping out in the kitchen. It will be easier now for the new group of kids who will be teenagers—because they all tend

to be in the same age range. With me, there were maybe two or three at nineteen and then one at seventeen and one at fifteen. It may sound like a very small age difference to you, but it makes a big difference. . . .

One sympathetic middle-aged woman expressed her concern that, although her mosque gave a good deal of attention to such activities as Sunday school for children and organized social groups for adults, little is provided for teens:

Over the years this mosque in particular has expanded quite a bit. They have a very large and well-attended Sunday school. They have a women's auxiliary, but they do not have enough programs for older teenagers. My children aren't that old, but I think it is important that the teenagers have some place to go and do things with other Muslim teenagers other than just at their homes. The mosque might be a good place for them to meet and have some types of discussions or learn chess or study politics of the Middle East region . . . etcetera.

Among the more obvious problems in planning for teen activities in the mosque are the lack of availability of interested leaders and supervisors, and the difficulty of keeping the facility open for teen gatherings. A more subtle problem is the question of the appropriateness of the mosque for the interaction of the sexes. It is clear that most young people wish social activities to be shared among boys and girls, and also that most Muslims encourage their youth to interact more with other Muslims than with non-Muslims as they approach the marriageable age. Nonetheless, the question of interaction between the sexes is a difficult one in the Islamic community, and many are apprehensive about whether or not—or how—the mosque should provide the context for this. Not all, by any means, would endorse the wish expressed by one person interviewed that their mosque institute "social activities to bring in the youth, both male and female together." And some members go so far as to say that the mosque should not provide social activities for any separate groups—children, teens, men, or women.

The difficulties of raising children to be responsible Muslims in the American context have led some to feel that an Islamic parochial education is preferable to public schooling. Muslims surveyed differed widely over the idea of sending their children to an Islamic school, in the mosque, Monday through Friday. Roughly a quarter strongly favored some such attempt, while somewhat less than half were opposed (see Table 2.2D). The majority of young adults or parents interviewed have either gone through the public school system themselves or have children who recently entered it and are pleased with the training and

TABLE 2.2D   Mosque Functions and Programs: Academic Schooling of Children

Questions	Percentage of Responses (Total number of Respondents)
Having an Islamic school in the mosque Monday through Friday replacing public school for children is:	
Very important	26
Quite important	13
Somewhat important	21
Not important	40
	100 (305 cases)
Place of birth of respondents saying this is *"very important"* (%):	
United States	18
Lebanon	31
Other Muslim Countries	39
Pakistan	18

the treatment they or their children have received in general and specifically as Muslims. They also are very concerned about the quality of education. As one said:

> We moved here because of the excellent public school system. Because to me my children's future life is very, very important. I can't take my children from a system like there is here and put them in any school because it happens to be Islamic, and it may help them Islamically, but on the other hand it may not help them with college. To me, college is very important, education is very important. So if the Islamic school were academically good enough I would probably send my children, but if it were not—I wouldn't.

It is not surprising to find that supporters of a mosque are those who generally maintain a more conservative approach to Islam and to the role the mosque should play. Immigrants are slightly more likely to want such a school than the American born, with the exception of the Pakistanis, who prefer that their children enter the public school system (see Table 2.2D). Very education-oriented, Pakistanis may question the quality of their children's training in an Islamic school and its adequacy as preparation for the better colleges and graduate schools.

Some respondents are apprehensive that the Islamic school might be too conservative or strict in its interpretation of Qur'anic injunctions.

Others feel that the tuition required for private instruction might be beyond their means. The most commonly expressed fear of those who indicated they would not send their children to Muslim schools, however, is that it would isolate them from American society. Assimilation in the American culture is a high priority for many Muslims in our sample, and they are eager to play down those elements that tend to label them as different. For them, commitment to living in the United States means a commitment to integration. Such a perspective is revealed in the following expressions of concern:

> I would not agree to putting my children in an Islamic school. I think what you are doing there is taking the child out of the context in which he lives to a large extent . . . it would isolate him.

> No, I would not send my son to an Islamic school because then it would label all kids going into this school being Muslims, and I know what the American feeling is about Muslims. I don't want to label my son. Maybe later I would if the view of Muslims changed in America.

> We discussed that in our mosque, and I was opposed to an Islamic school instead of public school for my children because I think that doing something like that would tend to alienate them from the rest of the community, instead of integrating them, and any lack of confidence they had about being Muslim would make it worse.

In sum, Muslims on the whole feel strongly that the mosque is an important source of support as they attempt to raise their children in the Islamic faith. Fully three fourths of those in our survey with school-age children or grandchildren said these children attend the mosque weekly, and the great majority highly value their children's involvement there (see Table 2.2E). Education in the fundamentals of Islam and courses in Arabic are identified as the central elements of the mosque experience for children and teens. On the whole, social activities are organized around whole families rather than for special age groups, partly because of limited resources in terms of space and leaders, and partly because of ambivalence concerning the extent to which the mosque should be a center for social and recreational activities.

This ambivalence carried over into the question of whether or not weddings and funerals should be held in the mosque. Because of the communal (and often, by implication, the social) as well as the religious nature of such events, some feel that it is not appropriate for them to be associated with what is essentially a house of worship.

In general, there is less conflict over funeral services than over weddings. One respondent reflected on what the practice used to be like:

TABLE 2.2E   Mosque Functions and Programs: Attendance by Children[a]

Percentage saying their children or grandchildren attended:	
Every week	79
A couple times a month	5
Several times a year and on Eids	13
Seldom or never	3
	100 (161)
Percentage saying attendance was:	
Of great value	70
Of much value	15
Of some value	13
Of little or no value	2
	100 (161)

[a]Eighty-seven percent of the sample had children or grandchildren under the age of seventeen and living in the United States. These adults were asked how often their children or grandchildren attended the mosque. Those whose children or grandchildren did attend the mosque were asked how valuable they believed this attendance was for the children in teaching them more about Islam.

> When there was a funeral there was nothing else because the body would be there. We would not go to the funeral home; it was strictly right there. And they used to sit up with the dead—all night. And the family of the deceased would have . . . boiled eggs and cheeses and olives and bread in the kitchen area. And whoever wanted to eat went in there quite a long time. After going to the cemetery the family returned to the mosque and had a dinner.

In the case of the death of a member of the community, the imam may take responsibility for securing a burial plot at a nearby cemetery and making the special arrangements for washing the body. The difficulty some Muslims have with the association of funerals with mosques seems to center on the *aza,* or condolence event, which they see as separate from either the religious rite or the practical arrangements for the burial. On other occasions certain practices common to particular nationalities may appear offensive insofar as they seem to reflect beliefs that are not normally considered part of Islam. It is a Lebanese custom, for example, to prepare a special pastry at the time of the funeral. "The people want this pastry to be as a sacrifice for their dead," said one Lebanese Muslim, "and so the people from Lebanon are still doing this here in the mosque. . . . It is usually offered for the soul of those people that died."

Another person provided this comment, which suggests quite clearly what the source of conflict is between those who want the mosque used for these occasions and others who do not:

> One group insists that the mosque "should be only used for worship, nothing else." And the people from Lebanon think that they should have a hall and a mosque for their activities . . . whether a wedding, or a meeting, or a funeral. . . . Anyway, a mosque is used for funerals in modern times . . . that is where they lay the body to be seen . . . it is nothing new . . . but the main conflict I think is the weddings.

Prayers can be said by any Muslim; it is not necessary to have a trained imam, though that is often the case. New imams of more conservative orientation do not generally object to having a funeral service in the mosque. They do object, however, to placing the body in the mosque to be viewed (although that is a common practice among some Muslims in the United States), and especially to serving food or observing other cultural customs of communal affiliation in the context of the mosque. Others object because they believe the body might defile the mosque.

It is also true, as the respondent cited previously indicated, that there is more conflict over the matter of weddings in the mosque. A wedding in Islam is a legal contract and not a sacrament, which means that there is no necessity from a religious point of view to have it in the mosque; often a wedding takes place in a home or a large private setting. In the United States the mosque has been used for this function in ways that it generally is not in Islamic countries. Again, new conservative imams do not usually object to having the wedding contract itself in the mosque but are loath to allow the celebration (singing, dancing, and eating) that commonly accompanies a wedding.

One young man reflected somewhat sadly that when he was a child mosque weddings almost always were accompanied by dancing outside the prayer hall, but that with the arrival of a stricter imam not only dancing but weddings in general were forbidden in the mosque.

A more moderate view is that having the wedding in the mosque is fine as long as it does not involve music or dancing, as indicated in these words of an imam:

> If you are talking about performing a wedding in the mosque, there is nothing in Islam which will say to you, "no." The Prophet used to do that in the mosque. But if you are talking about having the wedding in the form of music and dancing in the mosque, we will not allow it. Any one who wants to do that, he can go and rent a hall outside, but it will not be accepted in the mosque.

TABLE 2.2F   Mosque Functions and Programs: Weddings

Having a Mosque/Islamic Center with Space for Weddings[a]	Percentage of Responses
Very important	31
Quite important	22
Somewhat important	27
Not important	20
	100

[a]Those born in Pakistan were least likely to say that it was important for a mosque to provide this (17 percent very important) and those born in the United States felt it was most important for a mosque to provide this (41 percent very important).

There was a clear diversity of opinion in the group interviewed on the question of whether or not the mosque or Islamic center should provide facilities for weddings, with slightly more than half indicating they feel it should (see Table 2.2F). The issue clearly is not weddings per se, but that of a mosque being a center for social activities in addition to religious functions. Nearly three fourths of those surveyed said that mosque sponsorship of such events as coffee hours, teas, potluck suppers, and other social events is quite important, although far fewer than half felt it was very important (see Table 2.2D). (American-born Muslims seem most likely to encourage this social function, and Pakistanis are least likely.) Those who favor social events in the mosque see two purposes being served: (1) to allow and encourage Muslims to meet and interact with one another, increasing the likelihood of maintaining marriage within the faith, and (2) to bring relatively unmosqued Muslims into the mosque in the hope that they might be encouraged to also attend some of the religious and educational offerings. These opinions are reflected in the following comments. From a fifty-year-old woman born in the United States of Lebanese parents:

> I think the most important thing in this country is to have a place where Muslims can meet socially. That is the only way Islam is going to survive in this country . . . if they intermarry within the faith community. Once you begin to get mixed marriages, Islam will die in this country. That is very, very important that mosques have the social part of it so that the kids can meet each other.

From a thirty-year-old woman immigrant from Egypt:

> I think the duty of the mosque goes far beyond holding the regular services. . . . It should have social activities that get us all together.

Because if I have ties with the Muslim community, I feel more comfortable and I feel less isolated and my children will grow up to be good Muslims—better Muslims—if I have Muslim friends around me. The chances of keeping the faith will be better, maybe they will marry from the Muslim community here. At least the next generation will know each other better this way.

From a thirty-year-old male immigrant from Lebanon:

I would suggest the mosque have more social activities to attract more people. Let these gatherings be dinner or pastry and coffee, and maybe some entertainment. Just bring these people to the mosque, get them used to going there. Let them see that they have a nice place that they can come to and pray, and let them see that there is a place that they can bring their kids to and teach them their religion and their languages. Then once they get used to coming to the mosque, you will see them there regularly when they have the time.

There is no question that for a considerable number of Muslims today the mosque plays an important role in social integration. This is particularly true for women whose lives may be isolated and lonely and for whom events at the mosque provide a welcome opportunity to interact with others of the community. "Well, people they come from different states and different cities, and they don't know the place," said one, "and you introduce them to the place and a lot of them join . . . and we are together."

In addition to their interest in the strictly social side of mosque activities, women are particularly concerned about the role the mosque can play in the socialization of their children and in inculcating Islamic values. A twenty-four-year-old American-born woman reflects on early childhood experiences in a mosque:

Since it was so far back, all I remember is that everybody went there, everyone knew each other. . . . I just remember going into some little room and the Shaykh would come in and he would talk to us about religion, tell us stories, and then he would say things and we would just say them after him. And, after he would be done with that, we would go and have sweets and stuff. And then we would go outside and play . . . for the rest of the day. And the mothers would sit and talk and the fathers would sit and talk.

To some extent the differences in expectations of what a mosque should be and do are generational. For many of the older people in the community the new stress on a stricter and more pristine understanding of the functions of the mosque leaves them without a context in which to be part of a community of people interacting informally and casually. Recalling earlier days with nostalgia, one said about the time spent in the mosque: "It was fun, it was like a holiday. Every Sunday would be a holiday. We would get to go and see everyone and see all the kids that we would only see from week to week." And from another, a clear indication that the situation changed completely when a new imam arrived with ideas much more conservative than those of his congregation:

> It [social activity in the mosque] didn't conflict with the religion until we had the new imam coming into this. . . . It wasn't done in the mosque because the mosque for prayer is upstairs and we figure the basement is for social functions. They danced, they sang, they had weddings, they had showers, they had fund raising, they had all types of activities . . . liquor was not allowed . . . against the religion. They had the kitchen, they had brunches, luncheons, what have you . . . all that stuff. We didn't have conflict until the imams came over there and started telling us well this is a mosque and the basement belongs to the mosque and you cannot dance, you cannot sing, you cannot do anything . . . so that is it.

The reflections of one older Muslim respondent serve as an even more poignant reminder that for some people giving up any aspect of mosque activity can mean the loss of an opportunity to break the shell of loneliness that surrounds them: "You see, there is a lot of people that is lonely . . . and by that church [sic] being open seven days a week . . . it brings them a little hope, you know what I mean . . . because that loneliness is a worse disease than any kind of disease you can come across."

Liaison with American Culture

Historically in the Muslim world mosques have functioned as centers for political activity and debate as well as houses of worship. Although they normally do not play this role in the United States, some mosques do provide instruction in current affairs by engaging speakers on such topics as Middle East politics. A number of mosques are taking an active role in helping non-Muslim Americans understand more about Islam and what it means to be Muslim. Those mosque leaders who feel that the more Christians understand about Islam the better able they are to appreciate having Muslims in their community, have tried to make use of public media and have welcomed the opportunity to be interviewed by reporters for the press, television, and radio.

A number of other Muslims in our study, however, have assiduously attempted to maintain a low profile as Muslims in their communities. Apparently fearing that reporters might portray them or their mosque unfavorably, possibly damaging relations with the community and making their own circumstances more difficult, they much prefer that their mosque not receive much attention from the media. And some simply feel that it is inappropriate for a mosque or its representatives to be liaisons between its members and the community, either for the education of the American public or as a means of helping Muslims adjust to secular society.

Some mosques, like some churches and synagogues, actively try to help their immigrant members to adapt to American life and society by offering specific services such as job counseling or instruction in English. Nearly three quarters of the respondents felt that helping immigrants in this way is important, and an even higher number affirmed the need for mosque leaders to inform the public about Islam. Some indicated that assistance to immigrants is already being provided to some extent by American public services for those who need help in developing job and language skills. Only the mosque or Islamic center, however, is likely to make any effort to inform the general public about Islam or Islamic activities. One mosque in our study is organizing a letter-writing campaign to the state legislature to get official recognition of the *Eids* as legal holidays to be observed by Muslims in schools and offices.

Several mosques reported that they have members, often medical doctors, who provide their professional services to other Muslims for little or no charge. Normally this service is private and not an official function of the mosque. However, one mosque donated two of the rooms in its building to be used as a medical clinic, staffed by "some Muslim doctors who are volunteering say six hours a week to be here for blood tests, for blood pressure tests, and for some other services which are needed by the Muslim community on a free basis." Such services not only provide important medical care but also serve to introduce Muslims to the general functions of that mosque.

Financial Aspects

Unlike the situation in much of the Islamic world, where mosques typically are supported by the government, in the United States they rely on member donations and fund-raising events for their operating capital. Unfortunately, many immigrants are not aware of this different economic reality, and thus do not regularly contribute to the mosque in any significant amounts. As a result, many mosques have had either to adopt measures that are initially offensive to some Muslims, such as passing the collection plate at services and having bingo parties, or to increase their efforts to encourage their constituents to tithe or contribute substantially to the running of the mosque.

About two fifths of the Muslims surveyed in the present study reported that they had given over one hundred dollars in the last six months to their mosque or Islamic center. With the exception of a few who contribute large amounts of money, the average donation for Muslims to the mosque is only slightly more than two hundred dollars a year.

The Imam

The designation "imam" in the Islamic world has been used to indicate any of a number of leadership roles. To Muslims as a whole, it is an honorific title for one who is recognized as particularly learned in the Islamic sciences. It has been used more technically by Sunnis to refer to the Caliph as head of the community and by Shi'ites in different ways, including the designation of that individual who, through hereditary succession from the Prophet Muhammad, is the true leader of Islam.

Imam is also the title given by Muslims to the person who leads the congregation in the Friday prayer service. There is no counterpart in the Islamic tradition to the ordained clergy of Christianity and Judaism, and the one who is called imam in the sense of leader of congregational prayer may or may not have received specialized training in the study of Islam. In any case, in Muslim countries he would not have general "pastoral" responsibilities; other professionals carry out duties related to weddings, funerals, Islamic education, consultation in matters of Islamic law, and the like.

The Imam in the American Context

As is true with many aspects of the practice of Islam in the United States, the role of imam here often takes on dimensions not normally present in the Islamic world. Here he is often encouraged to assume responsibilities that more closely resemble those of the American pastor or rabbi than the traditional imam. To some extent, this is due to the different circumstances in the United States. Demands for instruction in Islam, for "pastoring" to a congregation many of whose members may be having difficulties adjusting to a new culture, for visiting the sick and bereaved and providing family counseling, all press the imam to enlarge the scope of his functions. And, in this country, the absence of those other professionals to whom individuals might go for specialized services—*shaykhs* (religious leaders), *qadis* (judges), *'alims* (persons learned in law and theology)—means that these responsibilities are added to what is expected of an imam.

The expansion of roles required of the North American imam is also due in part to the variety of activities engaged in by priests, pastors, and rabbis in their respective communities. Imams in some cities are asked to join ecumenical organizations, to speak at gatherings where presentations are also made by Christian and Jewish clergy, and to appear on local radio or TV programs to talk about Islam. As one imam in this country explained:

> The role of the imam in the United States is completely different from the role of the imam in the Muslim world. In the Muslim world the imam's job is just to lead the prayer, but when you come to the United States, the role of imam is several roles. For example, here the imam conducts the funerals, a job which the imam back home would not do, there is a special person to do the job authorized by the government to perform marriages. Here too the imam practices the job of marriage counselor, or an arbitrator between husband and wife, parents and children. This role of course is not practiced by the imam in the Muslim world. The mosque in America serves the Muslim affairs from cradle to death . . . a place where . . . all the necessary functions of society—economic, political, social, religious, . . . recreational—everything is being practiced here. The imam is the center of that place so he is the one to be involved with them, with all these things.

In the traditional Muslim family overseas, problems are shared with the extended family. The elder members of the group deliberate and adjudicate among the contending members within the family structure. In the American context young couples, separated from their traditional roots, resort to seeking help from the imam, the respected leader of the community. This is not because he is an imam, as such, but is rather in recognition of his knowledge of the Islamic faith and his ability to discern the proper means of resolving contentious issues. The demand for counseling seems particularly strong, as reflected in these remarks by a full-time imam:

> Counseling is almost a daily occupation here with me. I am constantly counseling people who are coming to me with various [kinds of] advice sometimes for marital problems, sometimes with finances, sometimes problems that they run into every day on the job, how they should conduct themselves on the job. I do a lot of counseling with converts.

And from a part-time imam:

> I do counseling, but my time is limited and I cannot do as much as I would like to do, or what is needed, because of my own personal responsibilities. Most of the counseling problems I deal with fall into two categories, one being economic, another being marital. Counseling takes up a lot of my time—too much. There is a great need in the Muslim community, and we need to get better organized to help here. Many of the Muslims new to this country do not like to reveal their private life to some stranger. But if the matter is tense and they have to do something about it, they will come to a place they trust, the mosque. If it is something confidential, it is easier to talk to the imam than to some social worker.

Part of the counseling function clearly involves helping fellow Muslims learn to survive in an environment that is often unsupportive of Muslim ideals and values. Our survey thus showed that a large majority of Muslims in this sample want their imam not only to be skilled in family counseling but to be well informed about American society (see Table 2.3A). For some, it seems that such expertise is desired so as to help members of the Muslim community to be better able to maintain a strict Islamic code in this culture in matters of dress, food, social interactions, and business dealing. For others, familiarity with the workings of American society on the part of the imam might, they feel, predispose him to understand how difficult it is for Muslims to follow Islamic law in this context (and possibly, by implication, to sanction less strict observance).

Only about a third of those surveyed said they consider it very important for their imam to maintain strict Islamic standards. Almost twice that number, however, do feel that they want the imam to make conscious attempts "to bring Muslims back to the fold," whether that means recalling the lapsed to stricter adherence to the law or simply bringing them back to the mosque for worship (see Tables 2.3A and 2.3B). It is mainly Muslims who have come to this country as immigrants who want the imam to interpret Islam more strictly, while those raised in the United States seem on the whole to favor flexibility. If the imam is more lenient and understanding, the latter assume, they and

TABLE 2.3A   What Is Wanted in an Imam: Important Characteristics

Characteristics	Importance (%)			
	Very	Quite	Somewhat	Not
Skills in family counseling	46	33	16	4
Understands American society	64	24	10	3
Tries to see that attenders maintain strict Islamic standards in dress, food, social interactions, and business dealings	31	29	22	18
Seeks to bring Muslims back into the fold	61	26	9	4
Full time (i.e., does not hold another job)	48	19	19	14
Had proper Islamic training in shari'a	73	15	9	3
Can speak English fluently	68	24	6	2
Can speak Arabic fluently	69	20	7	4

TABLE 2.3B   What Is Wanted in an Imam: Correlations of Items in Table 2.3A with Birth in the United States

Characteristics	Correlation with Birth in the United States
Skills in counseling	n.s.
Understands American society	.11 (p ≤ .02 level)
Maintains strict Islamic standards	−.17 (p ≤ .001 level)
Brings Muslims back to the fold	n.s.
Full-time imam	n.s.
Proper Islamic training in shari'a	−.18 (p ≤ .001 level)
Speaks English fluently	+.14 (p ≤ .006 level)
Speaks Arabic fluently	+.13 (p ≤ .007 level)

their children will feel more comfortable in the mosque and less at odds with the rest of American society.

The Imam as Professional

It should be noted, first of all, that although having an imam is desirable for most Muslim congregations, it is technically not necessary and some mosques simply do not have a person functioning in that capacity. (In the Islamic tradition, any believer can lead the prayer or give the *khutba,* or sermon.) For those who do have an imam, any of a variety of alternatives is possible. The mosques in our study thus vary widely in their arrangements.

In one of the mosques we studied, three men serve in the capacity of imam, on a rotating and voluntary basis with no financial compensation provided from any source. In another, the members annually choose from their own congregation one person who they feel is sufficiently knowledgeable about Islam to be the imam, again on a voluntary basis with no remuneration. Sometimes the imam is paid a small stipend for serving on a continuing but part-time basis, as is the case with one man in our study who is also supporting himself by a full-time job in industry. His father preceded him in the same mosque as a part-time imam.

This kind of volunteer or partly remunerated service is much like the "tent-making" ministry of some Christian clergy who serve low-income congregations in their spare time while earning all or most of their salaries in other occupations. Imams who function in this manner resemble Christian clergy in evangelical and independent sects more than those in mainline Protestant denominations, however, in that they are chosen by their congregations and are not formally designated or recognized by any external official Islamic bodies. Normally they have no special education for their task but are selected on the basis of general knowledge, character, and availability.

Some imams in the United States, represented in our study, do more closely resemble denominationally ordained clergy in terms of preparation and professional intention. These have formal training in the Islamic sciences and thus are prepared to give informed judgments about Islamic law as well as to preach and lead the prayers. Persons with this kind of background generally seek full-time positions offering sufficient salaries so that they need not be employed elsewhere. Many mosques in the United States do not have large operating budgets, however, and welcome the assistance of countries such as Egypt and Saudi Arabia as well as such international organizations as the Muslim World League. In some cases these outside agencies pay the salaries of the imams directly. In one of the mosques considered in this study, the full-time imam is salaried by the Muslim World League, although his rent and health insurance are paid by the members of the mosque.

The Muslim World League would be willing to secure more funding from Arab countries to support well-educated imams trained in the

Islamic tradition. Many mosques, however, do not wish to accept this help. Leaders of three of the mosques in this study refused the offer of a full-time paid imam, partly because they perceived there would be strings attached. The League, or the country that provides the funding, is responsible for the selection of the imam. Typically he is someone educated in a Muslim country whose first introduction to the United States is as the imam of a local mosque. Several mosque leaders expressed concern that such a "foreign" imam either would not fit in with the members, imposing a different interpretation of Islam than they wished, or would simply wrest control of the mosque from the leaders who currently enjoyed such influence. Such concerns are illustrated in comments from leaders in two different mosque sites:

> The Muslim World League wanted to send us an imam who speaks English, Albanian and Arabic, but the Albanian community in this mosque did not want that kind of help; they wanted to be themselves.
>
> I know there are imams in the U.S. sent by Saudi Arabia. But I think most people in our congregation, and I also speak for myself as part of the congregation, would like to continue to see an imam come out from themselves.

In one mosque/Islamic center used as a site in this study, the imam is both full time and paid by the Islamic center itself. This mosque is in an area where Muslims from Arab countries have been settled for several generations, and have established themselves as middle-class business people and professionals. The area experienced an influx of new professional immigrants from Pakistan and the Middle East. Their affluence and stability recently permitted them to build a magnificent new mosque and to take pride in being able to pay the salary of a highly educated imam of their own choice.

For many Muslims in less flexible circumstances even the inability to support a full-time imam does not mean they would trade the freedom to make their own selection for the financial advantages of accepting outside funding. In actual fact, only twenty-six imams in this country are supported by the Muslim World League. Most mosques either do not have an Islamically educated imam, or if they have one they are not able to enjoy his services on more than a part-time basis. Only a few are supported full time by their congregations. To make up for the lack of Islamically trained leaders in the local mosques, occasionally a volunteer or a student from overseas will provide instruction in Arabic or in essentials of the faith.

Cross-cultural Conflicts

Problems of various kinds have arisen in mosques in which the imam is from a different country or culture from that of most of his constituents. One imam interviewed identified the disparity in cultures between imam and mosque members as the major problem encountered by another mosque when its leadership, including the imam, changed. Especially galling to many members of the mosque was the new imam's refusal to allow women to pray in the same room as the men, occasioning a serious struggle within the congregation. As the imam we talked with explained:

> It depends on the leadership. You cannot have an imam from Egypt and compare him to an imam from Saudi Arabia. . . . Everyone has his own country. The one from Saudi Arabia does not see any women on the street there, in the streets of Mecca. Whereas the imam who is coming from Egypt has the common experience of seeing women on the streets. That type of culture will be affecting the behavior of the imam when he comes to America.

This imam went on to say that divisions among Muslims in America, whether a result of national origin, length of time spent in this country, or socioeconomic and educational status, usually can be overcome by the guidance of an imam "who is a qualified leader. . . . If there is leadership which everybody trusts, you will find people are regrouping around that leadership." The problem is that while the outside imam funded by another organization or government is normally well trained in Qur'an, *hadith,* Islamic law, and Arabic, he runs the risk of not having a neutral base of trust in the mosque. The imam who rises up from the membership, on the other hand, and who is known and trusted by that membership, often lacks the Islamic qualifications of his foreign counterpart.

Generally, however, it seems that even an imam who comes new to a congregation will be welcomed by that group as long as he attempts to understand the culture and expectations of his constituency and introduces any changes he might wish cautiously and diplomatically. Imams from abroad often find that Muslims born in America expect that they as members should have more direct say in running the mosque than members normally have in other cultures. It takes a particularly sensitive and diplomatic imam to successfully reprimand those whose behavior he feels is inappropriate for a mosque as well as to effect the kinds of structural, programmatic, or policy changes he may feel are necessary to make the institutions more Islamic. As one imam observed, "In Muslim countries you can issue orders to people as a religious leader; here you cannot."

Although nearly half the Muslims surveyed said it is "very important" for them to have a full-time imam who does not work at another job, about a third felt it is only "somewhat important," at best, that their mosque have someone in this capacity. In contrast, having an imam with the proper Islamic training in the law is "very important" to almost three fifths of those surveyed, while only a small number indicated it is only "somewhat important" at best, that their imam have these qualifications (see Tables 2.3A and 2.3B). Muslims who most wanted a full-time imam for their mosque also wanted an imam with training in shari'a, fluency in Arabic, and family counseling skills. All this suggests that many Muslims want an imam whose primary responsibilities are preaching and leading prayers, which often can be done on a part-time basis.

The Importance of Arabic

In a traditional Muslim service, the call to prayer and the *salat* (ritual prayer) are both in Arabic, a practice followed whenever possible in the United States. In most mosques passages from the Qur'an and *hadith* are also read in Arabic. In the sample of Muslims interviewed for this survey, more than two thirds wanted an imam who speaks both English and Arabic fluently. A bilingual imam can communicate with the English-speaking members of his mosque and can deliver the sermon in a language comprehensible to them. In addition, he can render the other parts of the service in the appropriate language, Arabic, and also offer instruction in the Qur'an and the Arabic language within the educational program in the mosque.

In our sample, finding an imam who speaks English fluently was said to be a bit more difficult than getting one well versed in Arabic. The importance of this facility in English for communication is expressed by two mosque members as follows. From a woman in her fifties born in this country of Lebanese parents:

> I enjoyed the imam because he spoke in Arabic and explained it in English. Let's face it, you have a lot of American born Muslims here who don't understand Arabic, and my sons don't understand that much Arabic because we were gone too long and they weren't exposed to it enough. In order for them to enjoy a sermon they are going to have to

understand it. . . . Even my daughter-in-law, she is not an Arab and does not understand Arabic, she enjoyed it. I am very well satisfied with the imam.

And from a middle-aged immigrant Lebanese male:

What a mosque actually needs, especially in a non-Muslim country, is an educated imam that speaks the language of that people alongside English—in order to be able to speak to other people, either non-Muslims or people who don't speak the Arabic language, and tell them what Islam is all about. I don't think we have an imam at our mosque who can do this, he still is not educated enough. He doesn't know enough words in English to get his points across.

Some studies have maintained that mosque attenders are increasingly rejecting the use of Arabic in prayer and sermons.[2] Nonetheless the importance of Arabic as a language of scripture, liturgy, and religious instruction clearly is felt in this country as well as in Islamic cultures, and our data suggest that an imam who had no facility at all in the language would not be desirable for most Muslims, whether they emigrated to or were born in the United States.

CHAPTER 3

Living in America:
Social Integration

In assessing the experiences of immigrants in the American context, one of the key issues to consider is the degree to which they are able to—or wish to—become integrated socially into the American culture. Recent studies have attempted to analyze questions of upward mobility for immigrants in this country.[1] To some extent their findings indicate escalating experiences of discrimination on the part of those who are more highly educated, particularly as they come into increasing contact with other Americans in the workplace.[2]

The situation of Muslim immigrants in the United States—who until recently have been primarily from Arab countries—seems to be somewhat different from that of the Irish or Italians or other immigrant groups because their numbers have been so much smaller. Muslim immigrants continue to be only about 1 percent of the population, not presenting the potential threat to the resident nationals that more sizable communities might pose. In the Midwest a large number of immigrant Muslims are from the unskilled labor class, although there is a growing number of professionals. Those who have moved into the professional class of the American-born are already fully integrated into this society. They generally have anglicized names and few if any characteristics distinguishing them as foreign or even Muslim.

Recently arrived professionals from various parts of the Islamic world have not been competing for scarce American jobs, but have filled open positions in such fields as engineering and medicine, again not posing a direct threat to Americans in the work force but rather contributing their special skills and training to American society. They are part of the brain drain various Muslim countries have recently suffered because of the inability of their underdeveloped economies to absorb highly trained professionals. Some are simply lured by the "glitter" of the West, while others opt to stay because of opportunities for training and advancement in their fields. This is not to say, however, that all Muslim immigrants to this country have been successful in finding employment. An estimated 40 percent of the Yemenis who came in the 1960s and 1970s, for example, are unemployed. In the Midwest, the slowdown in the automobile industry has had severe effects on many of the Arabs employed in the factories.

For the most part people who have had difficulty in the workplace were not covered in our survey. It is therefore not surprising that Muslims interviewed in our study report being satisfied with their success in finding jobs as well as in establishing some kind of social contact with Americans of other faiths. Although the great majority feel that Americans in general have negative stereotypes about Islam or about Arabs, for the most part they do not report having personally encountered much prejudice or hostility. Whatever hostility is evident in the media and the press they appear to feel is directed against Muslims overseas. There are several possible explanations for the fact that those in our survey did not report to our investigators significant experiences of prejudice in this culture, even though others outside these groups have indicated they do encounter it. If one has not personally experienced such prejudice, for example, one may not be aware of others who have had such experiences. It is also possible that in many cases other Americans do not associate these Muslims with Islam, or at least with the kind of Islam they hear about in the media. Those who have experienced prejudice in some form may be uncomfortable in admitting they have been so treated, denying it in the hope that it will not recur and at the same time maintaining a sense of personal dignity.

The very success in assimilation that Muslim immigrants have had is a source of concern to some who fear that it may cause members of the community to lose touch with their knowledge of and pride in their Islamic background. Although immigrant Muslims generally have expressed the desire to assimilate into American culture, some in the Muslim community now indicate a strong sentiment that it is of crucial importance to preserve the identity of the community by maintaining distinctively Muslim or ethnic characteristics. The success earlier generations of Arab Muslims achieved in assimilating into American society is a cause of concern to some who have arrived more recently. They object strongly to the attempt to merge into this culture by changing names and playing down characteristics or customs that would set them apart. They are concerned that once drawn into

American society, immigrants may be tempted to neglect the practices and values that distinguish Islam as a religion and a way of life.

This chapter will attempt to describe through their own narratives some of the experiences that Muslim immigrants and their children have had in this country and to draw ramifications of these experiences for Islamic identity and the integrity of the Muslim community.

Desirability of Location for Muslim Settlement

In the first chapter, brief descriptions were given of the three major sites investigated in this study: the Midwest, the East Coast, and upstate New York. Included in those descriptions was some indication of interaction of Muslims with other Muslims of different backgrounds, as well as with non-Muslim Americans. This kind of interaction, be it for reasons of choice or necessity, is one element in determining whether or not individuals feel their particular area is a good one for Muslims to settle in. In two of the three areas, a clear majority of those interviewed indicated that their area is in fact a good one for Muslims, whereas in the third, the East Coast, less than half were so persuaded. Following are some of the kinds of responses given by members of these respective groups.

Midwest

The most common reason given by Muslims in the Midwest for feeling that it is a good place for Muslims to settle is that groups of Muslims from Arab countries and their descendents are already living there. A number of mosques as well as social clubs for people of different national origins help in making new immigrants feel at home. In this area we studied three cities, some of whose Muslim residents appear to be related to each other through intermarriage. For the most part they are descendants of the early Islamic immigrants who came at the turn of the century. Records show that some had homesteaded as far as North Dakota, only to congregate in the late 1930s in industrial cities and form part of the labor force of the Midwest. In only one of the mosques studied was there a sufficiently high concentration of Muslims in a limited geographic area to be able to call it a residential enclave. In this context, however, it is clear that a high density population offers the opportunity for affirmation of the individual as a member of an already established group. Thus, one mosque member commented as follows:

> The area is a good one for Muslim families to settle in. It is nice to know that in a certain part of your neighborhood there are thousands of us. It really makes you feel good deep down inside. I mean all of us are like we were back home (in Lebanon); there are a large majority of us here in this neighborhood.

Another mosque member affirmed the built-in support that the community provides:

> This is a good place for new Muslim immigrants to come because there already is a Muslim community here. It will help you better to practice your religion if you live among the Muslim community, you will feel more secure, more comfortable among Muslim brothers. . . . Also for other activities (social and political—e.g., collecting money for Lebanon) it will succeed because there are a lot of Muslims in this area. Some other place I cannot do that, because Muslim people—they do not live there. Therefore, you can achieve more activity in this place.

And another expressed appreciation for community centers that are run by Arabs to help immigrants acquire language facility as well as skills such as typing, writing resumés, and otherwise preparing for the job market:

> This is a good area for new immigrants because it is a growing community. There are a lot of places where there are community centers for the Arab community and more if they wanted them. People wouldn't feel so left out if they immigrated to this area because you have so many Muslim families in here now.

For other midwestern Muslims, however, the fact that many Muslims live in close proximity and interact frequently with each other raises serious questions. They fear that in such circumstances the immigrants will be less highly motivated to learn English well or to make the kinds of accommodations that will aid in the process of acculturation and acceptance by non-Muslim American society. A few midwestern Muslims interviewed expressed concern that some of the newer immigrants such as rural Yemenis or displaced Palestinians and Shi'is from South Lebanon are perhaps less clean, honest, and orderly than members of the old-time Lebanese immigrant community. This anxiety over new immigrants not undoing the gains in social acceptance achieved by the Muslims who have been in this country for some time is expressed in the following statement by a midwestern Muslim:

This is a good area for Muslim families to come to from the old country . . . but I still feel that when they come over here they should Americanize a little bit. They should understand that they are not in the old country, that they have to teach their children to respect other people's property, and they should also take care of their property and keep it up, like everybody else does. Otherwise, people are really going to be upset. They should also learn the language. Because a lot of them have been here for years and still don't know how to speak English. They should also understand the laws of this country.

It is clear that Muslims from this area have mixed feelings about the desirability of living with large numbers of other Muslims. For some, the community provides a comfort and an antidote to the loneliness of living in a society in which Islam is not understood, as well as an opportunity to share concerns about the home country. It is also true that recent negative press reports about the situation in Lebanon have contributed to the feelings of isolation on the part of Lebanese immigrants. One young woman whose family now lives apart from the community of Muslims in the Midwest area finds herself drawn back whenever possible:

My area is not a good one for immigrants, because there are Americans all around us. And you feel very lonely, I still feel lonely and I have been here for seven years. I don't stay at home. I go more toward where the Arabs are, in the area where I work. I have always worked in this area. I have been coming here a lot lately.

For others, however, it is extremely important that Muslims make every effort to learn English well and to socialize with non-Muslim Americans:

It depends on the person whether or not the area is a good one. I think it is really up to the person himself whether he is going to have a hard time or not. A person might be in a particular community that has more Christians in it than Muslims; he might even be the only one there. Now, I have integrated very well into this. . . . The only thing that I can really see that might be a problem [in interacting socially with Christians] would be the pork problem. But once you get into that—and believe me, when they understand that you don't eat pork—they see that they have something else for you to eat.

East Coast

This area originally was populated by Muslims from the Middle East who eventually ended up working in the shipyards. Recent immigrants who have settled there represent a number of nationalities, many attracted by the large metropolitan area with its educational opportunities, medical services, and technology. In general, Muslims in this area have tended to assimilate fairly well, families integrating into suburbs where they may be the only Muslims in the neighborhood. Although they tend to take their children to a mosque or Islamic educational center to learn the fundamentals of Islam, as well as to go to the mosque at least for the Eid celebrations, they do not restrict their socializing to other Muslims. Most have formed social ties with non-Muslim Americans and feel themselves to be fairly well integrated into the society.

The East Coast is the most heterogeneous of the three areas we surveyed in terms of both the Muslim population and the other religious and ethnic/national groups located there. The metropolitan complex (sometimes called a megalopolis) and its suburbs is composed of a large number of quite distinct neighborhoods. This very heterogeneity may be a major reason that fewer than half of the Muslims surveyed there feel it is definitely a good area for Muslim immigrants to settle in. For some, the particular characteristics of the section in which they live may make it congenial, while quite different circumstances for others provide a mixed contrast.

Although both excellent educational opportunities and good jobs are available for those who are highly educated, others who lack qualifications in education or experience find it difficult to gain employment. On the East Coast it seems that upper-middle-class neighborhoods with higher income levels are relatively open to the presence of Muslims, while some persons we interviewed reported a sense of discrimination by persons in lower-middle- and working-class neighborhoods. There are, of course, exceptions to these generalizations. The following excerpts indicate some of the reasons given by the Muslims we interviewed as to why living on the East Coast is advantageous.

Availability of excellent educational institutions:

> This is a good area for immigrant Muslims. Education here is the best in the world. The medical, the technology, electronics—there is nothing in this area you can't get!

Availability of lucrative employment:

> This is a good area for an immigrant if he has the qualifications. If he is a hi-tech or medical person, a professional, he can find a good job; but if he is not, he will have a hard time.

Availability of institutions and facilities:

> The city is an ideal area. There is a good cultural mix, a university atmosphere, always something going on culturally and socially. There is a mosque and an Islamic center. Jobwise, with good roads and local transportation for commuting, I think it has a lot to offer immigrants.

Inherent flexibility of the city:

> The city is one of the greatest places. I love it, so I am prejudiced. Whether it is good for new immigrants may depend on where you live. In areas where there are conflicts between blacks and whites, it can be pretty tense. But it is a live and liberal city, and people will accept most anything—just because of the high student population here, they have to! Most of my non-Muslim friends want to know more about Islam than anything else—and most of them are dying to go to the Middle East.

Others are less sanguine about the possibilities for immigrant Muslims to be happy on the East Coast:

> The city is depressed, and of course in our area we have a heavy Negro population, plus Cubans and Latinos. In the [working class suburb] area we have some Islamic families living, and a lot of them are made unwelcome. I would not recommend this area particularly for immigrant Muslims.

For some, the city itself holds far greater possibilities for immigrants than the suburbs:

> The city is not bad for immigrants—there are a lot of Muslims there and a lot of activities for them. But this town is not growing or mobile. There are no universities in this area [suburb] and hardly any new Muslim families come to settle here. I don't advise it for new settlers either. It is not a good area for immigrant Muslims.

Upstate New York

As was indicated earlier, this area has received a recent influx of immigrants from Pakistan. In the main they are highly educated and employed in top business and professional positions, and they have come to the area primarily because of the professional opportunities available. Typically they do not live near one another but buy houses or rent apartments in the more exclusive urban or suburban areas. Thus, it is rare that Muslims, let alone Pakistanis, live in proximity to one another. Yet many make efforts to attend their mosques and to socialize with each other in their homes, even though it involves driving some distance.

While the majority of those interviewed said that upstate New York is a good place for Muslims to settle in, others were ambivalent. As is the case in the East Coast area, those with the right qualifications have little trouble finding employment, but there are few jobs for persons with minimal education and skills. Said one:

> I would say this is one of the better areas for immigrant Muslims to settle in . . . but then we as a Muslim community are privileged in that we have a well-educated group of people who are well established and doing very good. But it is an economically depressed area, and the chances of people getting jobs who do not have the education for a profession that is in demand here—such as doctor or engineer—are rather slim. But once you have a good joob, this is an excellent area to live in and raise a family.

Another cited the lack of a sizable Muslim community as a particular concern:

> No, I do not think this a good area for new immigrant Muslims to settle in. There aren't enough of us. We are a very small minority. Our voice is not heard at all. We just are so small that we don't count—politically, economically, everything.

Several of those interviewed were not only positive in their evaluation but specifically cited lack of discrimination as a reason why upstate New York is a good area for Muslims:

> There is no active discrimination against Muslims in this area at the present time. However, our number is so small it could be considered insignificant. And only time will tell if Muslims are tolerated in this area or not. However, I feel they will be tolerated well.

> I feel this is a good area for immigrant Muslims as far as our personal experiences have gone. We have been accepted as Muslims in the area. There has been no discrimination as such in day-to-day living, now that is why I feel it is all right for Muslims to come and settle in this area.

> I think the treatment here by Christians and Jews of Muslims has been good. There have not been any problems with any of these communities. We have lived as neighbors and as friends and as co-workers, very peacefully and very harmoniously without any problems. There are people who are saying their prayers at work in a non-Muslim environment and yet, people are respecting them in their religious beliefs.

One Muslim interviewed in the area believes both the climate and the general conservatism that predominate helps Muslims retain their proper Islamic behavior:

> This is still somewhat a "conservative" area and a cool one. Because of the climate, six months out of the year we are somehow forced to dress in the Islamic manner whether we like it or not. So for instance if we were in a hotter climate, we would be tempted to not dress in the Islamic manner. But here we can't do that! Also, the fact that the non-Muslim community is conservative is good in that the Islamic activity here is not hindered by any of the other communities.

A number of others feel that what makes this area a particularly good one for immigrant Muslims is the effort the Islamic center makes to bring new immigrant people into its membership, helping them to meet other Muslims and to adjust to the realities of life in America:

> This is really an excellent area for immigrants. The Islamic center is really striving to incorporate people into the Muslim community, to educate them and to bring them together. This might be considered a fairly new attitude [on the part of the Islamic center] to make this a good area.

Although in many cases the general characteristics of the three sites described above influence the views of those surveyed as to their desirability, it is also true that opinions on this issue are determined in part by individual characteristics and circumstances.

In none of the areas is sex, age, or educational achievement clearly related to opinions on the suitability of the area for Muslims. However, those born in America are considerably more likely than new immigrants to give a positive evaluation, and in two of the three areas surveyed, this likelihood is increased in proportion to the length of the respondent's stay in this country. For example, while only 35 percent of the immigrants who came to the United States in 1980 or later felt that their area is a good one for immigrant Muslims, fully 60 percent of the Muslims who settled in the United States before 1980 said their area is good (see Tables 3.1 and 3.2). An exception to this was registered by residents of the Midwest area. Immigrants who have settled there since 1980 are just as likely as those who have been in the Midwest since before 1970 to feel that it is a good place for immigrant Muslims. As in the other areas, however, the American-born are more likely than newcomers to favor this environment for Muslims.

Other factors come into play in determining responses to this issue.

TABLE 3.1   Satisfactions with Area for Immigrants and First- and Second-Generation Muslims (%)

Responses[a]	Immigrant	First Generation (American-born)	Second Generation
Agree	55	72	70
Mixed Feelings	31	24	26
Disagree	14	4	4
	100	100	100
	(212)	(53)	(69)
	Tau B	= −.15	
	Significance	= .001	
	N	= 334	

[a]To the statement "The general area in which I live is a good one for Muslims to settle in now."

TABLE 3.2   Satisfaction with Area and Years in the Country (%)

| Responses[a] | Year of Immigration to the United States | | |
	Before 1970	1970–1979	1980 or later
Agree	61	60	35
Mixed Feelings	27	26	49
Disagree	12	14	16
	100	100	100
	(69)	(106)	(37)
	Tau B	= .12	
	Significance	= .03	
	N	= 212	

[a]To the statement "The general area in which I live is a good one for Muslims to settle in now."

First, our sample shows that Muslims who go frequently to the mosque are more likely to favor the area than Muslims who go infrequently. So, second, are those who tend to dine with Muslims who are not members of their families. A third and apparently even more significant factor in favorably disposing respondents to their areas is that of dining fairly frequently with non-Muslim Americans. Eating with persons who are not members of one's faith or national group has been cited by other researchers as a measure of social assimilation into the host culture,[3] which supports the conclusion that both identity with a group of Muslims in the area and establishing social relations with non-Muslim Americans may work to help Muslims feel happy in a new environment. Our study in fact provides evidence that both these factors—social exchange with Muslims and with non-Muslims—when taken together provide a situation most conducive to immigrant Muslims feeling at home in their particular residential areas.

Integrating into the Community and Workplace

On the whole, those interviewed in our survey expressed satisfaction with their current jobs, most indicating that they are better off than they would be in their country of origin. Several who are in scientific fields said that they had been recruited by American corporations or universities to come to this country. Concern about possible discrimination as a factor in finding a job is more prevalent among graduate students who have not yet actually sought employment.

For the most part, Muslims we interviewed reported that they hesitate to ask their employers for time off to attend the Friday noon prayer service. This is due to the fear that such a request might hurt their chances of promotion or might be refused. One imam reported that his request for release from his job for two hours on Fridays to lead the Friday prayer was denied even though he was willing to have the necessary amount deducted from his salary. It is interesting to note that he did not see this as discrimination directed against Islam but as a discipline necessary in the factory where he worked to avoid setting a precedent for absenteeism. "Others," he said, "could then ask to be minister of this or rabbi of that."

Most of those interviewed, however, said that there is no problem taking the Eids as holidays as long as the time is made up or counted as vacation. No Muslim interviewed reported that he or she had ever experienced any personal harassment in the workplace or knew of any experienced by a friend or associate as a result of being either Muslim or foreign-born. Nor did any of those interviewed report any problems in buying or renting homes or apartments as a result of perceived prejudice. They feel generally accepted by their Christian and Jewish neighbors and report the normal kinds of local exchanges such as shared child care, occasional social interaction, borrowing of tools and household items, and the like.

One of the areas tested for possible prejudice is that of social interaction over meals. In most parts of the Islamic world eating is an extremely important aspect of social life; for Arabs especially, sharing a meal is a way of cementing social bonds. Eating with those who are not part of one's family or community is taken more seriously than is generally the case in American culture. Muslims in this country may therefore show some reserve in issuing or accepting invitations for meals with non-Muslims. In addition, some Muslims may be concerned about being put into a situation in which alcohol or pork products are served, and traditional Muslims may object to the women in their families being in the company of other males. One Muslim scholar pointed out that the Qur'an contains an injunction against eating with idolaters, and a *hadith* warns against eating with polytheists. While these have not generally been applied to Christians and Jews (People of the Book), some legists have interpreted them to mean that Muslims should not eat with people of any other faith. (Those who object to such a strict interpretation point out that the Prophet Muhammad had a Christian wife who cooked for him, legitimating such activity.)

Such concerns do not mitigate against social interaction with non-Muslims for all those in the Islamic community, of course. Hospitality is a very important part of Muslim culture, and eagerness on the part of many to be accepted into American society means that there is, in fact, a good deal of such social interaction. One fourth of those we interviewed said that they go often to the homes of non-Muslim American friends for dinner, although nearly half (46 percent) indicated that they eat predominantly with other Muslims. The incidence of dining with Americans of other faiths increases with each generation (see Table 3.3).

The area in which Muslims live also plays a part in determining the nature of the social interaction they have with those outside the Islamic community (see Table 3.4). In the upstate New York area, for example, Muslims generally dine socially only with other Muslims, whether or not they are family members, even though typically they must travel out of their neighborhoods to do so. The fact that they are predominantly conservative Pakistanis undoubtedly influences this kind of pattern. In the Midwest, respondents reported that they eat fairly frequently with non-Muslims. Here again, however, the nature of the community is a determining factor. On the whole they have been in this country for a longer time than those in upstate New York and are less conservative religiously. However, this area also has a high concentration of Arab Christians as well as Arab Muslims, and for many eating with a non-Muslim may simply mean eating with another Arab. Furthermore, the Midwest has the highest concentra-

TABLE 3.3   Percentage of Muslims Who Dine with Friends and Acquaintances (by Generation)

	Immigrant	First Generation (American-born)	Second Generation
Eat often with both Americans and Muslims	20	31	12
Eat some with both	15	27	40
Eat more with Americans	5	10	22
Eat somewhat more with Muslims	17	6	7
Restrict dining to Muslims (but do socialize with nonfamily Muslims)	31	16	10
Eat at home with family almost always	12	10	9
	100	100	100
	(217)	(52)	(68)

tion of first-, second-, and third-generation Muslims who have been socialized by the American public school system, where they have formed friendships with people of other faiths.

While the upstate New York Pakistanis are mainly upper-middle-class professionals and the midwestern Arabs are generally lower-middle-class blue-collar workers, the East Coast area represents a mixture of classes and ethnic backgrounds. They report a high degree of social interaction with Muslims, but we cannot tell from our present information whether or not members of the respective ethnic and national groups interact with those of other groups. Further study may reveal the extent to which, if it is true, the cosmopolitan nature of the city has broken down the ethnicity clearly observable in the other two areas. Evidence from this study would seem to suggest that the longer Muslims are resident in this country the more likely they are to establish friendships with other Americans, and that the very fact of living in a culture in which the vast majority of people are not Muslim will inevitably lead to this kind of increased social interaction. As an immigrant businessman in his forties indicated:

There is a lot of interaction of Muslim with non-Muslim families in this area. They interact, and have to interact, because they live in an environ-

TABLE 3.4   Percentage of Muslims Who Dine with Friends and Acquaintances (by Geographical Distribution)

	East Coast Dispersed	Upstate New York Commuter Enclave	Midwest Residential Enclave
Often with both Muslims and non-Muslims	20	8	23
Sometimes with both	20	12	26
More with Americans	5	2	12
Somewhat more with Muslims	16	27	7
Restrict eating nonfamily to Muslims	30	45	17
Eat at home	9	8	14
	100	100	100
	(75 or so)	(66)	(185)

ment where the majority of the people are non-Muslim. Your neighbors, your co-workers, your fellow students—a large number of whom will be non-Muslims you cannot avoid. You cannot just build walls around you and say, "I will not speak to them or meet with them." They are our friends, our neighbors and we respect each other and spend time with each other as appropriate. There is not much of an interaction with other Muslims, because I don't have any Muslim family in the neighborhood.

Our data shows that those who dine with Muslims as well as Americans of other faiths are more likely to perceive their area as a good one for immigrant Muslims (see Table 3.5).

There is, however, the possibility that for some Muslims such a mixing with American society is not the only choice. There are some Muslims who advocate as much social segregation from non-Muslim America as possible, emphasizing distinctive dress and particular attention to Muslim culture and tradition. This they see as the only way to preserve Islam for their children. In several U.S. cities there is conversation about establishing Muslim day schools where Islamic values are incorporated into the curriculum. It remains to be seen whether or not such efforts might result in a culturally distinctive Muslim in the sense that members of some of the Mennonite community, for example, are set apart from the rest of American society.

TABLE 3.5 Perception of Whether Area in Which One Lives Is Good for Muslims to Settle In (by Categories of Dining with Friends and Acquaintances)

Dining with Friends and Acquaintances Categories	Response to question: "Is area a good one for Muslims to settle in?" (%)		
	Agree	Mixed Feelings	Disagree
Eat often with Muslims and non-Muslims both	72	25	3 (65)
Eat with both Muslims and non-Muslims somewhat	60	29	11 (73)
Eat more with non-Muslims	61	29	28 (31)
Eat somewhat more with Muslims	65	28	6 (46)
Restrict eating to with Muslims	57	30	13 (84)
Eat only with family	46	36	18 (13)

Tau B = .12
Significance = .005
N = 332

Integration of Muslim Children

Almost all of the parents interviewed reported that their children play with non-Muslim friends from the neighborhood or the school. Often they see their Muslim friends only once a week or so at the mosque. This appears true even in the upstate New York area, where the adults are still most likely to maintain social relations as families with Muslims only. As one woman from this region described the situation:

There are several other Muslim families living in the area . . . well, within fifteen minutes' driving time. We know them very well. . . . We know less well also some families who are Christians and some who are Jews here. Because of their education, our children mingle with non-Muslim children. Although there are other Muslim children who are my children's ages and they do meet quite often, I think they mingle with non-Muslim children more so than with those who are Muslim because they go to school together.

The Pakistani Muslims in upstate New York tend to have slightly darker skin than do Muslims from other countries, and occasionally this has caused some temporary problems for the children in school.

My children play with white and black Catholic, Protestant, and Jewish children every day. There was a problem when my son started going to regular school, though. For the first couple of years, the neighboring children did try to bully him. I brought the sheriff's department into it. The sheriff did visit two or three families and it stopped directly. My daughter who has just started going to kindergarten says that older children do make comments to her . . . nothing too serious, probably would happen with any nonwhite children. But overall the effect of going to school with other children has been positive. Other children ask them questions about Islam and they give them very good answers. There has been no negative effect on my children because of this society.

Most Muslim parents in this area did not report any difficulties for their children at school because of either their nationality or their religion. Most of the children take the Eid days off from school, as one parent put it, "regularly, without any penalty or difficulty from the teachers or their schoolmates, as far as I know."

In other areas, parents also report that their children are making friends with non-Muslims at school and that their teachers respect them as persons, often asking the children to tell the class something about their faith or the land where their parents were born. School officials are typically lenient about children taking the Eids off from school as well. Parents interviewed repeatedly affirmed that being Muslim has not created any difficulties for their children at school, and that overall they are pleased with the quality of education their children are receiving.

While it is obvious that one of the functions of the public school system is to help mold children into responsible American citizens, some teachers seem to be sensitized to the fact that this need not mean depriving children of the right to claim their own distinctive heritage. Although little curricular material is available, individual instructors are attempting to provide a broader understanding of what constitutes American society, involving both parents and students in the effort. The following commentary from a Turkish immigrant mother in her middle thirties describes the experience of her children in one of the schools in the East Coast area:

My children were very Muslim in public schools, they always talked about it, and they were very proud to be Muslims. . . . We live in an area which is predominantly Jewish, and my children were probably the only Muslim children in school at that time. But they had programs on Islam in school and they made plays about it—just to introduce Islam to this society, and also to make my children feel good. . . . I also was invited by their teachers and went to their schools and gave lectures, and the teachers always called and asked if I had any slides on the Middle East that I could show and talk about. They asked me all kinds of questions. I think the school benefited from it, and my kids more than anyone. . . . And if there was a [Muslim] holiday and they wanted to take the day off, no problem. My children are very proud of being Muslims, they never hide it. If they want to pray, they will get up and pray; there is nothing holding them back.

Another mother in her thirties who was born in this country of Lebanese parents makes a similar observation about the way her children act and are reacted to in school:

So far my children seem very happy with their friends and their school. They have never come home and said this person said this or that. They are also outwardly telling people that they are Arabs and they are Muslims. They take time off from school for the big and little feasts whenever they fall on a school day. I always tell the teacher the reason. In fact, I was asked if in the future I would go in and explain to the class what the holidays were about because the teachers said the Jewish parents do this and they thought it would be nice for the children to know about the Muslim holidays.

A man who emigrated from Pakistan now living in the East Coast area proudly described how well teachers and neighbors respond to his children:

No one gives my children a hard time because they are Muslim. They are very well accepted and as a matter of fact, got the Eid holiday off when I asked the principal explaining this is an important day to the Muslims. My kids are very, very lovely kids and all the neighbors love them because they don't fight and they don't go for other kids like that. Sometimes my neighbors ask me, "How can you manage your kids to behave like that?" I tell them because it is part of their religion.

In one midwestern city, the public schools have such a high concentration of students from Arab backgrounds (in one instance 80 percent) that the Eids are automatically given as holidays by the school board. Instruction in the schools is bilingual, in Arabic as well as in English. Comments such as the following register the fact that local officials have taken note of the educational, religious, and dietary needs of Muslim children:

In this school system the majority of children are Muslim, maybe as much as 70 percent of them. When we have our holidays, our kids are given an excused day. In fact I don't even think they have pork on the school lunch menu now, ever.

If the Eids fall on a school day, we just call the school and tell them the children are not coming today because they have the holiday, and that is the size of it. . . . In fact my daughter's teacher asked to borrow our Qur'an and see what our religion is like, what it is all about.

How Muslim children integrate with American non-Muslim children depends on whether they were born here or whether they arrived here recently. If they arrived here recently, they tend to congregate with children like themselves. . . . After they have been here awhile, and have a little English, they work into the other group. . . . Now that they have bilingual teachers in the schools, I think it has been easier on the Arab children than it had been before the bilingual program. They are not having difficulties or the communication problems they formerly had. . . . On the big and little feasts, the children are all out of school. The school recognizes that this is an Islamic holiday and the children are allowed not to come to school. As a matter of fact, the school is practically closed because 75 percent of the children that go to the school are Arab children.

From this sample it is clear that Muslim parents have few complaints about the way the American public school system treats their children. Most parents of primary and junior high students seem to feel that, if anything, their children's pride in being Muslim has been strengthened through interaction with those of other backgrounds and religious beliefs. The following comment from a Muslim immigrant mother illustrates this point:

I don't think my children's being in public school and interacting with Christian or Jewish Americans has made them less committed to their faith. When I look at my children, I think they have more in them Islamically than I had in me when I was in my country, which was an Islamic country. I think it made my children stronger being involved with other beliefs and other nationalities.

Another parent, however, who does not see any evidence either that his children have experienced prejudicial treatment or that there is any visible lessening of their commitment to Islamic values, still expresses some concern:

I think that the one danger of interaction between my children and non-Muslim children is loss of Muslim identity. I think that integration into the non-Muslim environment has to be done with the sense that we have to preserve our Islamic identity. As long as the activity or whatever the children are doing is not in conflict with Islamic values or ways, it is permissible. But when we see it is going to be something against Islamic values, we try to teach our children that this is not correct to our beliefs and practices. They understand it and they are trying to cope with that.

This parent is trying to educate his children at an early age to the reality that their non-Muslim friends may be allowed to do things that they as Muslims will not, especially in their teen years. As the reminiscences of a young woman in her early twenties looking back on her school years indicate, Muslim youths associating with non-Muslim friends does present increasing problems as children move into the teenage years:

When I was younger I never had any problems with other children because I was Muslim, I was too young. I knew that I was Muslim and I knew we had a different religion, but I never got any trouble from kids or any questions because I was doing the same things they would do at that age. I think when you go to junior high and high school you start getting questions because maybe there are some events you can't go to at school—like proms—and then they ask you why, why can't you come to the dance with a guy?

Care of the Elderly

The Qur'an and traditions make it very clear that it is the responsibility of the members of the Muslim community to care for and respect the elderly. Parents in particular are held in esteem, and are to be provided for by children in their old age. One Qur'anic injunction is often quoted concerning this matter: "Your Lord has decreed that you worship none other than Him and that you show kindness to your parents. If one of them or both of them reach old age with you, do not grumble and do not rebuke them but speak to them kindly. And lower to them the wing of humility through mercy and say, 'My Lord! Have mercy on them as they raised me when I was small' " (S. 17:23–24).

Families in the Muslim world are generally large, both nuclear and extended, and traditionally family members have lived in proximity to one another. This has meant that there have been plenty of people available to look after those who are older. Women in the family have not normally worked outside the home, thus making it easy even for families with limited means to care for their elderly relatives. For those who can afford it, it is possible to hire someone at nominal cost to serve as a "nurse" for physically disabled older persons. Such nursing homes as do exist in most parts of the Islamic world are usually only for the indigent, with dreary surroundings and only minimal care provided. Putting one's parents in a nursing home in most Muslim countries, then, is generally unnecessary and considered tantamount to deserting them in their old age.

Muslims who emigrate to the United States, however, face a different set of conditions. Seldom are there members of the extended family living in the same area to help care for elderly relatives. Families must be ready to be mobile, both in searching for jobs and when they are transferred by the companies for whom they work. Often it is necessary for both husband and wife to work to support the family, leaving no one at home to care for older persons. This makes providing for elderly parents and family members difficult, especially if the family cannot afford some kind of household assistance such as a maid or nurse. At the same time, some of the nursing homes in the United States are far superior to anything in the Muslim world, providing not only twenty-four-hour care and nursing supervision, but good food, companionship, and pleasant surroundings.

The Qur'an stresses that parents must be well cared for in their older years, but it does not specify how or where that care should be provided. Although there is strong traditional and cultural pressure to care for the elderly in the home, it is certainly not "un-Islamic" to put physically disabled or senile parents into a nursing home that will give them excellent around-the-clock care. Unfortunately, the costs of such care may be prohibitive for some families. This, plus the pressures of custom to keep parents at home, leads to deep concern and ambivalence on the part of those trying to make responsible decisions about their elderly. The following quotations illustrate some of their concerns. From an imam:

> We always express our displeasure at the idea of nursing homes. Parents are not to be put in nursing homes, they are to be taken care of by their sons and daughters. The younger generation should respect their parents and keep them at home, give them company and the time and love and affection they need, rather than get rid of them by putting them in a nursing home . . . unless they are very sick and need hospitalization for an extended period, but not just because they happen to be old, that is not the Islamic way of life.

From another imam:

> It was very difficult for me, but I did have to put my father in a nursing home. He is unable to move, and my wife cannot move him. I wanted to give him a bath many times, and he would not let me. But at the nursing home, the nurses will move him and bathe him, and he is not used to that. We visit frequently.

From a young woman immigrant:

I personally could not put an elderly relative in a nursing home. But I can understand how Muslims do. I have seen women in this country going out and working eight-hour shifts, taking care of three kids, cooking dinner, doing the washing, and after a while also taking care of the person who is bedridden and needs constant attention. It gets to be . . . a lot of work. In cases where the persons doing the caring themselves begin to break down physically because of so much toil, then nursing homes may be the needed alternative. But personally, I just feel that a person in a nursing home is doomed to die, there is no reason to live. Whereas, if the older person is at home interacting with other people and family members, they would have something to look forward to tomorrow, be happier people. Plus there is all the guilt—parents might feel guilt because they are putting their children under a lot of tension, but the children on the other hand might feel a lot of guilt if they put their parents in a nursing home: "You took care of me when I wasn't able to do anything myself, and now it is my turn."

From an older first-generation woman:

I would never dream of putting an elderly relative in a nursing home. My mother was very ill and there were four daughters available to take care of her. Each week one of the daughters would pack a bag and go to stay with her . . . each week for two years. We would never put her in a nursing home. One of my brothers also lives close, and his wife helped out too. I do not believe, whether you are Muslim or not, you should put your parents in a nursing home—unless, God forbid, they are seriously ill and need the care of a professional person.

From a young immigrant male college student:

People put their elderly relatives in nursing homes in this country often because there is no strong relationship between family members. Back home, we see that all the family live together. For example, if there was something wrong with my grandparents, my father or I would help them, and the neighbors would help them. But here, people are often alone, they do not have family around. Also, the fact that there are no nursing homes back home like there are in this country is because people cannot afford them, so the older people must stay with relatives. I would put my father in a nursing home in this country only if he would be better off being cared for in such a home and if I could afford it. I might not be able to afford it.

From a young immigrant man:

Most of the immigrants I know would keep their elderly relatives at home. But they would look at it more from a family standpoint, not a religious standpoint. Religiously, I can't see any clear direction one way or the other, though you are always encouraged to take care of your parents.

From a first-generation middle-aged woman:

I am not totally against putting elderly relatives into nursing homes, but my conscience would bother me if I could take care of them and I didn't. We kept my mother-in-law at home until she was so senile that she had to have someone watching her twenty-four hours. But there were seven of us, seven people daily checked on that woman while she was at home. But she became so bad it was impossible to keep her at home. You couldn't bathe her because she was a heavy woman and would not cooperate in getting into the tub. She became worse than a child, because she was violent and more and more forgetful. You had to walk around after her all night long for fear she was going to run away in the middle of the night or fall down the stairs. It was hell, but it was done because you take care of your own as long as you are able to take care of them. But when they totally need professional care—and we even tried that, getting a woman who would watch over her, but it was just an impossible situation—and you cannot afford it or it does not work at home, then a nursing home may be needed. By the time we put my mother-in-law in a nursing home, she lasted there three years, but she didn't know what it was all about anyhow. And that bothered me even then, do you believe it?!

From a middle-aged immigrant man:

One can take a short-sighted view of putting an elderly relative in a nursing home, and that's under religious law that no, you never should. But Allah said that you should look after your elders and on the other side, He desires not hardship for you. To put an elderly relative in a nursing home simply from the point of view of avoiding them, Allah would forbid. Allah has mentioned again and again in the Qur'an that you should look after your relatives. But of course there are circumstances where they are going to need specialized medical care, and there are some technical facilities available only in nursing homes. When the care of elderly people requires special equipment or special nursing—then, of course, there is nothing wrong in nursing homes for an elderly relative.

Despite the ambivalent feelings expressed by many of those we interviewed, almost half of the respondents disagreed that "If it is too difficult or expensive to care for elderly parents at home, a good nursing facility should be found." As can be seen in Table 3.6A, slightly less than a fourth agreed, and slightly more than a fourth said that their feelings about it are mixed. Neither gender nor age seem to be related to opinions on nursing homes, nor is the factor of the amount of time spent in this country. Tables 3.6A through 3.6D, however, show that those born in the United States are slightly more likely to have favorable attitudes about the possibility of putting parents in nursing facilities if it is necessary. Muslims in upstate New York, where there is a large community of immigrant Pakistanis who interact fairly often with each other, are most likely to object to putting the elderly into such facilities, considering that, as recent arrivals, they have not yet had to face the problem.

One strong correlation seems to come between opinions on welfare

TABLE 3.6A   Statistics on Caring for Elderly Parents: Overall Responses (%)[a]

Response	Percentage
Agree	24
Mixed feelings	28
Disagree	48
	100

[a] Question: "If it is too difficult or expensive to care for elderly parents at home, should a good nursing care facility be found?"

TABLE 3.6B   Statistics on Caring for Elderly Parents: Response by Country of Birth (%)

	Country of Birth			
Response	United States	Syria, Lebanon	Other Muslim Countries	India or Pakistan
Agree	29	19	26	20
Mixed Feelings	33	24	26	25
Disagree	38	57	48	55
	100	100	100	100
	(117)	(74)	(85)	(64)

TABLE 3.6C   Statistics on Caring for Elderly Parents: Response by Area

	East Coast Area	Small City East Coast	Midwest Area
Percent who disagree	49	62	43

TABLE 3.6D   Statistics on Caring for Elderly Parents: Correlations with Selected Items and Statement in Table 3.6A

Factors	Correlations
Born in the United States	.10 (p ≤ .04 level)
Gender	n.s.
Age	n.s.
Eat dinner with *non*-Muslim Americans	n.s.
Eat dinner with Muslims (nonrelatives)	−.11 (p ≤ .03 level)
Belief that Islam should be observed strictly	n.s.
Frequency of mosque attendance	n.s.
Religious observance scale (frequency of attending Friday services, fasting during Ramadan, praying five times a day, reading the Qur'an, inviting another Muslim to join in prayer)	−.12 (p ≤ 0.02 level)
"If one needs financial assistance because they cannot work, they should be encouraged to apply for welfare."	+.24 (p ≤ .0001 level)

and on nursing homes; those who agree that anyone who cannot work should be encouraged to apply for welfare also tend to agree that a good nursing home is acceptable if care at home is too difficult. In general, the degree to which one participates in religious activities, holds conservative religious views, or attends the mosque does not appear to be related to opinions on nursing homes for the elderly. Those interviewed typically said that their mosques do not take a stand on the issue of nursing homes but rather leave it up to individuals to decide how best to care for their parents. As the following quotation suggests, this may also be because it is known that a number of mosque members have had to put relatives in such facilities: "Putting elderly relatives in nursing homes is frowned on in Islam in general, as well as in Arab societies wherever. But I don't think the mosque has ever come out with a strong stand, because I know some of them have relatives in nursing homes." Several of those interviewed questioned why Muslim communities do not work to develop nursing homes for Muslim elderly where they could be well cared for according to Islamic standards of food, dress, and religious observance, with special attention to the problems of being Muslim in the American culture:

I think we should be planning for a nursing home. We should build senior citizen homes for our Muslim families as they get older and have people take care of them in these homes, just like the Jews and every-body else does. I don't see why Muslims have to be different.

In my country, we are accustomed to have our grandparents with us all their lives. But in this country, this may not always be possible. Some service is badly needed here. If a center for caring for elderly were established and under Islamic supervision, it might be good. There is a nursing home nearby here, which is very beautiful and you would like to live there. If they put it under the auspices of the Islamic center, it would then be religiously oriented, and very good.

One of the mosques in this study is now trying to develop just such a facility for caring for elderly Muslims. The plans for the building are ready. Once the community locates the funds for the project, it will initiate the construction.

Celebrating and Coping with American Holidays

One of the realities of being Muslim in the American context is having to decide whether or not to celebrate holidays that are part of the American—and often specifically Christian—calendar. The Islamic new year, of course, is part of the lunar cycle and thus does not coincide with New Year's celebrations in the United States. Most Muslims interviewed, however, saw no reason not to observe the Western new year as long as it does not mean joining the celebrations "with a lot of alcohol and a lot of dancing and a lot of other non-Islamic behavior which goes on." Seeing the new year in with friends and family and perhaps having a family gathering on New Year's Day are activities many Muslims engage in.

A great many of those surveyed observe American holidays that stress family relationships, such as Valentine's Day and particularly Mother's Day and Father's Day. In large part this reflects an interest in participating in customs that are particularly American. As one man who regularly celebrates all three holidays explained, he does it "for their symbolic sense, because it is an American custom, and you are living in a Western environment, don't forget." And a Muslim woman of sixty-five reflects her appreciation of the chance to show a little family consideration: "Valentine's Day we exchange presents. My husband has never missed one Valentine's Day. He brings me home a big heart of chocolates, all these years and he has never missed." Several of those with whom we spoke applaud the idea of Mother's Day and Father's Day because the Qur'an enjoins respect and honor for one's parents. Others, however, object to their commercial nature and prefer to ignore them.

The Muslim community generally observes the two major national holidays, Memorial Day and the Fourth of July, much as other Americans observe them, by attending fireworks or parades, putting flowers on tombs, having picnics, and relaxing. Immigrant Muslims in our sample were more inclined to cite the symbolic purpose of the holidays as reason to observe them than were Muslims born in this country, as in this reflection on Memorial Day:

> Memorial Day is a good holiday. The people died for [the] causes of the country, even members of the family, you have a special day to do something, to pray for them, or to go to the cemetery and just remember, you know, the loved one you lost.

Like many other Americans, first-generation Muslims tend to describe it as an occasion for taking a holiday and getting together with family and friends.

> Memorial Day is a big day because the whole clan gets together. We tell everybody, OK, we are having a picnic at such and such a time, here is where it is, bring your food and come on! If they show up, fine, and if they don't, fine. We just have a ball. I think families should stick together. If you don't have a family, you don't have anything.

Similarly, Muslims born in this country are more likely to see the Fourth of July as an opportunity for picnics and fireworks, while more recent immigrants stress the symbolic value of the holiday as a time in which to identify as Americans.

> I celebrate Memorial Day and July Fourth. Being an American I think it is befitting to celebrate.

> The reason I celebrate July Fourth is that I want to be like other Americans. . . . I am living here, I make my living in this country, and I am with everybody who is for freedom.

Almost all Muslim parents and young adults interviewed said that their children celebrate Halloween with the other children in the neighborhood, dressing up in costumes and going door to door trick or treating. Most of the adults report gladly handing out candy and other goodies to the young children who come to their doorsteps on Halloween. One immigrant Muslim woman said that they used to have Halloween parties for the children in the social hall of the mosque until one member complained that it was inappropriate both for a mosque and for Muslims:

We used to celebrate Halloween in the mosque at one time. We had Halloween parties until somebody came and said Halloween was a Christian custom, so they did not have them anymore. I don't believe Halloween is a Christian custom. I don't think it is a Christian custom for a child to dress up and go door to door and ask for candy!

Generally those interviewed on the subject of Halloween, however, reported in ways similar to this immigrant Muslim man:

Halloween is fun for the kids. . . . I always liked Halloween. I love children and that is an occasion to show those children that we care about them. It is good, nothing wrong with that. If it is done in a light manner, it is great!

Most of those we talked to also celebrate Thanksgiving with turkey and trimmings at gatherings of family and friends. A few who think of Thanksgiving as a "Christian holiday" still celebrate it as a social and family occasion. Most, however, seem to feel that Thanksgiving is a religious as well as a social occasion, it is an American custom that transcends individual religions and can be used as a time for those of all religions to give thanks to God.

We do celebrate Thanksgiving. . . . I think Muslims view Thanksgiving as a general holiday for people all around the world, but I think it is practiced more widely here in America. It was started historically by the Pilgrims as offering their thanks to God for the blessing He gave them. So it is not in conflict with Islam.

I think Thanksgiving is celebrated among the Arabs living here just like any other Americans. Muslim Arab Americans celebrate Thanksgiving, they know what it is for. They know the reason for Thanksgiving is the act of giving thanks to God for the plenty that has been given to us.

Of all the widely celebrated holidays in America, Christmas seems to provide the greatest dilemma for Muslim families. Although it is clearly a Christian holiday, it now has become a very secular social and commercial holiday as well. Even the religious aspect of the occasion is not irrelevant to Muslims who recognize Jesus as a very important prophet (though not the Son of God or a divine being) whose birthday should be respected. However, a great deal of confusion and divided opinion was evidenced in this sample of Muslims in America over the degree to which they should celebrate Christmas, if at all, even as a secular holiday. Several Muslim men interviewed indicated that they recognize Christmas to some degree because their wives or mothers are Christian:

My wife is Christian-American. I don't want to celebrate Christmas but she thinks we should have some get-together with family. I don't see anything wrong in that.

We celebrate Christmas because my mother is Christian and she is very, very understanding in celebrating Eids with us. So we celebrate Christmas with her.

Some of the more recently arrived immigrant Muslims celebrate Christmas to the extent of having a tree and exchanging presents and cards with family members and both Muslim and Christian friends. They do so mainly because they want to be part of American society and see Christmas more an as American holiday than a strictly religious one.

We celebrate Christmas for two reasons. It is important to get involved with American society, and if you don't celebrate Christmas and if you don't celebrate Thanksgiving, to me really you are telling those people you are not part of American society, you are something else. How can you be effective, how can you affect those people if they think that you are completely different? You cannot. First of all you have to let them understand that you are just like them. OK, they are not better than you. Then you can do your own thing, that is fine. So you have to celebrate Christmas, which is very important to them. The second reason is that we do believe in Jesus. We don't believe that he was a god, but we do believe he was a prophet.

Many of those interviewed said that they try to observe at least some of the Christmas customs when their children are young, such as exchanging gifts and hanging stockings for Santa Claus, but that they gradually drop these practices as the children grow old enough to understand the distinction between Christian and Muslim holidays. Some Muslim parents do not celebrate Christmas in any fashion and try to explain to their very young children that this is not a Muslim holiday, with mixed results. The following quotes illustrate some of these experiences of Muslim parents and their children in the Christmas season:

When I was growing up, my mother would see that we had presents from Santa Claus. But we didn't do anything with the religious part. I think Santa Claus is a little dream that each child should have.

We did not celebrate Christmas. We were told, which was very hard to understand, that Christmas was just for other people. After a while you get to the point where you understand it, but it is hard—to see the other kids getting toys and things like that. In those days it was even harder because there weren't that many Muslims around.

Years ago, when we were between six and ten and so on, you were exposed to Christmas at school. Everybody is bragging about it—"I am going to get a G.I. Joe or a train set." You go home and say, "Ma, what is this holiday?" One of your parents will sit down and explain to you that this is not our holiday. . . . We always got a tree though, when we were kids, but as we have grown up, you know, just like any other day.

We used to have a Christmas tree every year until my dad died. We understand that this wasn't the Muslim religion, it was just for the fun of it that we did it. When we were younger we used to believe in Santa and everything, and we kept on believing it until we were old enough to understand. Then my mom said, "There is no Santa in our religion, this isn't our religion. It is just so you won't feel different from all the other kids. . . . We can have a tree every year and exchange presents and have a good time—as long as you know that this isn't part of our religion, not a holiday for our religion." When some people (other Muslims) would say, "Shame on you," my mom would say, "Well we just have it for the fun of it." It is just something we got used to doing.

For two years I did have a Christmas tree and my son and daughter exchanged presents with our neighbors, but now that my son and daughter are older, we don't have it anymore because they understand why.

We don't celebrate Christmas now. When we were kids, it was funny. My parents used to buy us presents and stuff, but we never had a Christmas tree. One day it really got to my brother and me that we never had a tree. So it was a few days after Christmas and people were throwing out trees, and my brother and I were walking home from school and we found this big Christmas tree. We lugged it all the way home and we brought it into the house and we decorated it and everything. My father came home and he saw this thing, and he said, "Don't you ever do that again!"

When we came to this country in 1973, one of my daughters was three years old. When she was four years old, that was the first Christmas for her. In our neighborhood there were no other Muslims. She was playing in other kid's houses and she saw Christmas lights and all sorts of things there. She asked me why our holiday doesn't have Christmas trees and lights. I tried to make her understand right there, saying, "Now look, they are Christians. They have their religion and they should celebrate it. We have our religion and we have our celebration at that time." From then on and until today, every Eid, even if sometimes I can't afford it, I buy each of my children a gift.

One of the questions put to respondents in this survey was whether or not they agreed that "it is all right to put up a Christmas tree or other decorations in December." Opinions in the total sample were divided: 33 percent agreed, 30 percent said that their feelings are mixed and 37 percent disagreed. Among those born outside the United States, 25 percent of the Lebanese, 18 percent of those from other Arab countries (e.g., Egypt, Saudi Arabia, Jordan, Yemen, etc.), and 12 percent of Pakistanis favored putting up a tree. More in the Midwest (45 percent) think such a custom is acceptable, due in large part to the high concentration of American-born Muslims and those of Lebanese extraction in that area. Fewer are so inclined in the East Coast area (25 percent), and only 6 percent of those from upstate New York, a community represented mainly by Pakistanis (see Table 3.7), agree. In general those Muslims who report frequent social interactions with Christians, such as sharing meals, are much more likely to favor having a Christmas tree than those who do not. And those who are stricter in observance of Islamic rites such as attendance at the mosque, praying five times daily, reading the Qur'an, and fasting during Ramadan are more likely than others to object to Muslims having a Christmas tree.

Pets

One of the aspects of American culture that is often difficult for Muslims to understand is Americans' enthusiasm for pets, especially dogs and cats. In many parts of the Islamic world dogs serve such purposes as protection and herding cattle but are never allowed inside the house because they are considered unclean and even defiling. There was some disagreement among the Muslims interviewed as to whether it is un-Islamic to have a dog live inside a house or apartment. Most were

TABLE 3.7   Tau B Correlation between Birthplace and Approval of Muslims Having Christmas Trees for Each Area

Place of Birth	Responses According to Place of Residence (%)[a]		
	East Coast Area	Upstate New York	Midwest
United States	54 (of 13)	33 (of 6)	54 (of 94)
Lebanon	25 (of 12)	0 (of 0)	41 (of 59)
Other Arab country	18 (of 33)	5 (of 21)	28 (of 25)
Pakistan/India	12 (of 17)	3 (of 59)	0 (of 3)
	Tau B = .32 significant to .0008 $N = 65$	Tau B = − 0.8 n.s. $N = 86$	Tau B = .18 significant to .003 $N = 181$

[a] Responses are to the statement: "It is all right to put up a Christmas tree or other decoration in December."

of the opinion that "the Holy Prophet has forbidden dogs inside the house" or that the "only kind of dog Islam allows is hunting dogs." One man said that he allows them "as watch dogs outside my home; I don't let them in, but they are my pets, I treat them good, which is all right for a Muslim." Some current Islamic literature suggests that the Prophet Muhammad discussed the question of hygiene and worms, which one of our respondents interpreted as the caution of the Prophet that dogs are likely to spread germs, which might even violate the area of the house used for prayer. One felt that not only did Muhammad prohibit dogs in the house because they are unclean, but that "the presence of dogs in the house stops the angels from being present in the home." Another felt that dogs are so unclean that if "the dog touches your clothes, you cannot pray in the same clothing. If one has to pray five times a day, one cannot keep on changing, you know."

A number of other Muslims interviewed said that they personally have no objection to a Muslim or anyone else keeping a dog inside the home as a pet but that they themselves simply do not like dogs inside for reasons of personal preference rather than religion. Others felt that dogs are not really banned in the Qur'an but just disapproved of, and that perhaps that was more relevant for the time the Qur'an was revealed or even now in Third World countries than it is in the United States. Dogs are cleaner in this country, and these respondents saw no reason they or other Muslims should not have one if they so choose. Many Muslims, they said, in fact do have dogs. More, however, said that they know of Muslims keeping cats as pets and that they themselves have less objection to cats because they are cleaner than dogs.

In the survey, 27 percent agreed that it is "all right to keep a dog as a pet," 22 percent said that their feelings are mixed, and 50 percent disagreed that this is either allowed or desirable. As with approval of Christmas trees for Muslims, those who approve of having dogs as pets are more likely to have been born in this country, to believe that Islam need not be observed strictly, and to eat fairly frequently with non-Muslim Americans. Frequency of mosque attendance, however, was not related to opinions on whether one should keep dogs as pets, perhaps because some mosques reportedly are more liberal on the subject than others. Muslims in the Midwest are considerably more likely to agree that it is acceptable to keep a dog as a pet (40 percent), compared with 7 percent on the East Coast and 12 percent in upstate New York. The largest percentage of those who actively disapproved of keeping dogs was in the New York area (74 percent), compared with 68 percent on the East Coast area and 36 percent in the Midwest.

CHAPTER 4

Islamic Laws, Muslim Praxis, and American Culture

Islamic law is designed to give specific guidance to Muslims for everything from the particulars of religious observance to some of the most mundane features of everyday life. It is based first on the legislation for the community detailed in the Qur'an. For guidance in areas where the Qur'an has no specific regulations the legists of Islam turned next to the traditions of what the Prophet himself said and did (the *hadith*), to the common consensus of the community, and to analogical reasoning. On the basis of these components, the structure of the law (shari'a) was established, with only minor differences among the major schools.

In theory the shari'a is meant to apply to all times and all situations. As many Islamic countries have come to terms with forces of Westernization and modernization in this century, however, they have in varying degrees made some modifications in the application of Islamic law. The issue of adaptation of the law is extremely complex and much too detailed to summarize here. It is obvious that some Muslim countries, such as Turkey, have gone far in adopting Western legal formulations in place of the shari'a while others, perhaps most notably Saudi Arabia, attempt to retain the shari'a as pristinely as possible. The current rising tide of Islamic conservatism, of course, encourages a return to the essentials of Muslim law.

As has been observed earlier, there is a wide range of responses among Muslims in the United States to the question of how strictly Islamic law should be observed in this country and whether or not it should be interpreted to fit the realities of this culture. In this chapter we will look at some of the specific problems raised when various elements of the shari'a are applied in the American context, and the degree to which Muslims in our sample feel that Islamic law should be observed or modified in varying circumstances.

Economics, Welfare, and Occupations

Economics have been a key factor in Muslim immigration to this country from the beginning. One of the primary reasons for coming here has been the hope of gaining lucrative employment and enjoying better economic circumstances than might have been possible in the home country. Almost unavoidably, then, many Muslims have had to modify application of the specifics of Islamic law as they have struggled to survive economically in the United States. It may well be that as the number of Muslims here grows, as American Muslims' consciousness of Islamic law increases, and as new and more conservative immigrants urge the community to stricter observance, there will be a more concerted effort on the part of many Muslims living in this country to try to reconcile the law with the exigencies of American culture.

Usury, Loans, and Interest

One of the issues that receives a great deal of attention both in sermons and in adult education discussion groups, according to imams and other mosque leaders, is that of paying and receiving interest. Islamic law technically forbids the earning of interest on loans on the grounds that it is usury. Most of those we interviewed agreed that in principle this prohibition should be observed, especially in the case of individuals borrowing or lending money to each other, but that it is far more difficult to do in terms of the American banking system. The question then becomes how to avoid accepting interest earned on a savings account, or paying interest on a mortgage or on items bought for credit.

Some feel that the Islamic injunction against usury means only that one should not pay or collect unreasonable interest, that is, that one should not engage in loan-sharking but that a fair interest rate is acceptable. Others believe that although the Qur'anic injunction does in fact apply to all forms of taking and receiving interest on loans, this is meant for Islamic countries and is not intended to make life impossible for good Muslims in a country where they are a small minority and the economic and commercial institutions do not operate in accordance with Islamic law. The following quotations from Muslims interviewed at each of the sites included in the study illustrate this point:

> There are two school of thought on interest. One school says that interest loans are completely forbidden. Another school says interest is all

right as long as it is within acceptable percentages. I believe it is acceptable, for example, to take our interest loans from American banks. We
talk about it a great deal at the mosque. The imam says that interest is
forbidden.

I don't believe that anyone here would collect interest on a personal loan
made to others. As a matter of fact, I don't believe any Muslim would
do that. . . . But as for paying interest on a loan . . . well, we had some
discussion on this earlier and we decided we are in a totally different
country that is not Islamic. We know that Allah said that interest is
haram and that we should not partake in that, but we are in a country
whereby if we don't, then the Muslims will be left behind. So many times
we have Muslims who are trying to buy a home, trying to get into
business, trying to compete with the business man in this country. Often
times we do have to take loans and we do have to pay interest on them. I
don't believe Allah will hold that against us. We are not the one making
the interest on that loan. It is those that have set up this system, we are
the victims of this system.

The question of taking out bank loans that require interest becomes
especially delicate when the issue is whether or not to seek a loan to
finance the construction of a mosque. One mosque we studied decided
to do so, and its members are still wondering if what they did was
wrong. Another mosque, as described earlier, took far longer to build
than would have been the case had they taken out a loan rather than
wait until they had saved all the money needed to begin construction.

Most Muslims opt to put their own money into American banks,
which automatically give interest on many accounts. The question then
becomes, should Muslims refuse to accept interest on their own money
which is held and lent out by the bank? As illustrated in the following
passages, most of those we interviewed felt that not to accept the
interest the bank collected for them was silly, though many knew of
other Muslims in the United States who do not:

Why should I not collect interest? I mean I put that money in the bank.
The bank then turns around and loans it to somebody else, and gives you
5 or 6 percent, and makes about 20 or 25 percent on everybody's money
for itself. Why shouldn't I have some of that?! Well, the Yemenis they
don't believe they should collect any interest, so they put their money in
the bank without interest. The bank takes it all. . . . Isn't that crazy?! If
you don't want that interest money, take it and give it to somebody who
needs it more than the bank needs it. That is the way I look at it.

The imam is always stressing that we ought not to take interest, it is
haram. Not taking interest on a loan you make to another Muslim, that

part I go along with. If I lend you money and you are a Muslim, I am going to get it back from you, but minus the interest. That is O.K. But if a stranger wants to borrow money from me, thousands of dollars, why shouldn't I take interest? That's the part I don't agree with.

If this were a Muslim society, not taking interest would be fine. If there is no Islamic banking system, you have to use the banking system you have. If you want to be extreme but not practical, you can just have a checking account and no savings account. A lot of Muslims don't have savings accounts here so that they will not receive interest—they keep all their money in checking accounts. But today they have checking accounts that give you interest . . . so it can all end up the same way. . . . Anyway, Islam is a practical religion. . . . It is supposed to give you comfort, not strain.

Some therefore argue against Muslims not taking interest on the grounds that the bank would get the money anyway. Others go even further than simply asking why the banks rather than the Muslims themselves should benefit from interest accrued on Muslim accounts, accusing banks of giving uncollected interest money on Muslim accounts to other religious groups:

You deposit your money in the bank, and if you don't collect interest from the bank, the bank takes it and gives it to the National Council of Churches in New York; they give it to them.

Dilemma on the taking of interest. . . . Collecting interest on loans made to others is strictly forbidden; no Muslim should collect interest from any other Muslim. . . . But if we do not take interest on accounts in banks, it will all go into the Jewish pocket. . . . Most of the financial institutions in America are worldwide and under ownership of Jews, who are contributing towards financing the Israelis. If you leave interest in the bank, you are putting interest into their pocket, which is all going into Israeli hands.

As a way of getting around the interest dilemma, one mosque instituted a small bank for members in which any interest collected was not given back to individuals who deposited it but instead put into a fund to help needy members of the mosque. This is unusual, however, and it is clear that most of those we surveyed used the American banking system, and in most cases do invest in savings accounts, often justifying the acceptance of interest on the grounds that the money accounts have earned will be spent as they wish it to be.

About half of those we polled agreed that "given the American economic system, it is all right to collect interest on money deposited in a bank or to pay interest on a loan and/or buy on credit." Only 18 percent disagreed, and the remaining third said they are ambivalent in their feelings about the interest issue. In two of the three major sites—the East Coast area and especially the Midwest—a majority agreed with the statement, and fewer than 15 percent in either site disagreed. Upstate New York Muslims, however, are divided almost equally into thirds among those who agree, disagree, and are ambivalent. Muslims born in this country are significantly more likely to feel that it is acceptable to collect interest on money deposited in their bank accounts and to buy on credit than those who are immigrants. However, the longer immigrants live in the United States, the more likely they are to agree that it is all right to collect interest on bank accounts and to buy on credit.

Neither sex nor education seem to bear on responses to this question, but the larger one's income (and the larger, therefore, the bank accounts and the possibility of significant interest accruing), the more likely one is to believe that accepting interest is all right. (This last relationship, however, though statistically significant, is not particularly strong; this suggests that it would not hold if the person with higher income, for example, had other characteristics.) Disagreement that it is acceptable to collect interest or to buy on credit is likely to come from those who favor strict religious observance such as fasting during Ramadan, praying five times a day, reading the Qur'an, and attending Friday noon services, although not necessarily those who attend the mosque frequently. Mosques themselves are often divided in the opinions expressed by mosque leaders on the appropriateness of receiving interest and taking out loans under any circumstances.

Muslims who socialize at the dinner hour with other Muslims outside their immediate families are neither more nor less likely to refuse to accept interest or to take out loans on which they must pay interest. However, the more frequently Muslims eat with non-Muslims, the more likely they are to believe that putting money in interest-bearing accounts and collecting this interest themselves makes good economic sense, as does taking out loans and buying on credit, in which case interest must be paid.

Welfare

Although very few Muslims in this study have incomes below the poverty level, and many are financially very secure, nearly three fifths said that they agree one should be encouraged to apply for welfare if he or she cannot find employment and needs financial assistance. Although a third described themselves as ambivalent on this issue, only a very small minority actually disagreed. Previous strong predictors—such as whether Muslims are born in America, whether they believe Islam should be strictly observed, mosque attendance, frequency of prayer, and frequency of dining with non-Muslim Americans—seem to have no relationship to an acceptance of welfare. A good reason for this is that accepting financial assistance in times of need is not contrary to Islamic codes. As was indicated earlier, the giving of *zakat* monies to the indigent is an integral and requisite part of Islam, whether or not a particular government in power has a welfare system. Even in this country, two thirds of the Muslims surveyed report "personally contributing *zakat* monies to impoverished Muslims directly."

At the same time, Muslims are opposed to anyone accepting welfare who does not need it. Some of the ambivalence about accepting welfare expressed by about a third of those we surveyed comes from the feeling that it is better to be self-sufficient, and that the availability of relatively easy welfare payment might undercut the motivation of some to be economically independent. The following comments are illustrative:

> If someone is unemployed, he should have the basic fulfilling of his needs. I really do not have any Islamic objection to food stamps or benefits from the social security, if he doesn't have any employment. Islam is really a religion which provides for the basic needs of its followers and is what you would call socialistic, as far as the economic policies and the welfare policies are concerned. It provides for the basic needs through the collection of *zakat*. Most of the Muslims in the Western countries have been paying taxes. So every Muslim who is living in the country is entitled to the social security and other basic needs.

> Nothing wrong with getting welfare. It is a matter of misuse—that is what is wrong. If you are out of work and you cannot find a job, you will have to collect unemployment checks. If you are truly poor and you cannot find a means of subsistence, you can take from the welfare. This is what is equal in Islam to having *zakat,* which will be collected and distributed to the poor. So it is exactly a welfare system in the Arab countries, but it is not called welfare, it is called *zakat,* the share of the poor.

> If you need welfare, food stamps or unemployment—then take it. I am not saying cheat the government. If you honestly do not need it, then you have no right to it. I personally would not take it unless I was in desperate need, then I would.

> Islam encourages hard work, encourages thrift, encourages management. Islam also encourages those who can help others who are at a

disadvantage. Now, if a Muslim owing to forces beyond his control is in need of help, then Islam provides for that help. The Islamic center here should work toward providing that help. If he is in genuine and dire need of help, then I would have no objection to this accepting welfare.

Those who are opposed to encouraging persons to apply for welfare if they cannot find work are probably much like the following young Muslim man in disliking charity of any sort:

> I am totally against accepting welfare, food stamps, and unemployment compensation. This is my own opinion. Some people accept charity, I will not accept [any]. I do not believe God created rich people and poor people, people are the ones who devised the system. Poor people have to wait for charity from the rich people. They say that the system is "dignifying." It is most indignifying to wait for charity from a rich man. I am against that. I have disagreements with religions, all of them—Christianity, Judaism, Islam—about the charity.

Appropriate Occupations for Muslims

Not all occupations are considered by strict Muslims to be appropriate ways for followers of Islam to earn their living. For example, some feel that banking is not an occupation Muslims should enter because it involves making loans for which interest is charged and paying interest to those who have bank accounts, as is shown in the comment below:

> No, we should not take jobs in a bank because money is loaned and there is interest on money. Where interest is involved we shouldn't be, according to our religion.

Most of those interviewed, however, indicated that working in a bank is fine for Muslims as long as they are tellers or work in positions that do not require handling loan transactions.

A number of Muslims indicated that they believe there is no job a Muslim should not take (providing it is legal according to the laws of the country) if he or she needs the money and cannot get other work. One exception that many make to this kind of generalization is bartending or owning or clerking in a liquor store because of the injunction against the consumption of alcohol and being around those who do.

> The only occupation I know about the Islamic center taking a stand on is bartending. My personal view is too that we should not encourage men even taking a part-time job in bartending.

Liquor is something *haram,* something you shouldn't even touch. I should abstain from this thing. I should not offer this even to a non-believer. I should not be a bartender.

However, a number of Muslims feel that, although it is far preferable to enter almost any occupation other than that of selling or serving liquor, even this alternative is preferable to starving or going on welfare. For example,

Sometimes you have to do whatever it is to feed your family. I don't think there should be any restriction. Some people say, "Well, you can't sell alcohol." But if it was me and it was the difference between feeding my family and selling alcohol, well I would. I wouldn't let my family or friends starve because I couldn't raise some kind of money somehow.

In the world we live in you have to do anything you can to earn a living. Even bartending.

A number of Muslims in the Midwest do own bars and liquor stores and enjoy doing so. Although they know it is against Islamic codes to sell or serve liquor, they seem to feel that it is much less serious than drinking it themselves, and they point to the good living that they and other Muslims who are also in this business make:

At our mosque we never talk about the kinds of jobs you can't have because of the religion. Many of the Muslims in this country . . . have liquor stores and bars . . . they are good people, Muslims, and they go to the mosque and they pray and all that. But they look at it as how they are making their livelihood. The don't drink it but they are selling it— they don't feel it is wrong. Religiously of course it would be wrong— serving it would be just like drinking it.

From a Muslim immigrant who has owned and operated liquor stores and bars in the United States for more than twenty years:

Myself, I know as a Muslim you are not supposed to serve or drink or be in the bar business. A Muslim shouldn't do those things. But I never stopped to think I shouldn't do that when I was working.

From a young man under thirty, born in this country of immigrant parents:

I used to have a bar. The work was satisfying. The money was good, the hours short. You are your own boss, you don't have to answer to anyone else. I was happy at that time. . . . It is *haram* in Islam they say to have liquor in your store, and selling it is worse that having it and drinking it, but it is a living. . . . I only sold out because I was offered about one thousand dollars more than I had paid for it.

A majority of the Muslims surveyed disagreed, however, that the occupation of bartending is acceptable for Muslims. In response to the statement "As long as a Muslim does not drink, it is all right for him to own a bar or be a bartender," fully 62 percent disagreed, with 17 percent reporting mixed feelings, and 21 percent of the total sample agreeing. It is only in the Midwest that a majority of Muslims who responded approve of a Muslim owning a bar; that is, while fully 85 percent of those on the East Coast and 86 percent of those in upstate New York disagree, only 41 percent of those in the Midwest disagree.

Muslims surveyed are significantly more likely to believe it is acceptable to own a bar if they have been born in America (although immigrants who have been in this country a long time are not more likely to endorse this as an occupation). The lower the educational level, the more likely Muslims are to feel bartending is acceptable, possibly because they see this as a way of upward economic mobility that their level of education would not preclude. Those who believe Islam should be strictly observed and who engage often in religious activity are very unlikely to endorse a Muslim owning a bar or serving liquor as an occupation. Frequency of mosque attendance is only slightly related to disapproval of this kind of job, suggesting, as some of the quotations indicate, that a number of frequent mosque attenders may be in the liquor business or have relatives and friends who are.

Dining with non-Muslim Americans seems to be related positively to belief that it is all right for Muslims to own a bar as long as they themselves do not drink. Part of this may be that some Muslim business people who entertain American business and professional people offer them alcohol, though they may not mix the drinks themselves. This is illustrated in the comments from the East Coast area and from upstate New York:

We were in business so we had to have liquor in our house. I never learned to mix a drink in my life and I never touched a drink in my life, and neither did my husband. We had friends that came in and business acquaintances who we entertained in our home. We would put the liquor and mixes out, and say, "There it is. Do what you want with it." That is as far as it went.

In our family ten years ago we used to serve liquor to our American guests. We would just put it on the table and leave it there for them to help themselves. But we stopped doing this as a result of comments made by my older daughter once—that when we don't drink, why do we serve drinks? . . . Since that time we have totally stopped serving drinks in our household.

Whether or not a Muslim serves alcohol to non-Muslim friends, it may be difficult for those who have friends who drink to oppose completely the idea of Muslims owning liquor stores or bars. The influence of dining frequently with Americans who are not Muslim probably has the most impact on Muslims in the East Coast and upstate New York areas; Muslims in the Midwest (where there is a higher proportion who eat frequently with non-Muslims anyway) do not seem much affected by what their non-Muslim friends do on this score, perhaps because a significant number of Muslims in this area are in the liquor business themselves. Although two thirds of the Muslims surveyed said that they never drink alcohol, those that do on occasion are much more likely to feel that the liquor business is appropriate for a Muslim. (More attention will be given to Muslims' own attitudes toward drinking a little later in this chapter.)

Muslims also serve as owners of restaurants, cooks, and waiters in eating places. This may pose problems insofar as pork or pork products, forbidden to Muslims, are served in such establishments. Several expressed personal distaste for taking any job that involved cooking or serving pork to others, as illustrated in the comments of one young Muslim woman:

> I think being a waitress is fun, but then I am not serving drinks. Also, I couldn't work in a place that serves pork, it would turn me off. I can't stand to touch the stuff.

Occupations for Women

Objection to certain occupations is sometimes even more stringent for women. For example, many Muslims object to a woman serving drinks as a cocktail waitress, in part because of the prohibition against having anything to do with alcohol, but also because a woman in this kind of work might have to wear indiscreet clothing and be the object of suggestive remarks from men. In fact, for some Muslims the latter may be a more important reason for women not to be cocktail waitresses than the fact that they serve alcoholic drinks. Muslim women do not differ much as a group from men in their opinions on this issue, as illustrated in the comments of these two women:

A Muslim woman has to take whatever she needs as long as she doesn't forget her religion and what it has taught her to do. What she does . . . for her living, unless it is something really bad, to me, it is not a big thing. Working in a bank is okay with me as long as you are properly dressed and you know what you are doing, and you are not really exposing yourself. . . . Serving liquor—that depends on where you are working. If she is not drinking and it is for her living to do this, I don't think there is any problem . . . if it is a restaurant. . . . But dress . . . if you are working as a waitress, you have to dress properly.

Women may certainly not become bartenders! . . . Because of the fact that there is a risk of being thrown into situations where she might not be able to control the others, you know—flirting with her, passing rude remarks, anything like that. She should certainly pursue an occupation where she can be mostly with women.

Most of the Muslims in this sample agreed that "a wife should work outside the home if she wishes" (73 percent), but there was a much greater range of response to the question of whether or not "a wife should work outside the home only in case of severe financial need." (There was 33 percent agreement, 48 percent disagreement, and 19 percent mixed feelings.) The fact that nearly half of the sample clearly disagreed that women should work only if there is severe financial need indicates a fairly flexible stance. Those who are more religiously conservative are more likely to agree that only in cases of extreme financial stress should women be employed outside the home. Muslims born in the United States are most open to women working, and women overall are slightly more open to the possibility than are men (see Table 4.1). Immigrant men, however, differ more from first-generation American men on this issue than they do from immigrant Muslim women.

The Muslim women respondents do differ in this sample on one significant variable—whether or not they themselves work outside the home (see Table 4.2). Professionals, both men and women, appear to

TABLE 4.1   Relationship Between Opinions on Women Working and Birth in the United States (Controlling for Gender)

	Percent Who Disagree with Statement[a]	
Born in United States	Men	Women
Yes	62 (of 39)	62 (of 77)
No	35 (of 116)	46 (of 108)

[a] "Women should work outside the home only in cases of severe financial need."

TABLE 4.2   Relationship Between Opinions on Women Working and
Occupation (Controlling for Gender)

	Percent Who Disagree with Statement[a]	
Occupation	Men	Women
Professional	57 (of 65)	83 (of 29)
Other occupations	32 (of 44)	59 (of 39)
Student	27 (of 30)	56 (of 36)
Retired (men)	50 (of 6)	
Housewife		395 (of 65)
	Tau B = −.15	Tau B = −0.25
	significant to .03	significant to .0001
	N = 145	N = 169

[a] "Women should work outside the home only in cases of severe financial need."

be more open to women working outside the home for other than
financial need. The relationship is stronger for women than for men,
however, and women who work are more likely than men who work in
both the professional and nonprofessional categories to disagree that
women should work outside the home only if they badly need the
money. (For example, 57 percent of the professional men disagree
compared with 83 percent of the professional women, and 32 percent
of the men in other occupations disagree compared with 59 percent of
the women in nonprofessional occupations.)

Although no survey question was asked regarding what kinds of
occupations women should be in, the fact that Muslims who agree that
women should not work outside the home unless it is financially necessary were also quite likely to be those with lower incomes suggests that
the occupations the more conservative Muslims see as appropriate for
women are probably more in the service and support area than in the
professions and sciences. Further, those who agree that women should
work outside the home only if necessary also typically believe that
"Muslim women should not go out on the streets unless their hair and
arms are covered and their skirts are well below their knees." This
association suggests that though few Muslims in our study would be
opposed to a woman working if the income she could produce is really
needed by her family, half of them would feel comfortable about it
only if the woman worked in ways and in environments considered
appropriate and safe for women. The following quotations further clar-
ify this, especially stressing the belief that an appropriate woman's

occupation is one in which she has little or no contact with men. The first comes from a young woman immigrant:

> We were having our discussions in the mosque school with the girls. They said there were certain jobs girls should not take. In one of the classes a girl asked if she could go and serve in the army. The answer to that was "No," because they would be involved with men. Maybe they could get jobs like teaching or nursing—but of course that was another problem. Even if you went and got a job nursing in the country—you become a nurse in any hospital, and you would be in touch with men. Also, in teaching, if you become a teacher you might have to go teach in colleges and teach men. They were saying that if you become a teacher, you should teach in an all girls' school or if you become a nurse, go to a hospital where there are all women. So, this is another rigid way of saying either do it this way or you go to hell. So this made a lot of the young girls leave the mosque.

> I would not want my daughters to choose just any career. I would try to persuade her that she should go in to teach, for instance, something that will enable her to teach in a girls' school, or something which will enable her to be a doctor in a women's hospital. In other words, I would try to get my daughter not to work where she has to work in a mixed environment, men and women together.

As indicated, there is likely to be a relaxing of this attitude toward women's work with each generation born in America, and with the length of time spent in this country, especially if individuals socialize with non-Muslims and if these non-Muslims are professionals. More will be said in the next chapter about the role of women in Islam and about their particular circumstances in this country.

Inheritance and Wills

Islamic law determines the range of inheritance for all members of the family. Legal scholars have worked out intricate charts determining the percentage of wealth various heirs are to receive. One is not allowed to disinherit legal heirs, which includes parents. According to Muslim law one can dispose of only one third of one's goods and property through a will. Technically, therefore, it is unnecessary to make a will except to specify small bequests. Under the Islamic system the daughter inherits half of what goes to a son, precisely because of the Qur'anic stipulation that it is a man's responsibility to provide for the financial upkeep of the women in his family. A woman, on the other hand, is free to dispose of her financial resources as she sees fit.

In the United States the situation is naturally somewhat different. If a man dies intestate, his wife has the right to claim a far larger share than she would be able to in a Muslim country. It is also possible for a husband to will to his wife a much larger share of his estate than is technically allowed under Islamic law. Data from our survey indicate that even those Muslims in this country who identify themselves as observing Islam in a strict manner—that is, those who are likely to believe that "Islamic inheritance laws should be followed in the United States"—are as likely as more liberal Muslims to believe that "it is a wise thing for a Muslim to write a will in the United States." They reason that writing a will is one way to ensure that Islamic laws concerning inheritance are carried out after one's own death.

Many Muslims born in the United States, as well as those who have lived here for a long time, either have little awareness of or have given little thought to the Islamic legal position in regard to inheritance. This may be because of a tacit acceptance of and trust in the justice of the American legal system, perhaps because their holdings are not substantial enough to make a sizable inheritance, or out of a reluctance to leave more to the male children than to the female children in this culture.

Thus, while only a little over half of those surveyed felt that Islamic laws of inheritance should be followed in this country, over four fifths agreed that it is a good idea for a Muslim to write a will here. Immigrant Muslims are far more likely to believe that Islamic inheritance laws should be followed in the United States than those born here, and the longer one stays in this country the less sure he or she tends to be about the necessity of following these laws. Table 4.3 indicates that those born outside the United States are twice as likely as those born here to believe that inheritance laws should hold in this context; it also illustrates that among second-generation Muslims there appears to be more mixed feelings than actual disagreement.

If we look at some of the other elements considered in this survey, we find that Muslims who eat fairly frequently with other Muslims who are not members of their families are likely to both favor following Islamic inheritance laws in this country and to feel that it is wise to write a will. However, Muslims who eat frequently with non-Muslim Americans are less likely to think that Islamic laws of inheritance should be followed. Table 4.4 shows that eating with Muslim non-

TABLE 4.3 Relationship Between Adherence to Islamic Inheritance Laws and Generation in the United States (%)

| Response [a] | Immigrant | Born in U.S. | |
		First-Generation (American-born)	Second-Generation
Agree	67	35	36
Mixed feelings	25	31	42
Disagree	8	34	22
	100	100	100
	(213)	(52)	(67)

Tau B = .28
significant at = .0001 level
N = 332

[a]Responses are to the statement: "Islamic inheritance laws should be followed in the United States."

TABLE 4.4 Relationship Between Adherence to Islamic Inheritance Laws and Who One Eats With

| Who One Eats Dinner With | Responses (%)[a] | | |
	Agree	Mixed Feelings	Disagree
Equally with both Muslims and non-Muslims often	48	32	20 (66)
Equally with both Muslims and non-Muslims sometimes	49	36	15 (74)
More with non-Muslims	23	43	33 (30)
More with Muslims somewhat	67	24	9 (45)
Only with Muslims	77	15	8 (82)
At home	46	37	17 (35)

[a]Responses are to the statement: "Islamic inheritance laws should be followed in the United States."

family members and not eating with those who are not Muslims seem to be more directly related to favoring adherence to Islamic inheritance laws than eating strictly with family members. It is clear from these figures that, as with other Islamic practices, insistence on the necessity of division of one's property according to Islamic law declines with the length of time spent in America and with increased social interaction with Americans who are not Muslim.

Dietary Restrictions, Alcohol Consumption, and Participation in American Culture

Islam is a religion whose laws and customs provide guidance for all of the activities that make up the day-to-day life of its adherents. Thus, even the most mundane activities such as eating, drinking, and clothing oneself can be subject to specific injunctions or recommendations. As in the other areas we have been considering, living in the United States presents particular problems and the necessity for specific decisions on the part of those Muslims who attempt to abide by the traditional guidelines for what one eats, drinks, and wears.

Dietary Restrictions

It has been noted that one of the things Muslims need to be on guard for in this country is inadvertently eating a product that has some elements of pork in it. Over 90 percent of those we surveyed indicated that they have not eaten pork at any time in the last six months. Several kinds of reasons are cited by Muslims for their abstention from eating any kind of pork product. Some say that the fact that it is banned in the Qur'an is reason enough to avoid it. Others feel that the pig is a filthy germ-carrying animal that should be avoided by all people, not just Muslims. And for many, the fact that they have never eaten it is sufficient to make them not like the idea and just not want to try it. Following are some of the kinds of comments interviewees made about the question of eating pork:

> None of my family ever ate pork or ever will. I have been involved in the medical world a lot, and one of the first things doctors take away from you if you have heart, liver, kidney, or ulcer problems is pork. They know themselves that it is a bad thing.

> Eating pork is one thing I never did and never will do. On a scientific basis, and I am a scientist, there are so many new findings every day relating diet to cancer. I do not have all the answers, but I will not take the risk of eating pork and then finding later it is carcenogenic.

> In our last adult discussion group meeting, Dr.———was talking about whether we should eat pork or not. Dr.———gave the example of him having the equipment to completely purify the piece of pork to the point where it didn't have any disease in it, and he could absolutely guarantee it. The question remained, should we eat it or not? And the answer he gave was no, because of other people who don't have the expertise to purify the pork like that, and follow his example, because Islam is taught by individual example. Because he is a director of Muslim World studies,

people will say, "Well, Dr.———is eating pork and so it is okay for me to eat pork." But they would not be eating the same purified piece of meat that he would.

Thus, for some, avoiding pork seems to be based primarily on health reasons, with the understanding that it may have deleterious effects on the human body. Some Muslims interviewed did indicate that if it was a choice of eating pork rather than starving, then it would be acceptable to eat pork.

A number of those in our survey believe that the major reason for avoiding pork is because it is banned by the Qur'an. The following was quoted by a Sunni imam from a book about Islam published by the Qadianis.

> Pork has been forbidden in the Old Testament. God forbad it to Moses. Jesus, may God bless and preserve him, he never ate pork, he never used it. As a matter of fact, it says in the Bible that he used to send the evil spirits on it. . . . Islam prohibits the use of the pig for the following reasons: male pig cohabits with male pig, and sodomy is in consequence expected naturally to prevail among pork eaters. Pig is too fond of cohabitations; excessive lust in men and women using pork is the result. Pig eats up its own young as well, and is abnormally greedy. . . . The hog is not a healthy animal . . . and to satisfy its internal craving for food, everything in field or gutter, however filthy, finds lodging in its capacious stomach. It is filth and it wallows in filth, and is itself a living mass of filth. . . . The use of this flesh is both harmful therefore for health and morals. But its effects are directly traceable; people have not so far appreciated the harm which is done by it.

The imam then continued with the following:

> I am sure, however, that the day is not far off when the flesh of swine will become banned. . . . It has been said that all things were created for some wise purpose, and this is undoubtedly true, but hogs were never meant to eat. We read that Christ used them to drown devils; they can never be appropriated to a more beneficial use.

The comments of another imam emphasized other aspects:

> On the question of pork, lots of people misunderstand why the Holy God prohibited pork. Lots of people will say to you it is a dirty animal, there is some kind of germ in it. But it is not that. I can wash it and I can put it under 400 below zero and it will kill the germ. It is the principle. In Islam, a Muslim is not supposed to eat any animal that eats meat, and the pig eats meat. I don't eat the dog, I don't eat the tiger or the wolf, and I don't eat pork—all these eat meat. Islam gives special attention to pork especially because there are other things about the pig. . . . The pig is the only animal

which eats its children. If your flesh and bones are brought up on that meat, what type of relationship will you have with your children? . . . Even our doctors say nowadays that when you are sick or have an upset stomach, don't eat pork. So God prohibited pork for the benefit of mankind.

Muslims who have been raised in households in which pork was never served are very unlikely to eat it as adults, even though intellectually they may not actually see anything wrong with it. Years of conditioning not to touch this kind of meat leave their indelible effect, as the following samples suggest:

> I don't see anything wrong in eating pork. There might have been once, but there isn't anymore. These technologies can cure anything. Half the world is eating pork, and they are healthy—their eyes come out blue and their hair color comes out yellow. . . . No, I don't eat pork very often. Maybe I don't like the meat or whatever.

> I don't eat pork, but not necessarily because of the religion. We always know that pork is not healthy food to eat, has more cholesterol than other meat and has more fat. We never had pork in our youth and now we won't eat it. . . . Also I am not really religious. I have had some pork, but I don't like it.

Even those Muslims who categorically refuse to eat the meat of a pig in any manner may inadvertently eat a pork by-product in some other foodstuff. Pork lard, for example, is often used in this country as shortening. Most Muslims report that now that they are aware of this they are careful to check labels on the products they buy; over three fourths of our respondents indicated that they often look over all grocery products that they buy for lard content. Sometimes mosques aid their members by putting out lists of particular products to be avoided. Some Muslims feel that such assiduous attention to label reading is going too far and that it is all right to eat a food product unless they specifically know it has pork in it. Some of these perspectives are illustrated in the following quotes:

> One of my jobs as chairman of the mosque Religious Committee is to publish a list of products containing pork. We check with the companies, with the people who make cookies, like Nabisco, with the bread companies—What bread has lard and what doesn't? What toothpaste should a Muslim use?

> I hate to say this, but when I came to this country I was not aware that pork by-products are existing in things like cookies and doughnuts. By going to the market and talking to people there, I realized that, so I don't buy them.

As a matter of fact, I check all the labels in the supermarket to make sure there is no lard. The only thing I am not sure of, and I don't want to find out, is how they cook in restaurants, for example, McDonald's and places like that. Do they use lard? I hope not, we would probably have to start eating at home.

According to Islamic law Muslims are supposed to eat *halal* meat, that which is killed according to proper Islamic practice. This means that the animal is slaughtered rather than stunned, that the blood is completely drained, and that the words "in the name of God, the merciful, the compassionate" must be said at the moment the throat of the animal is cut. The reality of the difficulty of obtaining such meat in a non-Muslim country has resulted in some widely accepted compromise: if *halal* meat is not available, then it is permissible to buy kosher meat from a Jewish delicatessen or butcher shop. And if that is not available, then one must make do with whatever one can get, as long as it is not pork. Two thirds of those we talked with agree that "*halal* meat should always be bought and eaten when possible," although nearly half admit to often buying meat in a regular supermarket. Mosque leaders sometimes make efforts to see that *halal* meat is available to Muslims in the area. The following comments are from leaders of two mosques studied in this survey:

> *Halal* meat is an educational process we have been working on in the mosque. Just in the last two years we have had some place where we could go and purchase *halal* meat. If you are out on a farm . . . you can go out in the back yard and get it, but if you are in the city, it is just not practical. Another thing, we have been buying kosher chickens or whatever. As long as the meat was killed in the proper way, I don't see anything wrong with that. If it is killed in the name of God (we only have one God in the world), I don't see anything wrong with that. But then you have some Muslims who say, "It is not blessed by Allah." If you can get *halal*, I think you should, but if you can't, you should go to the next best thing. If you can't get *halal* and there are no kosher markets around, then you go to the supermarket and you bless the chicken and you say, "Thank you, God," today in 1983 and half the world is starving. You know, we are not practical sometimes.

> In one of the mosque's monthly letters, it was stated that when they bring food to this mosque, to make sure that it is *halal* meat. If you want to bring a meat dish, it must be *halal*. We get *halal* meat by going to some farms around here and purchasing a goat, lamb, or cow. We talk to the owners and we tell them we are Muslims and that we have to take care of the meat a certain way. They do this for us because they appreciate our business.

Not uncharacteristic of the findings in other parts of our survey, Muslims who eat supermarket meat are most likely to be those who were born in this country, who believe that Islam should be adjusted to fit the reality of contemporary American life, and who dine fairly often with non-Muslim Americans.

Alcohol Consumption

Alcohol consumption of any kind, as we have seen, is strictly forbidden to Muslims. This is interpreted by some to mean that Muslims should not serve anyone else alcohol, or even be around those who are drinking. Although the stricture against drinking alcohol is at least as severe as that against eating pork, Muslims in our survey seemed, for whatever reason, to be somewhat more flexible in their own habits related to alcohol. Thus, while only 7 percent said that they had eaten pork at any time in the last six months, exactly a third indicated that they had taken an alcoholic drink in that time.

This disparity might be a result of the fact that drinking is so much a part of the social and professional life of this country that it is perhaps harder for Muslims to avoid it than it is to abstain from eating pork products. Few Muslims we interviewed indicated that they avoid places or parties because alcohol will be, or might be, served. They generally choose rather to attend and to sip soft drinks or water. Regardless of their personal preferences, most recognize that they are living in a culture in which alcohol is part of the fabric of everyday life. In one of the Midwest mosques a number of the members are themselves bar owners. New immigrant leadership in the mosque is putting a great deal of pressure on these people to change professions, which creates a very difficult situation insofar as they are not trained to do anything else and do not see themselves as being bad or irresponsible Muslims. Following are some of the kinds of comments made by mosque members who are trying to cope with the reality of alcohol in the American culture:

> I have a business in a restaurant, me and my wife. Sometimes I have to go to parties or business affairs where there is liquor. I try to avoid going, but sometimes we cannot because we have to earn a living. But if I do go, I never touch it. Even some of my Christian friends over here, when they come to our house as guests, they never expect any alcoholic drink because we don't have any. We have some good friends, Christians, when they invite us to dinner they check with us before what type of bread to eat, and what not. Out of respect, they don't drink that night.

I think if we go to parties and don't drink, that is fine. People who know us now don't even offer us any drinks. Someone, like —————, says that you have to leave the party if you are Muslim and drinks are served. If you leave the party, then I think you really isolate yourself. You really then would not be supposed to socialize with any non-Muslims. I think that would be hard living here.

If I go to a party and somebody offers me liquor, I don't find their offer offensive. . . . But if it is not part of our religion, we don't have to accept it. We have friends who are, for example, Christian Scientists, and their religion forbids them to drink any kind of alcohol. They are from this country, and they are living in it, and they have not found it to be difficult. . . . But I think we as Muslims living in this country will have to realize that we cannot live as an island. We are living in a context where alcohol and other things predominate.

The results of our survey do indicate that it is probably not the Muslim businessperson or professional who is tempted to drink at social gatherings, or even the person who has a number of non-Muslim friends who drink; rather, it is young American-born Muslim males. Muslims born in the United States are significantly more likely to have had an alcoholic drink in the last six months than are immigrants; this is true for both sexes, but somewhat more likely for men. Taking a drink often symbolizes a kind of rite of passage into manhood in this country, and young Muslim males are as likely as any others to succumb to this (see Tables 4.5A–C). Muslims born in the United States are more likely to drink on occasion than are immigrants, which may be related to the fact that they tend to socialize more with non-Muslim Americans.

Participation in Other Forms of American Culture

Conservative Muslims generally frown on activity that they perceive might lead to excitement of the passions. This is particularly true for those activities in which members of both sexes participate together. Therefore, such things as coed bathing (even in conservative bathing suits) at public beaches, dancing among couples who are not married to each other, and even listening to rock music are forbidden to many young Muslims. In recent years several Muslim summer camps have been organized by various umbrella organizations. Those supervised by conservative Muslims have segregated swimming, when available at all. This kind of strict interpretation does not hold for all Muslims in this country, however. Among those we surveyed, over half said that

TABLE 4.5A   Relationship Between Drinking Alcohol and Generation in the United States[a]

Generation in U.S.	Percentage Who Drank in Last Six Months
Immigrant	26 (of 219)
First generation	45 (of 53)
Second generation	49 (of 69)

[a]Responses in Tables 4.5A through Table 4.5C are to the question: "Have you had any alcoholic drinks in the last six months?"

TABLE 4.5B   Relationship Between Drinking Alcohol and Area of Residence

Region	Percentage Who Drank in Last Six Months
New England	17 (of 76)
Upstate New York	5 (of 66)
Midwest	50 (of 183)

TABLE 4.5C   Relationship Between Drinking Alcohol, Generation in the United States, and Gender

Gender	Percentage Who Drank in Last Six Months	
	Immigrant	Born in America
Male	24 (of 117)	62 (of 40)
Female	27 (of 109)	40 (of 77)

in the past six months they had been to a public beach to swim (with about a third going at least several times), and slightly under half said they had gone to an American-style dance in that time (with a fourth going at least several times). Those who swim in public places tend to be those who also dance and occasionally have an alcoholic drink. Young people are more likely to swim and dance than they are to have an alcoholic drink occasionally. While swimming at a public beach does not seem to be related to whether one is American born, going to an American-style dance clearly is. Muslims born in America, particularly those who are young, are more likely to listen to Western-style music.

Listening to music, even rock, in the privacy of one's home or car is not considered particularly unacceptable, and in fact is reportedly done at one time or another by most of those surveyed. In one group we studied, several young people had formed a rock group and performed for others at one annual convention of the group. Close to half of those in our sample indicated that they listen to Western music frequently. Attending rock concerts, or even listening to rock music on the radio, is discouraged by imams and the parents of young people, but apparently the objection is neither stringent nor consistent. As one imam put it, "music to motivate love and sexual feeling is forbidden." But one of the young adult members of his mosque said that "rock music is OK as long as you are not drinking or taking drugs." Another member of the same mosque indicated that "music and dancing are frowned on, but there is no public stance." In an even stricter mosque, leaders said that "listening to rock music at home is something we haven't talked about directly at the mosque or in our newsletters or sermons. But these are not really the preferred type of activities that a Muslim should engage in. It will be discouraged more actively in the future." This may not be very easy to effect, however, given the response of some of the members of the mosque such as the following:

> We do listen to rock music at home . . . having teenagers in the house we do . . . but it is not on twenty-four hours a day.

Two mothers in their thirties, trying to interest young people in attending mosque functions, were reprimanded for trying to bring music and dance there. In one instance the mother was told she could not have any music in the mosque building, even for children to dance and sing. As she relates it:

> Music was intoxication. . . . So you could not have music. It is against Islam to listen to music. At that time they said there will be no music downstairs (in the mosque basement) and I made the suggestion that I would hold the party in my house, and I would like to have music. The imam said no, I could not bring the boys and girls together and have them listen to music or dance as couples.

In another mosque, a mother upset the mosque leaders greatly by inviting a belly dancer as entertainment for a community dinner. The event was canceled before the dancer had a chance to perform. The woman reflected as follows on this experience:

> A lot of Muslims in the community, they all go to shows like this for which they pay eighteen or twenty dollars, they watch movies on television, and watch everything else, and I found it very contradictory. But I

realize now that it was a mistake on my part because after all the controversy and the thing was over, I came back and looked it up in the Qur'an, and there was a definite "no" about dancing and singing or any form of music at all. . . . Next time I will be more conservative. . . . I personally don't see anything wrong. . . . I mean I like going and attending shows, and I like the ballet and art in any form. . . . I guess I don't understand that aspect of it.

In some Middle Eastern cultures, such as Lebanon, folk dancing is part of many kinds of celebrations. For some Muslims who come to this country, then, it seems very natural to adapt to American forms of music and dancing. Muslim parents are likely to see danger in this only if they feel it might lead their children, especially their daughters, into dating non-Muslims. More will be said about dating and its meaning to Muslims in the next chapter.

Another aspect of American culture that has proven to be particularly appealing especially to Muslim women is watching soap operas on television. A full two thirds of those we interviewed reported watching them at least one or more times in the past six months, although fewer than a fifth said they do so often. It is, not surprisingly, housewives who most often look at these shows. It appears that to date soap operas have not been singled out by imams as un-Islamic, so those who enjoy them do so without compunction. However, it seems that some of the younger people who watch these shows are also likely to go to American-style dances. And, for whatever such a correlation might suggest, those who watch television in general and soap operas in particular are slightly more likely than others to eat dinner with non-Muslim Americans.

In one of the mosques we studied it was reported that an American convert from Judaism to Islam was upset by what he perceived to be nonadherence of Muslim students to the tenets of Islam. He used to visit their rooms or homes and ask them to dispose of their television sets and radios, claiming them to be agents for the dissemination of corruption and pornography in the world.

What effect does living in America have on the Muslim family and individual Muslims in particular? As we have seen so far, many of the stricter interpretations of Islam seem to decrease in proportion to one's stay in America, to interaction with non-Muslim Americans, and apparently as a general result of living in the American culture.

CHAPTER 5

Gender and Sex:
Roles of Muslim Women and Men

In the ongoing encounter of Islam and the West, one of the areas of clearest distinction between the two cultures is that of the structure of society, especially as it defines the roles of women and the relations between the sexes. As far back as the European-Islamic exchange at the time of the Crusades it became clear to Muslims that their foreign invaders had very different attitudes concerning sexual and social mores. Muslims in the Middle East understood their morality to be grounded both in the legal structure of Islam itself and in the Arab view of male honor as dependent on the responsibility of men to protect women from the public world of other males. Much of the astonishment by Arabs of that time at what they perceived to be a moral laxity on the part of the European Christians continues to surface today for Muslims troubled by what they see as the sexual freedoms of Western women.

The Western missionary/colonial adventure in the Middle East, as well as in other parts of the Islamic world, resulted in pressures both from within and without Muslim societies. Muslim reformers were struggling to find ways in which to bring their people up to what they saw as the higher educational and economic standards of the West. Many of them recognized that to do this would mean acknowledging a more active role for women in society. At the same time missionaries and colonial bureaucrats used their powers of persuasion as well as the resources of their educational institutions to alter Muslim attitudes, attempting to influence the leadership to bring about change in the roles and status of women. These efforts resulted in a number of reforms legislated in various Muslim countries by governments and urban notables.

This is not to say, however, that Muslims and their Western "advisers" saw eye to eye on issues involving relationships between men and women, or even on appropriate roles for women in society. Differences have not only continued but in many ways have deepened, or have been more sharply focused, as in recent years many Muslims have become disenchanted with Western approaches and have turned to a reappropriation of Islamic standards of modesty, honor, and morality. Among the areas in which Westerners and Muslims have traditionally differed, and in which therefore serious questions are raised for Muslims living in American society, are the freedom of male-female encounters, how marriage partners are selected, and questions of polygamy and divorce.

Early Muslim immigrants to the United States came from the mountains of Lebanon. The rural women from that area were hardy stock, used to active participation in the economic sector through involvement in various aspects of agriculture. Rural women have always dressed practically; while they may have covered their hair with a scarf, they did not wear a face veil. Such a covering would have been impractical in the field and was also unnecessary since there were no strangers in small rural villages and most people were related to one another through intermarriage.

Later waves of Muslim immigration to the United States reflect the changes that were occurring in various Arab countries. Western dress became more common and was adopted by a substantial number of urban people; it no longer was a sign of distinction and Westernization among the elite. Thus, the immigrants who came to the United States from the Arab world in the 1950s and 1960s did not need to change their dress nor did they find it difficult to adapt to Western culture.

In recent years this situation has changed, reflecting changing attitudes and responses both in the Arab world and in the United States. With accelerated modernization and urbanization, new leaders have assumed power in various Arab countries. Consequently, a great number of the traditional urban elite no longer control the wealth or have access to such privileges as government scholarships to study abroad. A growing number of Muslim students on American campuses are from the new urbanites, differing from the older ones in that the traditional values of Islam have a greater hold on their consciousness. Recent Muslim immigrants include a substantial number of Pakistanis whose women continue to wear the traditional sari and shalwar kameez. Furthermore, the present wave of Islamic revival that began to gain serious momentum in the early 1970s has focused on a return to traditional family values.

Other factors have come to play in the overall changing circumstance. One is the growing Pakistani influence on the interpretation of Islam in the Arab world. Another is the reaction of many Muslims to the American feminist movement, which is seen as having accelerated the breakdown in the social structure of the United States. Such things as the rising divorce rate, what is perceived as promiscuity, availability of pornographic literature, and more explicit sexual overtones in the media have had their influence on the American Muslim community as well as overseas. Thus, while Muslims throughout the world continue to seek Western technology, in growing numbers they reject Western social values, especially those associated with the relationship between the sexes.

The American Muslim community for many years had little access to traditional Islamic materials. Most publications on Islam written in English were by non-Muslims, the rare exception being some books made available by the Qadianis. Since the 1960s, largely as a result of the work of the Muslim Student Association, a growing body of English-language literature has become available in the United States, written from a normative perspective by members of the Muslim Brotherhood and Jamaati Islam.

This literature emphasizes the centrality of the family as the basic unit of society and the importance of maintaining and supporting the family structure. Accordingly, considerable attention is given to the relative positions of women and men in the family, and the ways in which they play different but equally important and supportive roles. It is clear that many of the traditional values, as well as the respective positions that men and women have in the family, are called into question in the American context. As we have seen in other aspects, responses to the pressures of American society differ widely among those in our survey.

The Position of Women in Muslim Society

The Qur'an has spelled out certain basic rights for women, granting them an equitable set of circumstances not available for women in other parts of the world at the time of the Qur'anic revelation. Much contemporary Islamic literature is devoted to the affirmation that this situation still pertains and that the guarantees the Qur'an gives to women mean they truly do enjoy a balance of freedom and responsibility, rights and duties. According to the Qur'an there is full religious equality between men and women, meaning that both are required to fulfill the basic duties of the faith and both will be called to account for their deeds and intentions on the Day of Judgment. In addition, the Qur'an establishes a series of individual rights and guarantees for women. Muslim jurists over the centuries have devised an intricate system using Qur'anic teachings as well as the practice and teachings of the Prophet Muhammad. Those things that might at first appear to contemporary Westerners as inequities for women, such as the fact that a daughter inherits half of what her brother does, are based on the premise that it is the man who has the specific responsibility to care and provide for the women of his family.

Certain developments in the early history of Islam had led to greatly decreased participation of women in the communal practice of Islam, such as attendance at the mosque, which was presupposed during the early days of the Prophet Muhammad, and before long to the virtual seclusion of the vast majority of Muslim women. Throughout most of the twentieth century various Muslim individuals and governments have been attempting to change this situation, to bring women back into full participation in Islamic society, which is understood to have been their original legacy. Thus, increased opportunities for women in education and in the workplace are a priority for many contemporary Muslim governments. At the same time, especially in the last decade in much of the Islamic world, some Muslims have been moved to rethink the importance of the Muslim family as a bastion of Islamic values, and the particular role of women in that context as the repository of these values. Thus, what might appear to the Western outsider to be a return to the traditional "bondage" of women, evidenced in such things as the adoption of specifically Islamic dress by some, can in fact be interpreted as the self-conscious choice of certain Muslim women to identify with Islam and to assume the responsibility of educating the males and the children in their families in the basics of Islamic life.

Contemporary Islam is subject to several different currents, each strong and with articulate advocates. While some reaffirm the importance of traditional Islam and the necessity of women remaining in the home to maintain these values for the sake of Islamic society, others stress the importance of full female participation in the public life of the Islamic community. The latter perceive the traditional position of women vis-à-vis men as alien to Islam and argue for equal rights in the workplace as well as equal participation in the outward manifestations of Islam.

These various trends of thought, along with a legacy of misunderstanding of Islam on the part of many Westerners, make it difficult for Americans to fully appreciate the position of women in Muslim society. Many of those we interviewed expressed their feeling that Americans in general do not understand the role of women in Islam and their own conviction that the Muslim woman does, in fact, have a better situation than women in other religious traditions (see Tables 5.1A–E).

TABLE 5.1A   Attitudes Concerning Women's Role in Islam Generally, in the Mosque in Particular, and Dress of Women

Responses to Questions	Percentage
Women in Muslim families here and in the Middle East are treated as well or better on the average than American women in Christian and/or Jewish families.	
Agree	47
Mixed feelings	33
Disagree	20
	100
	(338)
Women should be eligible for the presidency of the mosque/Islamic center.	
Agree	52
Mixed feelings	26
Disagree	22
	100
	(339)
Muslim women should not go out on the street unless their hair and arms are covered and their skirts are well below their knees.	
Agree	24
Mixed feelings	29
Disagree	47
	100
	(343)

TABLE 5.1B   Intercorrelations Among Attitudes Concerning Women's Role in Islam Generally, in the Mosque in Particular, and Dress of Women

Attitude	Are Treated Better	Eligible for Presidency of Mosque
Are treated better	—	−.18 (significant to .0001)
Eligible for presidency of mosque	−.18 (significant to .0001)	—
Islamic dress	+.28 (significant to .0001)	−.37 (significant to .00001)

TABLE 5.1C Attitudes Concerning Women's Role in Islam Generally, in the Mosque in Particular, and Dress of Women (by Country of Birth)

Statement	Percent Who Agree with the Statement			
	United States	Lebanon	Other Arab Countries	Pakistan
Women in Muslim families are treated well or better	34	49	49	65
Women should be eligible for mosque presidency	71	51	37	36
Muslim women should cover themselves	6	28	34	41

TABLE 5.1D Correlations of Attitudes Concerning Women's Role in Islam Generally, in the Mosque in Particular, and Dress of Women with Gender of Respondent

Statement	Correlation
Women in Muslim families here and in the Middle East are treated as well as or better on the average than American women in Christian and/or Jewish families.	not significantly related to gender
Women should be eligible for the presidency of the mosque/Islamic Center.	$-.14$ (significant at .006)[a]
Muslim women should not go out on the streets unless their hair and arms are covered and their skirts are well below their knees.	not significantly related to gender

[a]More women than men agree with the statement.

From a twenty-eight-year-old male immigrant from Lebanon:

The non-Muslim people think that Islam does not treat the woman and the man equally. They think Islam does not give the freedom and the right to the woman to decide her own life. I would like to clear this up for them. It is not the case, it is totally wrong. Islam gives the same freedom to the woman as it gives to the man. Islam treats the woman fairly and equally as it treats the man. There is no difference. Let me add this. Islam treats the woman with more respect than any other religion or any other doctrine. The reason women inherit half of what

TABLE 5.1E   Relationship Between Attitudes Toward How
Women Are Treated in Muslim Families and Gender of
Respondent (Controlling for Place of Birth)

	Percent agreeing to Statement[a]	
	Born in America	*Immigrant*
Men	70 (of 40)	32 (of 114)
Women	74 (of 77)	52 (of 106)
	Tau B = −.05	Tau B = −.23
	n.s.	significant at .0002 level
	N = 117	N = 220

[a]"Women should be eligible for the presidency of the mosque/Islamic center."

men do, is because the woman already has someone to take care of her.
In Islam she is not responsible for working and furnishing a house; if she
wants to work, that is fine, but if she doesn't want to, it's up to her. That
is why the woman inherits half of what the man does, because the man
has more responsibilities. It's not the way that the non-Muslims interpret
the case.

From a female immigrant from Egypt in her thirties:

Muslim women are independent, more than any other. A Muslim
woman is free to use her own money, she doesn't have to spend the
money in the house unless she does that voluntarily, while the man is
supposed to support the family, and he would have to spend his money
on that. Muslim women can manage their own businesses. Muslim
women have opportunities—certainly in Egypt—that women from other
religions don't have.

From a thirty-four-year-old male immigrant from Pakistan:

Islam has been dubbed by some a backward religion because of the way
it treats women. Islam gives a lot of opportunities and more basic rights
to the woman than other religions.

It is clear that as Muslim and Western attitudes about sexual morality and appropriate roles for women in society have long differed, so
too have perceptions about what constitutes proper treatment of
women. What one views as consideration for women's right to freedom
and equal access, another might see as disrespect and encouragement

of immodest exposure. For the Muslim, modesty as the highest virtue itself necessitates treating women with full respect; equality in that light implies a lack of basic consideration for the special quality that women are expected to preserve.

We therefore asked the Muslims in our sample whether they agreed with the statement "Women in Muslim families here and in the Middle East are treated as well or better on the average than American women in Christian and/or Jewish families." Slightly less than half (47 percent) agreed and only about one fifth actually disagreed with the statement, the remainder reporting mixed feelings. Place of birth is significant here, however; while only about a third of those born in the United States agreed, two thirds of Pakistanis said they feel it is true. It is interesting to note that there is no relationship between the gender of the respondent and agreement with this statement.

Belief that Muslim women are treated as well as or better than non-Muslim women does seem to be related to other attitudes about the appropriate role of women. Thus, those who hold this view tend to be those who also think that a wife should work outside of the home only when there is severe financial need. They are also the Muslims who participate regularly in religious activities such as praying five times a day, fasting during Ramadan, reading the Qur'an, and attending Friday services. They are unlikely to engage in behavior such as eating nonhalal meat, swimming at a public beach, going to an American-style dance, or drinking alcohol. Correspondingly, those Muslims who do engage in such activities are less likely to be persuaded that Muslim women are treated as well or better than Christian or Jewish women either in the United States or in other parts of the Islamic world.

One of the questions we posed to our sample was whether or not respondents feel that a woman should be eligible to be president of a mosque or Islamic center. In general, those who agreed that women are more favorably treated in Islam than in other religious traditions did not think that this is appropriate, although slightly over half of the total sample said that they should be eligible (with 22 percent disagreeing and 25 percent reporting mixed feelings). Country of birth is again clearly a factor here, with 71 percent of American-born Muslims in favor of women in this kind of capacity to only 36 percent of Pakistanis. Men and women born in America do not differ significantly from each other on this item but are far more likely than immigrants of either sex to agree. Among immigrants, however, women are quite a bit more likely to agree than are men.

In one mosque we visited, elections for a governing board were invalidated because some members protested the election of women to the board. When new elections were held, a new structure was devised in which membership to the *shura* (consultative) council that would oversee the administration of the mosque was restricted to men, while women were elected to a newly created committee to deal with social activities.

In most parts of the Islamic world women still rarely participate in mosque activities and in fact seldom attend the mosque at all. In the United States the situation is noticeably different. Because it is incumbent on males and not females to attend the Friday communal service, most of the women in our survey indicated that they do not go to the mosque on Friday. They do, however, attend Sunday events such as lectures, Qur'anic study circles, and prayer services. In some mosques and for some functions, women stay on the side, in others they are at the back, and in still others they are together with the men.

Women also have played and continue to play very important roles not only in organizing social events for the community but in planning and carrying out fund-raising activities crucial to the maintenance of an already established mosque or to collecting the monies to build a new mosque or center. They have also been extremely active in teaching in the Sunday schools, and attend the mosque services regularly.[1] Participation in these various activities has resulted in women acquiring a good deal of informal and formal influence in the decision-making structures of the mosque. Newly arrived immigrants, many of whom hold a more conservative view of the appropriate role of women in the mosque, have tended to be less appreciative of the active part women in this country play, a circumstance that has occasionally led to tension and conflict.

The longer Muslim men and women live in the United States, the more likely they are to feel that it is appropriate for women to play active roles in the functioning of the mosque and, as previously indicated, to believe that women should be eligible for top lay leadership positions such as the presidency of the mosque governing board. In several of the mosques in our study, women are recognized as playing significant roles; in a number of instances they are on governing boards, although no woman as yet has been president of a mosque board. The following reflections from mosque members representing all the major areas in our study indicate some of the general responses to the role of women in the mosque.

From an immigrant Pakistani Muslim, who is a past president of a mosque in upstate New York:

> The sisters have an equally important role to play in the activities of the Islamic center as do the men. Sometimes I feel that without them we probably wouldn't exist. They are the ones who essentially are planning the day-to-day activities and are a lot of help in bringing their families to the mosque functions and activities. They do perform a significant help in making sure that the social aspects are a full part of the Center's activities. We do not have any female members on the board this year, but we have had some in the past, and they have been a lot of help. The Islamic School was really started by the women.

From the president of an East Coast mosque:

> Women are very active in the mosque. How much more active can the women be who are the secretary and treasurer of the mosque board? They participate in everything, and the secretary and treasurer are two of the mosque mainstays.

From the imam of a Midwest area mosque:

> Although initially men formed the organization of the mosque, it wasn't long, just maybe a few months, before the women's auxiliary was formed by necessity because the men didn't do much cooking or household chores in those days, and at some of the mosque functions they wanted to serve Arab cuisine. But the women, God bless them, did not take long before they realized that they had a function superior to that of just cook . . . or providing food for the men. The auxiliary began to have a separate treasury and they elected their own president, secretary and treasurer—and all of those things that go with a society. They began acting independently. In some cases they would obstruct programs initiated by the men, or themselves initiate programs that weren't too liked by the men.

A woman member of this same Midwest area mosque, which has been established for a long time, had this to say:

> The board is now divided almost equally in terms of the amount of men and women sitting on the board. I think we are setting an excellent example to other Muslim groups in this country, and if the people in this community want to stay Muslim and keep their identity they are going to have to go about it in different ways, not having only men sitting on the boards and only men making the decisions. Men can't possibly consider the whole picture. Besides, the days when you can keep women in the house cooking bread and cleaning are over.

Women's Clothing

A good deal of attention across the Islamic world today is being paid to the question of appropriate dress for women. As was indicated earlier, while many Muslim women cherish the advances made by their mothers and grandmothers in abandoning the veil and traditional forms of Islamic dress, others are finding it appropriate to adopt the kind of conservative clothing that identifies them as Muslim and they are proud to do so. Still others have not yet come to the point where they are free to make such choices themselves. Conservative clothing for a Muslim woman generally means covering all parts of the body except the face and hands. The hair should be completely covered. Few if any of the Muslims born in the United States dress in this fashion, and most immigrants who come wearing it gradually change to more typically American-style clothing. In one place, however, traditional dress is considered the norm—that is the prayer room of the mosque. Women who do not put on conservative dress there often find themselves rebuked by the imam or other members of the mosque.

The degree of strictness in adhering to "Islamic" dress varies from mosque to mosque. In some places women attend Sunday services in Western knee-length dresses with no headscarves. Pakistanis often come in native saris. In other mosques one can see a variety of clothing. When an imam repeatedly urges the necessity for specifically conservative dress, it seems that the women gradually give in and begin to adopt it. In one mosque, after five years of hearing the imam insist on such dress, the last of the women capitulated. In another, however, a substantial number of women seem to have formed a kind of resistance group and continue to appear without scarves. Occasionally mosques provide special wraps for women to put on for services.

In one of the mosques in which women do, in fact, play very active roles, the imam expressed his opinion that "women should dress Islamically by covering their hair and body, allowing face, hands and feet to show only and that this dress code should be observed regardless of place." Despite his opinion, however, the great majority of women in this mosque cover their hair and bodies in the Islamic fashion only in the prayer room. When the field researcher for this mosque asked whether the women typically changed into regular street clothes before leaving the mosque, meaning into conservative but knee-length dresses, the women responded that of course they do because it is awkward to wear Islamic dress on the street and people tend to stare at them. The following is an excerpt from the comments of an American-born woman interviewed at this mosque:

> Women are always encouraged in and out of the mosque to cover their hair and wear long dresses. . . . Men can wear what they please pretty much but they are fussy about clothing of the women in the mosque. Now I think women who go to the mosque to pray should be covered; I don't think any woman would go in there with a short skirt or short sleeves, or what they call these saris with so much showing or not have their head covered. But—how women dress outside of the mosque is their own private business. I don't want to go to college with my head covered, and wearing a short skirt does not make me a bad Muslim. I am a Muslim and I am proud to say it, but I want to say it in ways other than dressing in obnoxious clothing. I want to blend in as far as my clothes go. I want to look normal.

Similar statements were made by women at other mosques in this study, indicating that they feel Islamic dress should be adopted in the prayer room of the mosque but that outside they have no hesitation in dressing in short sleeves and knee-length skirts, especially in warm weather. Younger Muslim women, especially first- and second-generation American-born, often wear miniskirts and shorts in hot weather as do their non-Muslim friends.

Some of the women, however, especially those who are older or who have immigrated more recently, did indicate that they take care always to cover their arms, legs, and head; in some cases this means putting on pantsuits and scarves more appropriate to the American situation. There is no apparent consensus, however, on whether a pantsuit is really modest dress. While traditional Pakistani dress includes the sharwal, and thus pants are considered acceptable by Pakistanis, many Arabs condemn pantsuits as too suggestive of the shape of the female body. People in several different mosques reported that recently arrived imams have publicly exhorted women to dress Islamically. It is interesting to note that recent publications on proper Muslim dress available in Muslim book distribution centers now suggest that men should wear bathing suits that cover from the navel to the knee, and that women should be totally covered. It is perhaps not surprising, then, that some young people are questioning modesty and proper behavior in terms of specific clothing styles.

We asked members of our survey to respond to the following statement: "Muslim women should not go out on the street unless their hair and arms are covered and their skirts are well below their knees."

Only about a fourth agreed, and nearly half disagreed. Those who agreed are also very likely to agree that women in Muslim families are treated as well as or better than women in Christian and Jewish families and to disagree that women should be eligible for the presidency of a mosque. Gender has no bearing on opinions concerning street dress, but country of origin clearly does. Only 6 percent of those born in America agree with the above statement, while 41 percent of those born in Pakistan feel that it is correct.

In general, the Lebanese are the closest to the opinions of American-born Muslims on all the issues relating to women. Since the sample of Muslims from the Midwest area is heavily represented by U.S. and Lebanese-born Muslims, it is not surprising to find that the midwestern Muslims reflect the most liberal responses. They are also less likely than others to participate regularly in Islamic religious duties such as regular prayer and fasting, and more likely to participate in some of the recreational activities that are avoided by more conservative Muslims, such as swimming at public beaches and dancing. However, the very fact that there are so many Muslims in the Midwest area, with new and more conservative immigrants coming in at a faster rate than in other areas, also creates a greater potential for conflicts about the appropriate roles for women than exists elsewhere. The most settled midwestern Muslims, those who eat fairly frequently with non-Muslim Americans, tend to favor a woman being president of the mosque and are less likely to feel that women in Muslim families are treated as well as or better than other American women. They are also relatively unlikely to think that it is necessary for women to have their hair and bodies covered when they are out on the streets.

Relations Between the Sexes

As was indicated earlier, the family unit is central to Islam, and relations between the sexes are defined exclusively in terms of that unit. This has the practical outcome for conservative Muslims of a very strict limitation in the kinds of interaction possible between men and women who are not in the same family. In some countries—for example, Saudi Arabia—the restriction on women interacting with, or even being in the company of, males who are not family members has posed grave difficulties for women who wish to enter the work force. In many other parts of the Islamic world interaction between men and women who are not married or part of the same family is much freer, although in no place are extramarital sexual relations in any way condoned.

The Qur'an, (S. 24:30–31), enjoins both women and men to dress modestly, a verse that has sometimes been interpreted to support the kinds of total covering that certain Muslims have worn and continue to wear in some places. This injunction, along with the concern that women not dress in such a fashion as to evoke sexual or romantic ideas in the minds of men they come in contact with outside their families, has supported the wearing of conservative dress in most parts of the Islamic world. This is also the reason why many Muslims, even in this country, object to Muslim women exposing themselves in ways that might engender sexual thoughts in men, such as by swimming at public beaches or wearing short dresses with no sleeves, even on very warm days.

For many Muslim women, however, especially those who were born in the United States or have lived here a long time, such restrictions are not welcome. It is not surprising to find that many of the newer immigrants to this country, especially those from Pakistan, frown on what they feel is lax behavior in dress on the part of many who have been here for a longer time. This, as we have seen, can be a source of tension between various groups of Muslims in the areas we have studied.

Shaking Hands

In a strict interpretation of Islam, men and women who are not spouses or relatives should avoid being alone together, since they might be tempted to adulterous feelings. A popular saying attributed to the Prophet Muhammad is that "when a woman and a man are alone together, Satan is their third." Actual adultery is still punished by death in a few very conservative countries, and is met with extreme disapproval everywhere in the Muslim world. For some, touching hands between unrelated men and women is dangerous for its possible sexual overtones, which is why many Muslims object to young people dancing together in the American style. An extreme version of this concern about touching results from the refusal of some Muslims even to shake hands with members of the opposite sex.

The Muslims in our sample who have settled in the United States are not that conservative. In response to an item in the survey that reads "Muslim men should not shake hands with Muslim women to whom they are not related," it can be seen from Section A of Table 5.2 that fewer than a fourth agree, and fully 61 percent disagree. A very high proportion of Muslims born in Pakistan agree with this item

TABLE 5.2   Attitudes on Sex, Dating, Marriage, and Divorce

A. *Touching Between Adults of Opposite Sex*

1. *Responses to the item:*   "*Muslim men should not shake hands with Muslim women to whom they are not related.*"

    a. Total sample response (%):

Agree	Feelings Mixed	Disagree
23	16	61

    b. Percentage who say they *agree* with above statement by where they were born:

United States	Lebanon	Other Arab Countries	Pakistan
5	16	27	61

2. *Some correlations with cross-gender hand-shaking*

    Should not *Shake Hands*

    a. Muslim women should cover hair, arms, legs — +.59 (significant at .00001 level)
    b. Women should be eligible for mosque presidency — −.39 (significant at .0001 level
    c. Women in Muslim families are treated as well as or better than in U.S. Christian or Jewish families — +.26 (significant at .0001 level)
    d. Muslim women should remain single rather than marry non-Muslims — +.38 (significant at .0001 level)
    e. If Muslim couples desire no children, they should use contraceptives — −.28 (significant at .0001 level)
    f. Young Muslim men should be allowed to date — −.49 (significant at .00001 level)
    g. Arranged Muslim marriages are a wise practice — +.44 (significant at .00001 level)

B. Percent Distribution of Other Attitudes Concerning Sex, Dating and Marriage, Divorce

	Agree	*Mixed*	*Disagree*
1. Muslim men should *not* be allowed to marry Christian or Jewish women.	21	30	48
2. It is preferable for Muslim women to remain single rather than to marry Christians or Jews.	48	21	31
3. Muslim couples should not get divorced just because they are unhappy living together.	22	24	54
4. If Muslim couples desire no children, they should use contraceptives.	55	27	18
5. Abortion is permissible for Muslims in the first forty days following conception.	22	28	50
6. Young Muslim men (eighteen and older) should be allowed by their families to date.	39	22	38
7. Young Muslim women (eighteen and older) should be allowed by their families to date.	31	20	49
8. Arranged Muslim marriages are a wise practice.	26	39	35
9. Marriage between first cousins is a wise practice.	11	39	50
10. In case of divorce, Muslim women should be allowed custody of their children until they are eighteen.	45	40	15

C. *Intercorrelations among Attitudes and with Other Characteristics*

	1	2	3	4	5	6	7	8	9	10
1. Men should *not* marry non-Muslim women	—	.37	.15[b]	n.s.	n.s.	−.15[b]	−.19[2]	n.s.	n.s.	.16[b]
2. Muslim women should stay single rather than marry non-Muslims	.37[c]	—	.28[c]	−.15[b]	−.20[b]	−.56[c]	−.59[c]	.26[c]	.12[a]	n.s.
3. Not get divorced	.15[b]	.28[c]	—	n.s.	n.s.	−.21[c]	−.21[c]	.23[c]	.14[b]	n.s.
4. Use contraceptives	n.s.	−.15[b]	n.s.	—	.36[c]	.27[c]	.29[c]	−.23[c]	−.22[c]	n.s.
5. Abortion OK in first forty days	n.s.	−.20[b]	n.s.	.36[c]	—	.23[c]	.31[c]	−.12[a]	−.12[a]	n.s.
6. Young men should be allowed to date	−.15[b]	−.56[c]	−.21[c]	.27[c]	.23[c]	—	.83[c]	−.36[c]	−.21[c]	n.s.
7. Young women should be allowed to date	−.19[b]	−.59[c]	−.21[c]	.29[c]	.31[c]	.83 [c]	—	−.33[c]	−.14[b]	n.s.
8. Arranged Muslim marriages are wise	n.s.	.26[c]	.23[c]	−.23[c]	−.12[a]	−.37[c]	−.33[c]	—	34[c]	n.s.
9. Marriage between first cousins is wise	n.s.	.12[a]	.14[b]	−.22[c]	−.12[a]	−.21[c]	−.14[b]	.34[c]	—	n.s.
10. In divorce, Muslim mothers should keep children until they are eighteen	.16[b]	n.s.	n.s.	n.s.	n.s.	n.s.	n.s.	n.s.	n.s.	—
Eat often with non-Muslim Americans	−.15[b]	.29[c]	−.19[b]	.23[c]	.21[c]	.37[c]	.34[c]	−.14[b]	n.s.	.11[a]
Male	−.17[b]	n.s.	n.s.	n.s.	n.s.	n.s.	n.s.	n.s.	n.s.	−.13[b]
Born in the United States	n.s.	−.30[c]	−.16[b]	−.10[a]	.10[a]	.41[c]	.34[c]	−.39[c]	−.25[c]	n.s.

[a] = correlation significant at .05 to .01 level.

[b] = correlation significant at .009 to .001 level.

[c] = correlation significant at .0009 to .0001 level or higher.

(61 percent again), compared with a fourth or fewer of those born in other countries or in the United States. Those who hold this position on hand shaking also tend to have the most conservative attitudes concerning women and relations between the sexes. They believe that women should cover their hair, arms, and legs on the street, that women on the average are treated better in Muslim families, and that Muslim women should not be mosque presidents. They also strongly disapprove of free interaction between young men and women and favor arranged marriages.

Dating

The issue of dating between young Muslim men and women is a particularly sensitive one in this country. Dating is generally discouraged and often forbidden for both sexes, largely as a holdover of customs in Islamic countries and because of a concern for the apparent license in sexual relations among many American youth. Those Muslims who take a liberal position on contraception and abortion are more likely to feel that young Muslim men and women (eighteen and older) should be allowed to date, and those who take a conservative position are more likely to feel that they should not be allowed to date. The American custom of dating is clearly one of the most difficult issues faced by immigrant Muslim parents in raising their children in this country.

Muslim youth are expected to meet prospective marriage partners through their parents or relatives at mosque/Islamic center events. Social interactions are generally allowed among young people of the opposite sex only in the presence of others, preferably chaperoning adults. Parents interviewed insisted that they have the same standards for their sons as they have for their daughters in the matter of dating, although several of the Muslim women who grew up in this country clearly recalled that their brothers were at least tacitly allowed to date (and did), while they were not. Section B of Table 5.2 indicates that, in the total sample surveyed, there is a good deal of difference in attitudes toward young men dating versus young women dating. For example, 11 percent more felt a young Muslim woman should not be allowed to date than that a young Muslim man should not date (49 percent to 38 percent, respectively).

Immigrant Muslim parents of preteen children generally said that they would be opposed to their dating. Quite a few of those interviewed who had been in the United States for some time, however, indicated that they would allow their children to invite other children of the opposite sex (especially if they were Muslim) to the house when the parents were at home, or to go out in a group with proper chaperoning. As one immigrant mother from Pakistan, in her thirties, explained:

> I would not mind if my children "dated"—but by that I don't mean going out alone with a boy or a girl. If they have friends at school, especially if they have Muslim friends, I would rather they invited them to come over to my house and sit there and talk and just keep an open friendship. If in the process they started liking somebody as a girlfriend or boyfriend, I would have to take it from there. Although I think girls and boys should be treated alike, I think with the girl I would be a little extra strict. I don't think I would allow either my son or daughter to go out alone [with someone of the opposite sex] though until they are twenty or twenty-one, at least while they are living with me.

Most of the parents interviewed indicated that if their young people (especially girls) were allowed to date at all, marriage would have to be a clear possibility. In other words, there is to be no frivolous dating, as illustrated in the comments of another mother in her thirties, born in the United States of Lebanese parents:

> I don't like the word "dating" and I would hope that my daughter especially, but also my sons, don't take up this habit. I don't mind them going out in large groups with other Arabs or Muslims, but this idea of one-on-one with Americans—I don't like it. You are so easily influenced when you are young, and you can get attached to someone emotionally. . . . But if they are older and are very compatible in many ways, and it was time for them to get to know each other, and it was done—not in a shop-around manner but in a very natural way—I wouldn't be against that.

Similarly, a Lebanese father in his forties who has been in this country for about twenty years commented as follows:

> Dating is not our way of life, the way I was brought up, not part of culture, but it is a part of the American culture. . . . The way it is done is ridiculous. I see some people who date one person for three days, then drop them and say "no good," and then date someone else for two days, then someone else—that is what I am against. I am not against finding yourself a partner, but I am against the way they abuse this "dating." I don't have as much problem with boys dating girls as I do with girls dating. If a woman or girl has to date somebody to see if he is going to be her future husband, all right—but I don't agree with the practice of a girl dating somebody for a few days, and then kicking him out and going with somebody else. I don't like it for boys either.

Since youths between seventeen and nineteen years of age are seldom ready for marriage, at least in the United States, Muslim parents usually prevent their high-school-age children from dating at all. Some hope that this can be accomplished by gentle instruction rather than through command, as reflected in the comments of a mother in her late thirties, born in Turkey:

> I have talked about dating with my children and I do not believe they will be allowed to date. My sons have friends in school, but I have never had any of their friends who are girls come to the house, though boys come. I have explained to the boys that if their sister cannot date, it is not fair for them to date. My older son is seventeen and a half, and he has no dates and is not looking for it. My sons do not really feel they are missing anything. In fact a lot of the time they will talk about their friends who are dating and they think it is silly at that age to commit yourself, and be unhappy most of the time for something that won't last a lifetime.

Whether or not her sons, or daughter, for that matter, will continue to be content with not dating as they move into the senior year and senior prom time and finally into college, is questionable, given the experiences of some other Muslim families. Many of the young Muslims will not date, at least until they are beginning to settle on a marriage partner, but this does create strains in families living in the American culture when their children's classmates are dating simply for the fun of it.

Although responses to the two items on dating attitudes were negative for nearly two fifths or more of the Muslims surveyed, a third or more of the sample did favor dating among unmarried persons eighteen and older, and another fifth or so were undecided. Since the two dating items are so highly correlated (and can really be used interchangeably in analysis), the following analysis will be done primarily with the attitude toward young men's dating, since the responses provide a better spread than the item on women's dating (i.e., in regard to young men's dating, 39 percent agree, 22 percent are mixed, and 38 percent disagree that they should be allowed by their families to date). As depicted in Figure 5.1, favorable attitudes toward young men (and women) become more pronounced with each generation in America.

Birth Control

Slightly over half our sample agreed that "if Muslim couples desire no children they should use contraceptives," and fewer than a fifth dis-

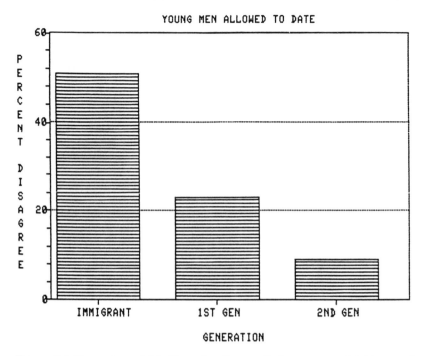

FIGURE 5.1 Percentage of Muslims who *disagree* that young men (eighteen and older) should be allowed to date.

agreed, with the rest reporting mixed feelings. Among those interviewed at each site there seemed to be some confusion as to what the Islamic stance is on birth control, and few seemed certain what the position of their mosque was or whether it had even taken one. Some felt that the Qur'an forbids any attempt to control the number of births, whereas others citing a *hadith* on the use of coitus interruptus by the Prophet—said that the Qur'an approves of some form of birth control. The situation becomes still more confusing when the question extends from the coitus interruptus kind of birth control to newer forms developed by twentieth-century technology, such as the pill and the intrauterine device (IUD). Various opinions were expressed about whether it is Islamic even among married couples to use birth control, taking into consideration economic factors, health hazards in having children, and the reality of an already large family. According to one imam interviewed, permanent means of birth control such as a vasectomy or tubal ligation are not permissible, although other forms are, including the pill or the IUD. Given this lack of consensus and differences of opinion often expressed within the leadership of a single mosque, it is no wonder that few of those interviewed believed their mosque had an official stance on birth control. Following are some of the kinds of comments offered:

From a young Pakistani immigrant man:

> I do not believe Islam is as strong on its stand on birth control as is Catholicism. To tell you the truth, in Islam, I do not think it is that clear-cut; most people just follow their own direction.

From a young female immigrant from Egypt:

> I am not sure what the Islamic position is on birth control. Some say you should control the number of births, some say you shouldn't. In Egypt, the government is trying to limit the number of births; some are trying to find the *hadiths* that say there shouldn't be too many of us. But there are also people who believe that there are passages in the Qur'an that say no to birth control.

From a middle-aged male from Pakistan:

> Birth control is a controversial issue. Some type of birth control is permissible, such as using the safe periods of the cycle, as well as coitus interruptus. But the more recent, more sophisticated birth control are considered not proper.

From a young first-generation woman of Lebanese parents:

> I did not know what the stance of my mosque was on birth control. So I asked the imam. He said that if the contraceptive is not long term, like when they tie the tubes, it is not *haram*. But if you do something long term that would permanently destroy your chance to have children, that's *haram*.

From an older immigrant male from Lebanon:

> In our mosque, we do not agree on birth control. Personally, I think it is all right. Look, in Egypt by the year 2000 there will be 75 million Egyptians, and now there are close to 45 or 50 million people. But many, many Muslims like large families.

From a middle-aged immigrant Pakistani male:

> Birth control was practiced to some extent by the companions of Muhammad. To the extent they knew how to use birth control, they did. If there is

one benefit from the technology in birth control, my opinion is—use it. Using any birth control simply to limit the number of children, of course, is not right. Birth control should be practiced if there is some economic hardship or some health consideration between husband and wife.

Abortion

While there is obvious confusion and some mixed feelings about birth control, nearly everyone interviewed agreed that abortion is forbidden in Islam. At the same time, many Muslims take the position that there are instances when abortion is permissible, such as when the woman's life is at stake or in cases of rape or incest. There is still some confusion about what the Islamic position is on abortion in the minds of a number of those interviewed, with some believing that Islam permits, or is at least quite lenient about, abortions performed in the first forty days of pregnancy. Others, more likely first-generation Muslims than immigrants, believe that (whatever the Islamic position may be on abortion) strict interpretations should be avoided in today's world, and more liberal standards applied concerning when abortion is permissible or desirable.

From an immigrant Pakistani man in his forties:

> Abortion is prohibited in Islam, except in the situation where a mother's life is in danger; in that case, medically it would be necessary and hence allowable.

From a middle-aged immigrant Pakistani man:

> I think there is a four-week limit when the pregnancy may be aborted. But after four weeks, the spirit enters the body and abortion is not permitted by Islam.

From an immigrant Pakistani man in his late thirties:

> When the life of the mother is threatened, then certainly treatment of the mother takes precedence. However, abortion by intent at any stage is equally prohibited, because it certainly does not make any difference if the fetus is four weeks old or thirty weeks old—conceptually speaking it is the same thing.

From an older first-generation woman born in America:

> According to our religion, abortion is forbidden all the way. But you know, it is a tough question. Let me tell you why. I have searched my

heart. I have young granddaughters. If they ever really made a mistake, at the early, early stage of pregnancy, dear God! I don't know. I do not know how I feel, and I pray that God does not test me. When there is a life and formation of a child—no to abortion. But right at the very start of nothing—I wonder under the circumstances.

From a first-generation woman in her thirties, born in America:

I don't know what stance the imam takes at this mosque on abortion. I have read contradictory arguments, some people saying it is forbidden in Islam and others saying, well, it depends on how soon you have it. I personally would not say that I am against it. It depends on the situation. I think for a girl of fourteen or fifteen who is pregnant, if she were my daughter, I would not want her to have the child—she is just not capable of raising the child, so it depends on the situation. . . . And for a married couple, if the husband did not want the child and she did not for one reason or the other, her career or just did not want to be tied down, maybe they shouldn't have the child if they didn't want it. Even if abortion is forbidden in Islam, I think it would have to be left up to the couple. It is something they are going to have to carry the burden of for the rest of their lives.

Half the Muslims in the total sample clearly disagreed that "abortion is permissible for Muslims in the first forty days following conception," with about a fifth agreeing, and somewhat more reporting mixed feelings. As can be seen in Section C of Table 5.2, those Muslims who believe it is all right for Muslim couples who desire no more children to use contraceptives are also significantly more likely than those who are ambivalent or opposed to contraceptives to feel that abortion is permissible for Muslims in the first forty days following conception. As indicated before, more Muslims agree with the use of contraceptives by far than agree to abortion (55 to 22 percent, respectively). Gender is unrelated to attitudes on these items. However, those Muslims who dine with non-Muslim Americans are more likely to take a liberal position regarding the use of contraceptives and abortion, as are those who are born in this country (this correlation is only slight).

Marriage

Homogamy, in terms of selecting a marriage partner based on common religion, race, ethnicity, and nationality, is a major means for all subgroups in the host society to maintain their particular identity, distinct values, and way of life. Hence, it is not surprising that Muslim immigrants stress marital homogamy as a way of preserving their religion. The following comment from a first-generation American-born Muslim woman reflects a common feeling among immigrants of any religion and culture about the importance of marrying within the faith:

> Others' cultures are entirely different. Not only their religious beliefs, but they don't have the same values, and I just don't think that it [marrying non-Muslim Americans] makes for a good relationship, makes a happy marriage.

Any minority group in America with its own distinctive values and approved behavior needs to be concerned about transmission of these values to subsequent generations, particularly as they go to school and then work in places where they are exposed to people of other faiths and origins. It is partly for this reason that Muslims stress intermarriage in America only within their faith, as can be seen in the following comment from an imam:

> One reason why we encourage members within the Muslim community marrying one another is that when you are living in America, you are up against so many pressures, so many influences of the society which are un-Islamic, and the father and the mother are the only hope for the children's maintaining their identity as Muslims or knowing about their religion. If the mother is non-Muslim, then there is very little hope that the child will maintain his identity as Muslim. Now I know some couples where the wives are Christian, but the families are trying to raise the children Muslim, and are doing very well. But I would think those are exceptions.

All of the imams and most of the other Muslims interviewed for this study understand that Islamic codes permit Muslim men to marry women who are Christians or Jews (People of the Book) even though they maintain their faith after marriage. Although the Qur'an is less explicit on Muslim women's marriage, most interpret Qur'anic passages as opposing a Muslim woman marrying anyone but a man who has been raised as a Muslim or has converted to Islam prior to his marriage. This difference traditionally has been accepted because of the assumption that the husband has the final say in how the children are raised. According to this understanding, it does not matter if a Muslim man marries outside the faith, but a Muslim woman cannot do so since her children would have to be raised in the faith of her spouse. Some Muslims in the United States believe that this principle holds with the same force today, particularly since they perceive that Muslims are tolerant of the religion of Christians and Jews and that this tolerance is not reciprocated by members of those two religions. This would lead to a grave situation since Christian or Jewish men would not allow Muslim women to raise their children according to the tenets of the Islamic faith. As one Muslim woman put it:

> For Muslim men, marriage to non-Muslims is allowed, but for Muslim women it is not allowed. As Muslims, men recognize non-Muslims as "People of the Book." The reason it is prohibited for women is because Christians and Jews do not recognize Muslims as "People of the Book" and would not recognize a woman.

Many of the Muslims interviewed, whether or not they agreed in principle with the sex differences in freedom of marital choice, expressed a concern about the likelihood of a Christian or Jewish woman married to a Muslim man being willing to bring up her children as Muslims simply because her husband wished it. Some noted that greater care is taken in the United States than is generally the case in Islamic countries to ensure that the non-Muslim prospective wife agrees to her children being raised Muslim before marriage. But they fear that even this may not be enough, especially since it is unlikely that the non-Muslim wife would agree to Islamic law, which says that the children go to the husband at a relatively young age in case of divorce. Later discussion will show that the Islamic law concerning custody of the children in case of divorce is not adhered to by many Muslims in America either.

Some Muslim women whom we interviewed expressed the opinion that the man's freedom to marry outside the faith is neither fair nor conducive to preserving the Islamic faith in future generations born in America, as illustrated in the remarks of one young Muslim woman:

> In Islam, marriage to non-Muslims is forbidden for a woman of course, but allowed for a man. I personally think that if it is forbidden for a woman, it should also be forbidden for men because the women are really the ones who raise the children, and if the wife is not Muslim, how are the children going to be Muslim?

A very practical reason for Muslim women, especially the unmarried ones or those with unmarried daughters, disliking the freedom of choice permitted to Muslim men is that the limited number of suitable grooms diminishes if men marry outside the group, especially in a country where Muslims are a minority. This concern was also sympathetically expressed by an imam:

Although it is permitted for a Muslim man to marry a non-Muslim woman provided she is a Christian or a Jew, there is a general feeling in our community that we should persuade our young men to marry inside the community. If you have a nice Muslim boy, educated, and he goes and marries outside the community (and we have a small community) then you have girls looking for husbands—and who can they marry? It presents a big problem.

One solution, of course, would be to restrict men from marrying non-Muslims, and another would be to allow Muslim women to marry outside the faith. Neither of these accords with Islamic law and thus both are problematic. In our survey there were some who favored one of these alternatives, and some who were uncertain, but far more took the traditional Islamic position. Nonetheless, there seems to be considerable uncertainty and disagreement on the issue of whether or not women, as opposed to men, should remain single rather than marry outside the faith.

As can be seen in Section B of Table 5.2, in items 1 and 2, almost half of the Muslims surveyed disagree with the statement that "Muslim men should not be allowed to marry Christian or Jewish women"; again, nearly half agreed that "it is preferable for Muslim women to remain single rather than to marry Christians or Jews," which is the standard Islamic position. However, the lack of consensus on either item, with a fifth or more of the sample taking the un-Islamic position of definitely agreeing with the first and disagreeing with the second, would seem to indicate a belief on the part of some that perhaps in America Islamic law and traditional attitudes need to be changed to fit other cultural values and realities.

It becomes evident why the previously discussed American practice of dating is so hazardous to the Islamic prescriptions and prohibitions concerning marriage partners. If Muslim youth are free to date anyone—even if the date is properly chaperoned—the likelihood is that they will marry non-Muslims, especially given the fact that Muslims are a minority. Fear that there will be no Muslim young men to marry the Muslim girls in the United States has led even some strict Islamic parents to question whether following the Islamic law that young Muslim men may marry Christian and Jewish girls is wise in America. Although belief that Muslim women should remain single if they cannot find a Muslim husband declines with time in America and across generations (see Tables 5.2, Section C), the same is not true for the issue of whether or not Muslim men should marry Christian or Jewish women. For example, those who are opposed to dating for young men and women are not only likely to agree that Muslim women should stay single rather than marry Christians or Jews, but are also somewhat likely to feel that Muslim men should not marry Christians and Jews despite the fact that it is approved by Islamic law.[2] It would seem that the principle of religious homogamy demands for many Muslims in America, even if Islamic law does not, that Muslim men not be allowed the freedom to marry outside the Islamic faith. Women are especially likely to believe that Muslim men should not marry outside their faith, a gender difference that does not appear on any of the other items concerning dating and marriage.

Although we did not ask our respondents how many Muslim men in their immediate families had married Christian or Jewish women, we did ask the somewhat "touchier" question of how many Muslim women who were close relatives had married men raised as Christians or Jews, and how many of these men had converted to Islam prior to or after marriage. A little over a third said that there had been such marriages in their families, and of these nearly half said that the husband had not converted to Islam. Muslims who have close relatives married to non-Muslim men are indeed more likely to be open to women marrying outside the Islamic faith; this may well be because Muslims born in the United States report a higher proportion of Muslim women married to non-Muslim men than do immigrants, and many of these marriages have taken place in the Midwest. Whether or not the Muslim respondent has female relatives married to men outside the faith has no relationship to attitudes concerning women's religious intermarriage and dating.

Twenty years ago, Elkholy[3] reported in his study of Muslims in the Midwest that the restriction that Muslim women marry only Muslims was an area of contention for Muslims born in the United States. He said that in cases in which Muslim women did marry non-Muslim men, they were generally ostracized by the Muslim community, and most eventually converted to Christianity. Elkholy found that 61 percent of the Muslims he surveyed in the Midwest felt that if a Muslim girl falls in love with a Christian boy and wants to marry him, her parents should advise her against it, try to prevent the marriage, or, if all else fails, at least get him to convert before the marriage. Using Elkholy's question, we found a slightly higher number of Muslims from all sites (74 percent) who would take such actions; however, a high proportion of Muslims in this current study double-checked response categories and wrote comments to the effect that though they prefer to take the firm stand, if necessary they would be willing to try to get along with the son-in-law and exert influence on the grandchildren to adopt Islamic values and practices.

Muslims who attend the mosque fairly often are more likely than those who are Eid Muslims or attend infrequently to disapprove of the marriage of Muslim women to non-Muslim men and dating for young unmarried persons. This seems to hold true even when other predictors are taken into consideration, such as whether the person is an immigrant or first- or second-generation American-born Muslim, and whether he or she believes that Islam should be observed strictly, moderately, or adjusted to fit life in the United States. Muslims who never or infrequently attend the mosque are more likely to feel that women should marry outside their faith if they want and that young men eighteen and over should be allowed to date. However, the Muslim respondents' personal beliefs about how strictly Islam should be observed were somewhat more important than the number of times they attend the mosque; the more strictly Muslims believe Islam should be observed, not surprisingly, the more likely they are to agree that women should not marry outside the faith and disagree that young men should be allowed to date.

The degree to which Muslims socialize with non-Muslim Americans has a significant effect on how strongly they adhere to the Islamic position on dating and freedom of intermarriage with Christians and Jews for Muslim women as well as for Muslim men. Whether Muslims eat with non-Muslim Americans at all appears to have a greater effect on their attitudes than whether they also eat with Muslims (not family members) fairly frequently. At the same time, as Figure 5.2 indicates, Muslims who eat frequently with other Muslims outside of their own families tend to be more rigorous in observance of Islamic regulations and duties than those who eat only with family members.

Those who believe strongly that Muslims should marry only Muslims are also highly likely to favor the custom of arranged marriages widely practiced in the Muslim world. There is quite a division among the Muslims surveyed over the advisability of arranged Muslim marriages. Responses to this item ranged from 26 percent agreement to 35 percent disagreement, with 39 percent reporting mixed feelings. There are no differences in response by gender to the question of arranged marriage, but there are strong differences according to place of birth. For example, no more than one fourth of the immigrants surveyed, whether

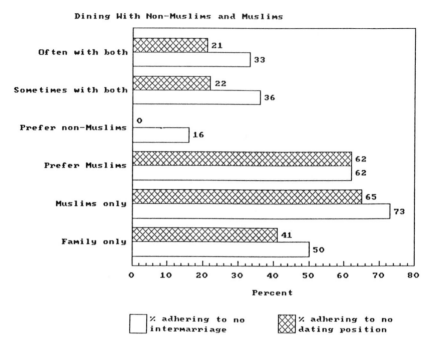

Figure 5.2 Adherence to the Islamic position on dating and women's intermarriage with Christians and Jews as a correlate of frequency of dining with non-Muslims and Muslims.

male or female, disagreed that arranged marriages are preferable, but about 60 percent of both men and women born in America believed that having parents choose their children's spouses is not wise.

Many of the immigrant Muslims in the survey are themselves partners in arranged marriages. Their support of their system would appear to depend at least in part on whether or not they feel their own marriages have worked. Muslims born in America are far more likely to believe that they should have the freedom to make their own choices, even if their parents have or had a happy arranged marriage. This is based partly on the concern that the parents might not understand enough about American culture to make wise selections. Even immigrant Muslim parents realize that though they personally may be in favor of arranged marriages for their children raised in the United

States, they are going to have to allow their children much more say in whom they marry than they might have in their home countries; this is indicated by two mothers from the subcontinent:

> Mine was an arranged marriage, and although I would like to have arranged marriages for my children, one of whom is a senior in high school and one who is in college, I think "influenced" marriage is more like it. I don't think I could really arrange the marriage and just have them see each other for the first time on the wedding day and have them accept it. It would at least be proper, I think, to introduce them and let them see and meet each other before they commit themselves to a marriage.

> Although the risk is high for a girl marrying a complete stranger, in the long run I do feel that arranged marriages do work out better. In the arranged marriage, you both start out from scratch and you are both aware that you have to give each other a chance to get to know each other, and that you have to love your husband. Even though you do not know the man on marriage, you are automatically assumed to develop love for him. You are more patient and more tolerant, I think, in an arranged marriage than you are in a love marriage. In a love marriage, I think you expect more, and when the infatuation is over, the marriage has more problems than the arranged marriage. But I would like my children not to have a completely arranged marriage, but a partially arranged marriage. I would encourage them to mix with Muslim children, and kind of push them, consciously or unconsciously in the direction of some Muslim young person I liked and they liked. But if they found someone they liked and I didn't, I am not sure I would have too much influence on who they married. I was raised in a society where parents can control their children and choose who they marry. But in this country you have to kind of ease off. My children are raised here— so I think I will try to control them without their . . . really knowing that I am, not openly choosing their future husbands and wives, but more gently nudging them in the right direction.

In Muslim countries, many of the arranged marriages have been within the family, often to first cousins. Among Muslims we interviewed, those who advocate arranged marriages are significantly more likely to also advocate marriage between first cousins than those who are ambivalent about or opposed to arranged marriages. However, in the total sample there is far more support for arranged marriages than there is for marriages between first cousins; while only about a third clearly oppose the idea of arranged marriage, fully half oppose the practice of marriage between first cousins.

Divorce and Child Custody

A commonly cited saying of the Prophet Muhammad is that nothing is more to be hated than divorce. Nonetheless, Islamic law clearly recognizes that in some circumstances it is unavoidable, and the law is clear about what steps are to be taken in initiating a divorce. (Although it is technically possible for a woman to divorce her husband, it is considerably easier for a man to obtain a divorce.) Actual divorce statistics in most parts of the Islamic world are considerably lower than they are in the United States, but most Muslims do recognize that despite the emphasis Islam places on family life there are times when it is preferable to contemplate divorce than to remain in an intolerable union. In fact, over half of the Muslims surveyed disagreed with the following statement: "Muslim couples should not get divorced just because they are unhappy living together." Only about a fifth clearly agreed; the remainder reported mixed feelings. Although those born in America take a more liberal position on divorce than immigrants, the latter also express a range of responses. The following excerpts illustrate some of the positions taken on the question of divorce:

From an immigrant male Pakistani, who is the leader of a mosque:

> Divorce for men or women is allowed in Islam. If two people are not getting along together, they should try to make an effort to resolve differences by trying to get consultation following the Islamic principles . . . but if everything fails and they cannot resolve their differences, divorce is permissible in Islam and is encouraged to be carried out in the best possible manner. The couple would leave each other, but the husband would have to take care of the needs of the wife still in a fair and equitable way.

From a young male Egyptian immigrant:

> Divorce gives you the sense of freedom, you are not in prison for life. In Christianity, if you are married for life, you are not supposed to break it. That is like a prison—suppose you don't get along together? Suppose you want to have children and your wife does not or cannot, or you cannot have children and she wants children. You can divorce and she can go and marry another man who will give her children; and you can get another woman who doesn't want children. So there is flexibility—and that is one of the good things about Islam—freedom!

From a middle-aged woman, born in the United States of Lebanese parents:

I believe in divorce if two people aren't getting along, and you cannot change them. I do not believe that you can change adults. So, either you live with a person if it is all fine and dandy, or if you can't, I think you should divorce. I don't feel you should be miserable for the rest of your life. Life is too short, you should be happy.

From an immigrant imam:

> Divorce is permitted in Islam, but not at all liked. It is the worst of all things which are allowed or permitted. Divorce should be the last resort and only done in very necessary cases. It is allowed for the man and woman alike and both may ask for divorce. Custody of a boy is with the mother until he becomes seven years of age and a girl may stay with the mother until the age of nine, and then both children go to the father for custody, unless a judge decides that either the father or mother can't care for the children.

The stipulations in Islamic law as to the reasonable causes for divorce mean there is not a great deal of disagreement among Muslims over the necessity, on occasion, to dissolve a marital union. When it comes to questions of child custody, however, the situation is quite different. The traditional Islamic pattern of giving the children to the father at a young age is apparently not considered acceptable in this culture by many of those we surveyed. Only 15 percent disagreed with the statement: "In case of divorce, Muslim women should be allowed custody of their children until they are eighteen." Fully 45 percent agreed and 40 percent described their opinions on the matter of child custody in divorce as mixed or ambivalent.

There is no correlation between opinions on whether Muslim couples should get divorced if they are unhappy living together and what the child custody arrangements should be in case of divorce. Interviews with Muslims in the different sites surveyed revealed that although a number feel that Muslims should follow Islamic law in regard to child custody, some women themselves were not absolutely certain whether they would or could have been able to do this if they had been divorced when their children were under eighteen. Some questioned the viability of giving custody to one parent or the other based on the gender of parent and of child. The following quotes illustrate the range of opinion on child custody:

From a woman in her thirties born of Lebanese parents:

> Child custody in Islam has been discussed many times at our mosque. In Islam, the child can stay with the mother until the age of seven and then

the father takes custody. Because I am a Muslim, I can understand. But I don't know what I would do if I were divorced and my husband wanted the children, I don't even want to think about that. I understand the Islamic position and I would probably go along with it—but I can't be one hundred percent certain.

From a young woman from India, in her thirties:

I would think that if a Muslim couple is getting divorced they should follow the Islamic law as far as child support and child custody go.

From a young immigrant woman from Qatar:

I think that what the Islamic religion says about men having custody of the children after the first seven to nine years is wrong. The women teach the kids the religion, not the men. The women are around the kids the most, and the women give them their first moral basis.

From a young male immigrant from Lebanon:

I am against Islamic law concerning the father having custody of the children soon after they become school age. Why should the father have the child? At the same time I would ask the identical question, why should the mother have the child? I would say that when the parents divorce, they divorce for a reason, Islam should better ask that the parents go to our courts and let them decide who should have the child.

As might be expected, women were significantly more likely than men to agree that in the case of divorce children should stay with the mother until they are eighteen. Although there was no significant difference between immigrant women and women born in American (almost half of the women agreed regardless of place of birth), almost twice as many American-born as immigrant men said that women should keep custody until the children are eighteen. This may be because of the reality that American judges in divorce court tend to award custody to the mother if she so desires. It is also true that Muslim men born in America are more likely than others to marry non-Muslim women, who would probably not be willing to abide by Muslim custody laws. The fact of dining with non-Muslim Americans apparently has less correlation with flexibility on the custody question than does watching soap operas; the more frequently Muslims watch such shows the more likely they are to agree that Muslim women should have custody of their children until the age of eighteen (keeping in mind the fact that far more women than men watch soap operas).

CHAPTER 6

Muslims in America: Apprehensions, Associations, Aspirations, and Achievements

One of the realities of contemporary Islam of which Muslims through-out this century have become increasingly conscious is the fact that Islamic minorities are to be found virtually all over the world. Attention is being given to the presence of Muslims not only in China and in the Soviet Union but also in places such as Japan, Australia, and South Africa. There are substantial minority communities in the heart of Europe in Germany, Belgium, France, and Great Britain, and in both the South and North American continents. The Organization of Islamic Conference (OIC), whose forty-three member nations are almost all Islamic states, is taking special interest in the circumstances of Muslim minorities throughout the world.

What then are the most crucial issues faced by these minority groups? The key concern is how to live an Islamic life in a non-Muslim country, especially in light of recent strong reaffirmations of the essential unity of religion and state. Islamic ideology makes it clear that the state, by definition, must organize itself around the needs of the believers in order to help them maintain the faith. And the believers in turn have the responsibility to hold the state to its task, to see that religion impacts on public policy and that society lives up to the will of God. This kind of mutual relationship and accountability is, of course, not possible where a Muslim minority exists in a non-Muslim country.

This is by no means a new problem in Islam, and classical texts contain instructions for believers on how to live an Islamic life in a country in which they are a minority population. The understanding is that it is acceptable to live in a non-Muslim country if it is necessary for some purpose, such as earning a living, but that one must plan to return to the home country. In no case should a Muslim give allegiance to a non-Muslim government. These texts also give the believer some leeway in interpreting and carrying out the specific responsibilities of the faith; the absolute necessity of maintaining all the tenets of Islam may be suspended in such extraordinary circumstances where there is no overarching state protection.

Obviously most Muslims who immigrate to America do not return, and the majority opt to become U.S. citizens with the understanding that allegiance is to be given to this nation. Many have come to this country with the explicit intention of returning home, particularly because some of them believe traditions teach that one should be buried in a Muslim country. It may be that a turning point in affiliation came when Muslim communities purchased land to establish cemeteries in America. Clearly one of the issues with which many immigrant Muslims must deal is the dual, but now not mutually reinforcing, relationship between their allegiance to Islam and their responsibility to their newly adopted country.

One of the fundamental concepts in Islam that is being highlighted in contemporary thought is that of *hijra* or emigration. Beginning with the flight to Ethiopia of a group of Muslims during the time of Muhammad and epitomized in the emigration of the Prophet and his followers from Mecca to Medina (marking the official beginning of the Islamic calendar), the idea of *hijra* legitimizes the necessity of leaving a country, even a nominally Islamic one, if it is impossible to live an Islamic life because of oppression on the part of the rulers. Here again, however, the expectation is that one will return to the home country to work for the establishment of a truly Islamic state. Members of the Muslim Student Association (MSA) often advocate this understanding of *hijra;* they are here for the specific educational training that will help them bring about change when they return home. Many of them have tried, relatively unsuccessfully, to affect local communities of earlier immigrants in America. Some are working with African-American Muslim groups, and in the geographic areas considered in this study three are serving as imams in immigrant mosques.

The immigrants who first brought Islam to this country were young men from rural areas who were often illiterate and with little knowledge of English. When immigration officials anglicized their Muslim names on entry into the country, most were too dazed to protest. Concerned with economic survival in a new land, they attempted to maintain a low profile and not draw attention to themselves or their religion. For the most part they had little Islamic consciousness or even knowledge of the fundamentals of the faith. Not having attended the mosque regularly at home they did not look to do so in the new land.

Life for the early immigrants was extremely difficult, and one may wonder that they were able to retain allegiance to their faith at all in what was often a very hostile environment. Muslims in the early days of this country were few, very dispersed, and often unable to communicate with Americans because of a lack of knowledge of English. Their fundamental concern had to be for economic survival. Those who served as pedlars, for example, trudged back and forth across areas of the Middle West selling small items to farmers for whom they served as a kind of lifeline to the outside community. Often little integrated into American society, they had to bring young women from overseas to be their wives. It was only after having children that they felt the necessity for providing some kind of structure in which to pass down Islamic values. Slowly the importance of maintaining the faith and perpetuating its belief system led to the organization of religious centers. Nonetheless, individual Muslims in this country were not called to account to family, tribe, or any overriding Islamic authority, and as time passed many of the children of immigrants married outside the faith and converted to Christianity.

Throughout this century different waves of immigrants have brought to America different ideas and expectations of what it means to be Muslim. They come representing the consensus of what their fellow Muslims overseas think Islam is and should be at any given time. In the 1950s, nationalist Muslims emigrating to America brought a rational interpretation of Islam in which the particulars of Islamic observance such as regular prayer and attendance at the mosque are considered less important than living an ethically responsible life. At the same time, a few imams came holding up the ideals of specific Islamic practice with a stress on law and ritual. More recently there has been an influx of Muslims from abroad with financial support from Saudi Arabia representing what they understand to be "official" Islam. These people are generally unwilling to compromise what they see as the incontrovertible principles of Islam in its pure form. All of these perspectives continue to characterize the whole picture of Islam in the United States and make it very difficult to generalize about "American Islam." One must take into account differences in nationality and ethnic affiliation, in educational level and economic status, in the interpretations of Islam current at the respective time that immigrants arrived in this country, and in the adaptations that occur over the years as a result of interaction with the American culture.

One of the realities of American immigrant Islam, perhaps because of this kind of extreme diversity, is that it has not yet developed institutions for training persons to occupy leadership positions. In the whole country there are at present two imams (of whom we are aware) who are the sons of imams (one of them is American-born), and their training in Islam is not extensive. American Muslims are not producing Islamically educated imams, which is the reason many of them are coming from Islamic institutions abroad. Because North American Muslims have not yet developed anything like a theological institute and have little indigenous scholarly production, they are often dependent on current interpretations by Muslims from overseas as to what Islam is and how it should be practiced.

Some evident changes in this situation, however, point to a rising sense of Islamic consciousness on the part of American Muslims. In the last fifteen years a small group of immigrant Muslim scholars in this country has taken on the project of writing Islamic texts for immigrant Muslims. New mosques are being built with the specific intention of representing Islamic forms of architecture. Even existing mosques are being dressed up in ways that illustrate Islamic symbolism, such as the addition of minarets. The use of mosques is often restricted to what is Islamically acceptable, and where social functions are allowed in connection with the mosque, new structures are being added to accommodate them so that the area of worship is restricted as specified by Islamic law. The growing transformation of Islamic consciousness means that small ethnic enclaves are in some cases learning how to share their institutions with more recent immigrants, in the process gradually dropping their ethnic particularities and moving toward a more common Islamic identity.

This rise of Islamic awareness, as well as the influx of immigrants who are self-consciously conservative Muslims concerned with maintaining Islam in its pure form, has brought about a new sense of what it means to be Muslim in this country. Adding to this a general concern—expressed by many we interviewed in our sample—that recent events in the Middle East, from the revolution in Iran to bombings in Beirut, may be helping to perpetuate a negative image of Islam. Many indicated their desire that Americans see Islam not as a religion of terror but a religion of peace and that the American populace somehow be educated to the fundamentals of Islam and the ways in which it is a sister monotheistic religion to Judaism and Christianity.

Three quarters of those surveyed believe that wars in the Middle East have had a negative impact on the ways that other Americans treat Muslims and have in fact made Americans actively dislike Islam. To a question of one thing Muslims in this country wish Americans better understood about Islam, the largest single response was to have people in this country see it as a religion of peace. For example,

Islam is a religion of peace and acceptance. The majority of Muslims are not terrorists or religious fanatics as the American media portrays.

Muslims are not warmongers. We are a peace-loving people.

Islam professes peace and not war. The majority of the Muslims, like the followers of other religions of the Book, seldom practice the basic tenets of Islam.

Consistent concern is expressed that Americans will come to dislike Muslims, Arabs, or those from Middle Eastern countries because of what they see as distorted press coverage of recent conflicts. Sometimes this is put in terms of a worry that people here will fail to differentiate between Islam as a religion and as a way of life, and will judge the whole by the actions of particular Muslim individuals and groups.

I would like to change the stereotyped image that people have of Muslims. If somehow we can tell the world that Muslims are no different than anybody else. There are some good Muslims out there, some bad Muslims out there, just like everybody else. If we as Muslims try to lead our lives according to the way that is taught by the Prophet and the Qur'an, there wouldn't be any bad Muslims out there. We would all be excellent human beings and excellent Muslims.

Another concern often brought up is that Americans, because of general lack of knowledge about Islam and distortions in reporting on the part of the American press, may believe that Muslim terrorists are good examples of what it means to be an adherent of Islam. Many of those responding indicated that they feel the American press is too sympathetic to the Israeli perspective and Israeli interests in the Middle East, with the result that it does not do justice to the Arab perspective.

Islam is a good religion. It is the religion which came to Moses and Jesus and was completed by Muhammad. To be against Islam is to be against Judaism and Christianity. Still, Americans are against Islam, and this is based on their ignorance, selfish lobbies, and the Zionist-dominated media. Americans should know that whatever is happening in the Middle East is by and large the result of Western influence in that part of the world.

Muslims have beliefs which make them sincere and reliable colleagues in faith, with no hatred toward Christians. They represent the most misrepresented faction of the world community, and Americans owe it to themselves to at least try to understand this, to see just in their own interests what are real costs and the reasons behind unqualified support to Israel.

It is commonly believed among Muslims (and probably quite correctly) that non-Muslim Americans have no idea that Muslims accept the teachings of Moses and of Jesus as well as the other prophets revered in the Judeo-Christian tradition. The following comments illustrate a general feeling among Muslims that Americans are generally quite unaware of the teachings of Islam, or that they seriously misunderstand them:

I have spoken to a lot of non-Muslim people who don't know much about our religion. I stress that we do not drink and do not eat pork and the reasons for this and for why we do not believe in premarital sex—it sort of changes their attitude. They say, "What a beautiful religion," or "I didn't know that!" Americans on the whole really do not know much about our religion. They say, "You believe in Allah." I say "You know what Allah means—Allah means God, the same as yours. Your God is my God. He is only one God, and Muhammad is his follower." People say we are "Mohammedans." We are not "Mohammedans," we only believe in one God and no other gods. Americans are amazed to hear that we believe in the Virgin Mary when I get through telling them that. They have no idea what we believe in. . . . When big shots get on a podium all over the United States, I would like the day to come when they all will say "Catholics, Protestants, Jews, and Muslims." I would love to see Islam included every single time that someone speaks about religions in America. Let us be included with them.

Many people believe that Islam is an off-brand of Hinduism, because they shove Oriental religions into one category, and Islam is an Oriental religion, so they think of it as having many gods and believe that it is totally different from Judaism and Christianity. We actually accept the Bible and the Torah and we believe in all your prophets, but most people don't know that.

I was at an ecumenical session with Catholics, Protestants, and Jews at Harvard University, and surprisingly, some of the ministers with doctor or masters of divinity degrees and doctorates did not know that Islam believes in the immaculate conception of the Virgin Mary and in Jesus as a prophet. Americans should be made more aware of some of the different things about our religion and also that our religion and Christianity are similar in many respects. For example, the Jewish people do not believe in Jesus at all, whereas Islam does. We try to educate the American public about these things when we send out our speakers to various colleges or schools in the area or when they come to us for information.

Muslims from Arab countries are particularly eager to show that the God they worship is the God of Christianity and Judaism. The grounding of Islam in the same prophetic line legitimates their part in the monotheistic tradition. A few Pakistanis, on the other hand, prefer to use the term Allah for God. For them, to give God any name other than the one given in the Qur'an—Allah—is somehow to take away from the being of God.[1] Arabs find this difficult to accept, feeling that the use of the term Allah is perpetuated by American scholars writing about Islam as a further prejudicial attempt to cast Islam as a religion foreign to the Judeo-Christian heritage.[2]

The term Judeo-Christian as used and misused in the United States is seen by many Muslims as an attempt to prove by including Judaism that one is not prejudiced; the result, however, seems to provide an exclusive definition of what it means to be American. Every time an official of the government uses the term he is excluding Muslims and members of other faiths from American pluralistic society. Whether this is intentional or not, it is noted in Muslim circles as a way of keeping them from participating in the formulation of the future of American society. They question whether or not it may in fact be serving notice that they do not belong at all.

The indifference to or apprehension about Islam most Muslims attribute to Americans they see as a result of past and present political situations as well as of long-standing confusion and ignorance in the minds of many as to what Islam really is. Muslims generally perceive Americans as little motivated to learn more about this sister religion and believe that such indifference can often lead to apprehension about the spread of Islam in the United States. When specifically asked about this in our survey, only 7 percent said they feel that Americans are open to such a spread, 34 percent indicated they think Americans are either completely ignorant of or simply indifferent to the possibility, and the remaining 59 percent said they feel people in this country are apprehensive about the spread of Islam.

Muslim perceptions of American attitudes on this issue do not seem to be related to factors such as age, sex, education, or place of birth, or to the amount of social interaction they have with Muslims outside their immediate families. However, those who "read a magazine or newspaper from a Muslim country" quite often are more likely than those who do not to assume that Americans are either apprehensive about or opposed to the spread of Islam (see Table 6.1A).

Also apparently unrelated to feelings about American concerns vis-

TABLE 6.1A   Distribution and Correlation of Perception of Openness to Islam and Reading Magazines or Newspapers from a Muslim Country

Questions and Responses	Percentage
1. From your experiences and what you have heard, do you think that most Americans are	
Open to the spread of Islam	7
Mostly indifferent to whether or not Islam spreads in the U.S. (or totally ignorant about Islam)	34
Somewhat apprehensive about the possible spread of Islam	31
Very apprehensive and opposed to Islam	28
	100
	(335)
2. Do you read a magazine or newspaper from a Muslim country	
Often	21
Sometimes	34
Rarely	26
Never	19
	100
	(343)
3. Correlation of 1 and 2 above	.13 (significant to .008 level)

à-vis Islam are such things as mosque attendance, involvement in religious activities, and the degree to which one feels Islam should be observed. Those Muslims who hold more liberal attitudes on questions of dating and who themselves sometimes participate in such activities as mixed-sex swimming, dancing, and drinking alcohol are slightly more likely to believe Americans are indifferent to the spread of Islam. The fact that the East Coast Muslims live in a liberal area with various educational and cultural establishments and a tolerance for different life-styles and values may help explain why nearly half of them feel that Americans are either open to or are at least indifferent to the spread of Islam, as opposed to only about a third who believe this in the other two areas (see Table 6.1B). None of these correlations, however, is strong. On the whole nearly three fifths of those surveyed said they believe that Americans are apprehensive about the spread of Islam.

Many of those interviewed expressed the feeling that Americans tend to look on Arabs as being backward and ignorant. This obviously causes a great deal of pain to Arab Muslims. Some, such as a young

TABLE 6.1B   Other Correlations with Openness to Islam's Spread on the Part of Americans of Other Faiths

Frequency of eating dinner with non-Muslim Americans	.13 (significant to .008 level)
Young men should be allowed to date	.12 (significant to .01 level)
Young women should be allowed to date	.10 (significant to .03 level)
Deviant activity scale (low scores = high frequency of engaging in behavior considered *haram* by most Muslims)	.10 (significant to .04 level)

Lebanese man who has lived in America for five years, manage to see it with a touch of humor:

> When I first started working at the company where I work now as a quality control engineer, my co-workers used to ask me first of all about the camels, do they have one hump or two in Lebanon—things like that. Now I have seen a camel twice in my life—once in Lebanon and once in a U.S. zoo! Another at the company asked me if we ever had a radio in my house, and one asked me if we ever had a car, and did I ever drive one back in Lebanon? And I asked him, "What kind of car do you have?" He named a '78 Dodge or something like that. I said, "Are you proud of it?" and he said, "Yes, I work hard and I bought it." I said, "You know, back in Lebanon I had a Mercedes 280." Please tell the American people we are not camel jockeys anymore. And yes, we do have radios and cars back in the old country.

Others are understandably bitter:

> Non-Muslim Americans are not at all open to the expansion of Islam. They have such negative feelings toward us, mainly because they don't know anything about us and just think we are a bunch of freaks. You know—women with veils, men can marry four or five times, have a harem, ride everywhere on camels—all the crazy things you see in the movies.

The comments of one young immigrant woman from Egypt reflect a not uncommon fear that Muslims in this country may experience discrimination, or even retaliation, on the part of non-Muslim Americans, especially as a result of recent events:

> I don't volunteer saying I am a Muslim. And it is not because I am not proud of being a Muslim—I am. It is just the propaganda that is in the United States. I would assume it is basically as a result of what happened

in Iran. By saying you are a Muslim, you are a bad guy (to Americans) and by saying you are an Arab, you are also a bad guy. So the thing to do is to say you are Egyptian—then you are OK.

And from an American citizen of Pakistani background:

When people ask me "Where are you from?" I always tell them that I am Indian. That way it is safer. I do not want to be an object of anti-Muslim hostility.

Few if any of those we interviewed reported having themselves experienced discrimination either in the workplace or the housing market, and with only a couple of exceptions they did not indicate that their children have had unfortunate experiences at school because of being Muslim. In private conversation, however, some did admit that they know Muslims who have experienced incidents of discrimination. And, in fact, we do know of some very unhappy occurrences at several of the sites in our study.

After the 1982 bombing of the Marine headquarters in Lebanon, carloads of American youths rode past the mosque in one city and threw trash and garbage at it, screaming obscenities and shooting BB guns at the building. A group of people from a church down the road finally stopped them. In other areas Muslim children were harassed by their classmates after school.

Another incident illustrates the apprehension under which many Muslims are living. A city in which an Islamic center is located was hit by a rash of arson fires in synagogues and in the houses of a rabbi and a prominent Jewish citizen. The whole town was deeply concerned that this was the work of anti-Semites; churches held services to purge themselves of the vestiges of anti-Semitism. The Jewish Defense League came into town and threatened to attack any suspect. Muslims were very apprehensive, and did not venture anywhere near the Jewish area. When it was finally discovered that the perpetrator was a young Jewish man, he was dismissed as disturbed and referred for psychiatric help. The rabbi, who had known about the suspect and withheld evidence, was not tried even though it cost the city thousands of dollars for extra security on all Jewish institutions. One Muslim mother commented, "I breathed a sigh of relief. Had it been my son who had started the fire, he would have been tried and jailed as a terrorist; had it been the imam who held the evidence he would have been jailed for withholding evidence. And everyone would have condemned Islam as a religion of violence."

Part of the apparent reluctance on the part of many Muslims to talk about the occurrence of incidents of discrimination and the presence of some real fear in the Islamic community, is a result of their desire to keep the issue as low key as possible. Another reason is the tendency to depersonalize, to see that incidents are not directed toward individual Muslims but are aimed in a generalized way at the larger community of Islam. This becomes a kind of safety mechanism for dealing with situations of tension and fear.

This fear is conditioned by several factors. One is the distorted image of Islam that is presented in the media. (Recent books about Islam have included titles such as *Militant Islam*[3] and *The Dagger of Islam*[4] and an article by Joseph Kraft in *The Washington Post* was entitled "The Dark Side of Islam.") Another is the lack of any substantial political or economic clout on the part of the Muslim community. Aware of the prejudice of Americans against Islam and against Arabs (who are often depicted as lustful, bungling polygamists in the movies and on television), Muslims must depend on the goodwill of their non-Muslim neighbors for survival.

Despite these very real concerns, integration of Muslim immigrants in the American context professionally and economically seems to be proceeding fairly smoothly. It is in the interests of American capitalism to accept those whose services contribute to the smooth functioning of the system. Our data show that cultural integration is somewhat slower, particularly when the immigrant is from a totally different culture. Westernized Arabs committed to a nationalist ideology have found America easier to adjust to than have Pakistanis committed to an ideology of an Islamic order. Complicating the assimilation of Pakistanis is their racial background. While Arabs can pass as members of other Mediterranean groups, such as Italians or Greeks, the Pakistanis cannot. Coming with a tradition of color consciousness in the Indian subcontinent, where light skin is generally associated with higher class standing in society, they often find this reinforced by experiences of color prejudice in America. Confronted by a great predominance of fair-skinned people here they subscribe to a religious consciousness that places the universal of Islam over the particular of national identity.

Several mosques in the various geographical areas we studied do define themselves specifically in terms of ethnic association, and national identity has certainly served and continues to serve several important functions. Such identity is extremely important for the psychological survival of new immigrants, especially those who speak nothing but their own native language, and serves as an integrating agent as the community slowly adopts various American customs.

These ethnic groups can serve to keep alive customs from the home country, especially if they are supported by fresh waves of immigrants. Nonetheless, it is also important for Muslims in America to view Islam as an overarching identity, linked with and yet finally independent of ethnic and national associations, a common bond holding together those of different backgrounds and customs.

Residence in North America does influence Muslim communities. Our data indicate that children are Americanized as a consequence of attending public schools, a process that also affects parents. In most areas Islamic activities related to the mosque are a family affair, including women's attendance at prayer services, potluck dinners, the education of children, study circles, and women serving on boards of the mosque. Even in the most traditional mosque there is a sense of ownership of Islamic institutions that is a direct consequence of the process of democratization. This is apparent in such things as the writing of constitutions and lay administration of institutions.

Furthermore, over the generations a process is evidenced by which Islam is identified to accord with the basic tenets of American civil religion, leading to a deemphasis of its distinctive features. Our data show that with each succeeding generation there is a decline in strict adherence to those values that are identified by Muslim leadership as specifically Islamic. These are the values on which this study focused, not the overarching philosophical and ethical values, such as justice and truth, that are the foundation of all world religions (see Tables 6.1A–C and 6.2A–F).

It is clear that Muslims who have been in this country for a long time, and whose children have gone through the American school system, show a great deal of heterogeneity in terms of Islamic practices. Even those groups composed of members of one national iden-

TABLE 6.1C   Area of Country and Perceptions of America's Openness to Islam's Spread

Perception by Muslims of Most Americans	Percentage Responses		
	East Coast	Upstate New York	Midwest
Open/indifferent	49	35	39
Somewhat opposed	22	35	33
Very opposed	29	40	28
	100	100	100
	(71)	(65)	(74)

TABLE 6.2A Behavioral Scales of Religious Activity and Deviant Activity: Distribution of Scales

Description	Scores	Percentage in Category
1. *Religious Activity Scale*		
Very active	5–8	25
Somewhat active	9–12	28
A little active	13–15	23
Not very active	16–20	24
		100
		(320)
2. *Deviant Behavior Scale*		
Deviant	4–9	25
Somewhat deviant	10–12	29
Rarely deviant	13–14	22
Almost never, never deviant		24
		100
		(338)

[a]*Religious Activity Scale:* Additive scale composed of the following items: (1) went to a Friday prayer service at a mosque/Islamic center; (2) fasted during Ramadan; (3) read the Qur'an; (4) invited a Muslim to join you in prayer; (5) prayed five times a day (response possibilities to all items: often, sometimes, rarely, never). Possible scores range from 5 to 20; 5 is the highest score or the highest degree of religious activity.
Deviance Scale: Additive scale, composed of the following items: (1) eat meat bought at a regular supermarket; (2) went swimming at public beach; (3) went to an American-style dance; (4) had an alcoholic drink (response possibilities: often, sometimes, rarely, never). Possible scores range from 4 to 16; 4 is the highest score or highest degree of engagement in deviant activities.
The scales, as collapsed above, are correlated negatively, as might be expected: tau beta −.32; significant to the .00001 level.

TABLE 6.2B Deviant Behavior Scale by Religious Behavior Scale (Controlling for Birth in U.S.)

Deviant Behavior Scale	Percentage Not Active Religiously (Scores 16–20)		
	Born in United States (+)	Foreign Born (−)	Difference
Deviant	63 (of 35)	37 (of 46)	+26
Somewhat deviant	28 (of 39)	20 (of 54)	+ 8
Rarely deviant	24 (of 25)	5 (of 44)	+19
Almost never, never deviant	27 (of 11)	7 (of 61)	+20
tau beta	−.24 (significant to .001)	−.32 (significant to .0001)	

TABLE 6.2C   Correlation of Areas of Country, Nationality, Religious
Behavior, and Deviant Behavior

Place of Birth	Percentage Very Active Religiously (Scores 5–8)	Percentage Somewhat Deviant at Least (Scores 4–12)
East Coast		
United States	15	69
Lebanon	33	58
Other Muslim countries	29	64
Pakistan, India	13	29
Upstate New York		
United States	20	17
Lebanon	none	no Lebanese in area sample
Other Muslim countries	47	0
Pakistan, India	53	0
Midwest		
United States	12	75
Lebanon	21	63
Other Muslim countries	23	82
Pakistan, India	67	33

tity become more diversified in their beliefs and practices the longer
they stay in this country. Many Muslims are increasingly aware of the
influence of the public schools in the process of Americanizing their
children. This has led to efforts to organize Muslim day schools in such
areas as Chicago, Seattle, Los Angeles, and other metropolitan
centers. Muslims surveyed in our study generally did not favor sending
their children to Islamic schools, but the issue is a real one for many in
this country. The tension comes in reconciling the desire for an aca-
demically excellent education, which is possible in some American
institutions both public and private, with the fear that such exposure to
different value systems may lead their children away from the principles of Islam.

Many of the more recent immigrants are appalled at what they see as
the moral chaos of American society with its high crime rate, drug
problems, and ready availability of pornography. They see such things
as products of a Christian culture that has lost touch with its basic
values. These Muslims find little here worth emulating, and consequently turn energetically to the alternative of an Islamic system of
values as infinitely superior. Thus they see it as their mission to call

TABLE 6.2D Behavioral Scales of Religious Activity and Deviant Activity (Uncollapsed) with Selected Variables

Variables	Religious Activity Scale	Deviance Scale
Born in America	−.25 (significant to .0001 level)	+.23 (significant to .001 level)
Date of Birth	+.13 (significant to .01 level)	−.16 (significant to .002 level)
Gender	not significant	not significant
Low Educational attainment	−.17 (significant to .002 level)	+.11 (significant to .02 level)
Low income	−.14 (significant to .008 level)	not significant
Infrequent mosque attendance	−.52 (significant to .00001 level)	+.16 (significant to .002 level)
Muslim women should stay single rather than marry non-Muslims	+.37 (significant to .0001 level)	−.36 (significant to .0001 level)
Young men should be allowed by their families to date	−.50 (significant to .00001 level)	+.56 (significant to .00001 level)
Women in Muslim families are treated as well as or better than American women in Christian and Jewish families	+.29 (significant to .0001 level)	−.28 (significant to .0001 level)
Eat often with non-Muslims	−.30 (significant to .00001 level)	+.38 (significant to .0001 level)

TABLE 6.2E Social Integration to Communal Involvement and Effects on Religious Activity and Deviance

Social Interaction	Percentage Very Active Religiously (scores 5–8)	Percentage Often Deviant (scores 4–9)
Dine with both Muslims and non-Muslims *fairly often*	22 (of 67)	43 (of 65)
Dine with both *sometimes*	14 (of 70)	30 (of 73)
Dine *mainly* with *non-Muslims*	0 (of 28)	39 (of 30)
Dine *somewhat more* with Muslims	58 (of 43)	15 (of 47)
Dine *almost exclusively* with Muslims	29 (of 76)	6 (of 83)
Eat at home, seldom socialize at dinner	19 (of 31)	19 (of 36)

TABLE 6.2F   Effects of Social Integration and Birth in America on Religious
Activity and Deviant Behavior

Eating Dinner with Non-Muslim Americans and Behavioral Scale	Born in America	Immigrant
Religious activity—percentage not very active religiously (scores 16–20)		
Often	53 (of 34)	27 (of 52)
Sometimes	31 (of 52)	15 (of 71)
Rarely, never	29 (of 24)	12 (of 84)
	Tau B = −.19	Tau B = −.03
	significant to .01 level	n.s.
	N = 110	N = 207
Deviant behavior—percentage fairly often deviant (scores 4–9)		
Often	44 (of 34)	44 (of 50)
Sometimes	31 (of 54)	21 (of 77)
Rarely, never	17 (of 24)	8 (of 96)
	Tau B = .23	Tau B = .35
	significant to .002 level	significant to .00001 level
	N = 112	N = 223

America back to faith in God and to work for the establishment of an
equitable and just Islamic order in the world, which is above tribal,
racial, and linguistic affiliation.

Islam in this country obviously takes many forms, and even in the
relatively small sample we were able to study, a wide range of ideas
and responses was evidenced. Recognizing the risky nature of generalizations, we have tried throughout this report to illustrate the wide
variety, both by giving a summary of the responses to survey questions
and by citing in their own words some of the reflections of individuals
at the several sites. We recognize that what generalizations we have
made are applicable to persons in the three areas we studied and may
or may not pertain to the broader community of Muslims in the United
States. Clearly, as was indicated in Chapter 1, considerable further
study is needed before responsible commentary can be given on the
overall picture of the Islamic community in this country.

Broader speculation, however, suggests that there are possibly five
major worldviews operating among Muslim immigrants in America.
First, there are those who can be called liberals; these are probably the
most Americanized of the Islamic community. This group has no recognized religious leadership. Adherents of the liberal worldview tend

to be American-born of Lebanese parents or Westernized unmosqued immigrants. Another group is conservative, Westernized, but adhering to the minimum requirements of Islam dealing with personal piety, dietary restrictions, and prescribed practices. The third group is "evangelical," putting great emphasis on scriptural foundations and the example of the Prophet Muhammad defining the perimeters of the faith. Advocates of this perspective are concerned with the daily living of an Islamic life, taking special care to fulfill *all* the minute prescriptions and proscriptions of Islam. They tend to be isolationist and centered in the small group of like-minded Muslims. Often they hold meetings led by itinerant missionaries from overseas who lecture on the necessity of faithfulness to Islam. The fourth group is neonormative, similar to the third in all respects, yet with an additional dimension. They affirm the necessity of supervision of public life by Islam and Islamic principles. Thus, their goal is to strive to alter society so that Islam may rule. And finally, there are the Sufis (the majority of whom are converts), who focus on the mystical dimension of Islam.

It is clear from the results of this study that our sample was limited to the first two of these groups and that, at the present, given the climate in this country, it is difficult if not impossible for a non-Muslim study team to get access to the others.

When a draft of some of the findings of this study of Islamic communities in the United States was released to the public in 1985, it was picked up by the press. An article by John Dart in the *Los Angeles Times* carried this headline: "Assimilation Perils Immigrant Muslim Values." This was understandably alarming to the Muslim community in Los Angeles; one mosque leader referred to it as "the bomb you dropped." Then a condensed version of exactly the same copy appeared in the *Chicago Sun Times,* but with the headline "U.S. Moslems Feeling at Home, Assimilation into American Way of Life Found Remarkable." As a result of the Chicago article two persons from two different mosques in Chicago asked whether their institutions could be studied. It is obvious that in both places the headlines set the tone for the perception.

In actual fact, the data the study has collected supports both headlines. Some Muslims are feeling at home and welcome assimilation into American life, while others are genuinely concerned that it will jeopardize the maintenance of Islamic values. Both kinds of responses relate to one's image of what it means to be Muslim in America. The future of Islam in this country will depend to a large extent on several key factors. One is the general trend of thought in Islam overseas in terms of leadership, articulation of the faith, and the flow of immigrants who will both challenge current consensus on compromise and help to reformulate it. Another is the degree to which American society itself acknowledges and welcomes the presence of a growing Islamic community in this country, the government formulates policy in the Middle East and other Muslim areas, and the press chooses to deal with issues sensitive to Muslims. And finally, Islam in this country will be expressed, appropriated, and lived as Muslims continue to search for and discover ways to be true to a faith that, in its universal nature, will find expression as a truly American phenomenon.

NOTES

Chapter 1

1. The estimates range from 9 million, as suggested by Warith Deen Muhammad, leader of the American Muslim Mission, down to 600,695, as given by Max Kershaw. Kershaw states that he actually counted 600,695 individuals but estimated that "additional uncounted numbers of Muslims would bring the estimated numbers to perhaps one million." Warith Deen Muhammad, "Muslim Demographic Survey" (June 1982), unpublished.

2. M. Arif Ghayur, "Muslims in the United States: Settlers and Visitors," *Annals* AAPSS, 454 (March 1981). A demographic survey of the community conducted by Dr. Raquibuz Zaman produced the same estimate.

3. As estimated by Dr. Raquibuz Zaman, at the request of the authors.

4. *The Harvard Encyclopedia of American Ethnic Groups* (Cambridge, Mass.: Harvard University Press, 1980) has essays on various Muslim groups including Arabs, Afghans, Albanians, Azerbaijanis, Bangladeshis, Bosnians, Fijians, Indonesians, Iranians, Kurds, Pakistanis, Tatars, North Caucasians, Polish and Lithuanian Tatars, Turkistanis, and Turks.

5. Yvonne Y. Haddad, "The Muslim Experience in the United States," *The Link,* 12, no. 4 (Sept.–Oct. 1979).

6. See, for example, *Arabic Speaking Communities in American Cities,* ed. Barbara Aswad (New York: Center for Migration Studies, 1974); Abdo A. Elkholy, *The Arab Moslems in the United States* (New Haven: College and University Press, 1966); Emily Kalled Lovell, "A Survey of the Arab-Muslims in the United States and Canada," *The Muslim World,* 63 (1973); *Arabs in the New World: Studies on Arab American Communities,* ed. Sameer Abraham and Nabeel Abraham (Detroit: Wayne State University Press, 1983); Earle Waugh et al., *The Muslim Community in North America* (Edmonton: University of Alberta Press, 1983); Ali Abdul Jalil al-Tahir, "The Arab Community in the Chicago Area: A Comparative Study of the Christian Syrians and the Muslim Palestinians," Diss., University of Chicago, 1952; *The Arab-Americans: Studies in Assimilation,* ed. Elaine C. Hagopian and Ann Paden, (Wilmette, Ill.: The Medina University Press International, 1969).

Chapter 2

1. Yvonne Y. Haddad, "Muslim in Canada: A Preliminary Study," in *Religion and Ethnicity,* ed. Harold Coward and Leslie Kawamura (Waterloo: Wilfrid Laurier University Press, 1978), p. 83.

2. Earle H. Waugh, "The Imam in the New World: Models and Modifications," in *Transitions and Transformations in the History of Religions,* ed. Frank E. Reynolds and Theodore M. Ludwig (Leiden: E. J. Brill, 1980), p. 147.

Chapter 3

1. Richard D. Alba and Mitchell B. Chamlin, "A Preliminary Examination of Ethnic Identification Among Whites," *American Sociological Review,* 48 (April 1983):240–47; Alejandro Portes, "The Rise of Ethnicity," *American Sociological Review,* 49 (June 1984):383–97.

2. See Portes, "The Rise of Ethnicity."

3. Gerhard Lenski, *The Religious Factor* (New York: Doubleday, 1961).

Chapter 5

1. Yvonne Y. Haddad, "Muslims in America," in *Islam: The Religious and Political Life of a Community,* ed. Marjorie Kelly (New York: Praeger Press, 1984).

2. Even more to the point, the two attitudinal items are significantly (at .0001 level) *positively,* not negatively, correlated regarding restriction of marriage of *both* Muslim men *and* women to other Muslims.

3. Abdo A. Elkholy, *The Arab Moslems in the United States* (New Haven: College and University Press, 1966), pp. 30, 35, 124, 149.

Chapter 6

1. See, for example, Anis Ahmad, "The Miracle Called Qur'an at the Mercy of Charlatans," *Al-Ittihad,* 15 (1978):53. He writes, "Strictly speaking, one does not have to be a genius to know that proper names like *Allah* cannot be translated, while attributive names may always be translated."

2. Complicating the issue of the use of the term Allah is the growing Muslim community of African-American heritage that, since the middle 1970s, has undergone a transformation of its theology. This has brought about a great interest in Arabizing terms used by the believers as a conscious separation from their Christian past. They refer to God as Allah and use a number of Arabic and Islamic terms in everyday conversation.

3. Godfrey Jansen, *Militant Islam* (New York: Harper & Row, 1980).

4. John Laffin, *Dagger of Islam* (New York: Bantam, 1981).

BIBLIOGRAPHY

I. General Studies

Abed-Rabbo, Samir. "The Neglected Focus." *Journal Institute of Muslim Minority Affairs,* 5, no. 1 (1983–84).

Abugiedeiri, el Tigani A. *A Survey of North American Muslims.* Indianapolis, Ind.: Islamic Teaching Center, 1977.

Aijian, M. M. "Mohammedans in the United States." *The Muslim World,* 10 (1920).

Ali, Kamal. "Islamic Education in the United States: An Overview of Issues, Problems and Possible Approaches." *The American Journal of Islamic Studies,* 1 (1984).

Bogardus, Emory S. *Essentials of Americanization,* 3rd ed. Los Angeles: J. R. Miller, 1923.

Bosquet, G. H. "Moslem Religious Influences in the United States." *The Muslim World,* 25 (1935).

Braden, Charles S. "Islam in America." *The International Review of Missions,* 48 (1959).

Darrat, Ali F. "Are Checking Accounts in American Banks Permissible Under Islamic Laws?" *Islamic Social Sciences,* 2, no. 1 (1985).

Ghayur, Arif. "Demographic Evolution of Pakistanis in America: Case Study of a Muslim Subgroup." *The American Journal of Islamic Studies,* 1 (1984).

Gottesman, Lois. "Islam in America: A Background Report." Prepared for Institute of Human Relations, The American Jewish Committee, 1979.

Graves, T. *The Muslim in American Stories.* [Printed in separate pamphlets by the U.S.I.A.], 1959.

Haddad, Safia. "The Woman's Role in Socialization of Syrian-Americans in Chicago." In *The Arab Americans: Studies in Assimilation.* Ed. Elaine C. Hagopian and Ann Paden. Wilmette, Ill.: Medina University Press International, 1969.

Haddad, Yvonne Yazbeck. "The Impact of the Islamic Revolution in Iran on the Syrian Muslims of Montreal." In *The Muslim Community in North*

America. Ed. Earle Waugh et al. Edmonton: University of Alberta Press, 1983.

———. "Islam in America: A Growing Religious Movement." *The Muslim World League Journal,* 9, no. 9 (1984).

———. "Islam in Canada." *The Canadian Encyclopedia.* Edmonton: University of Alberta Press, 1985.

———. "Islamic Institutions in America: Adaptations and Reform." In *Arabs in the New World: Studies on Arab American Communities.* Ed. Sameer Abraham and Nabeel Abraham, Detroit: Wayne State University Press, 1983. Reprinted in *Taking Root, Bearing Fruit: The Arab American Experience.* Ed. James Zoghby. Washington, D.C.: A.D.C., 1984.

———. "The Muslim Experience in the United States." *The Link,* 22, no. 4 (1979).

———. "Muslims in America." In *Islam: The Religious and Political Life of a Community.* Ed. Marjorie Kelly. New York: Praeger Press, 1984.

———. "Muslims in Canada: A Preliminary Study." In *Religion and Ethnicity.* Ed. Harold Coward and Leslie Kawamura. Waterloo: Wilfrid Laurier University Press, 1978.

Hamdani, D. H. "Muslims and Christian Life in Canada." *Journal Institute of Muslim Minority Affairs,* 1, no. 1 (1979).

———. *Muslims in Canada: A Century of Settlement 1871–1976.* Ottawa: Council of Muslim Communities in Canada, 1978.

———. "Muslims in the Canadian Mosaic." *Journal Institute of Muslim Minority Affairs,* 5, 1 (1983–84).

Hoffert, Andrew T. "The Moslem Movement in America." *The Muslim World,* 20 (1930).

Holmes, Mary Caroline. "Islam in America." *The Muslim World,* 16 (1926).

Irving, T. B. "The Islamic Heritage in the Americas." *Our Effort,* 5 (1976).

"Islam in the United States." *The Muslim World* [Notes of the Quarter], 48 (1958).

Kettani, Ali M. *Al-Muslimun fi Euroba wa Amrika.* Vol. 2, Dar Idris, Iraq, 1976.

Lovell, Emily Kalled. "A Survey of the Arab-Muslims in the United States and Canada." *The Muslim World,* 63 (1973).

Makdisi, Nadim. "The Moslems in America." *The Christian Century,* 76 (1959).

———. "The Muslims of America." *The Islamic Review* (England) (June 1955).

Muhammad, Akbar. "Muslims in the United States: An Overview of Organizations, Doctrines and Problems." In *The Islamic Impact.* Yvonne Haddad, Byron Haines and Ellison Findly. Syracuse: Syracuse University Press, 1984.

———. "Some Factors which Promote and Restrict Islamization in America." *The American Journal of Islamic Studies,* 1, no. 2 (1984).

"Muslim Students in the United States." *The Muslim World* [Notes of the Quarter], 52 (1962).

Nyang, Sulayman S. "Islam in the United States of America: A Review of the Sources." *The Search: Journal for Arab and Islamic Studies*, 1 (1980).

Nyang, Sulayman S. and Ahmad, Mumtaz. "The Muslim Intellectual Emigre in the United States." *Islamic Culture*, 59, no. 3 (1985).

Nyang, Sulayman S. and Cummings, Robert. "Islam in the United States of America." A report submitted to the King Faisal Foundation, Riyadh, Saudi Arabia, 1983.

Simsar, Mehmed A. "Muslims in the United States." *Twentieth Century Encyclopedia of Religious Knowledge.* Vol. 2. Ed. Lefferts A. Loetscher. Grand Rapids, Mich.: Baker Book House, 1955.

Speight, Marston. "Christian-Muslim Dialogue in the United States of America." *Islamochristiana,* 7 (1981).

Thomas, Katrina and Tracy, William. "America as Alma Mater." *Aramco-World,* 30, no. 3 (1979).

Tunison, Emory H. "Mohammad Webb, First American Muslim." *The Arab World,* 1, no. 3 (1945).

Waugh, Earle H. "The Imam in the New World: Models and Modifications." In *Transitions and Transformations in the History of Religions.* Ed. Frank E. Reynolds and Theodore M. Ludwig. Leiden: E. J. Brill, 1980.

Waugh, Earle; Abu Laban, Baha; and Qureishi, Regula. *The Muslim Community in North America.* Edmonton: University of Alberta Press, 1983.

II. Immigrant Islam

A. Studies of Immigrant Communities

Abraham, Nabeel. "Arabic Speaking Communities of Southeastern Dearborn: A General Overview." University of Wisconsin, Madison, 1975. Mimeograph.

——. *Arabs in America: An Overview. The Arab World and Arab Americans: Understanding a Neglected Minority.* Ed. Sameer Y. Abraham and Nabeel Abraham. Detroit: Wayne State University, Center for Urban Studies, 1981.

——. "Detroit's Yemeni Workers." *MERIP Reports,* 57 (1977).

——. "National and Local Politics: A Study of Political Conflict in the Yemeni Immigrant Community of Detroit, Michigan." Ph.D. diss., University of Michigan, 1978.

——. "Rejoinder to Detroit's Yemeni Workers." *MERIP Reports,* 60 (1977).

——. "The Yemeni Immigrant Community of Detroit: Background Emigration and Community Life." In *Arabs in the New World: Studies on Arab-American Communities.* Ed. Sameer Y. Abraham and Nabeel Abraham. Detroit: Wayne State University, Center for Urban Studies, 1983.

Abraham, Sameer Y. "Detroit's Arab-American Community: A Survey of Diversity and Commonality." In *Arabs in the New World: Studies on Arab-American Communities*. Ed. Sameer Y. Abraham and Nabeel Abraham. Detroit: Wayne State University, Center for Urban Studies, 1983.

————. "A Survey of the Arab-American Community in Metropolitan Detroit." In *The Arab World and Arab Americans: Understanding a Neglected Minority*. Ed. Sameer Y. Abraham and Nabeel Abraham. Detroit: Wayne State University, Center for Urban Studies, 1981.

Abraham, Sameer Y. and Abraham, Nabeel, eds. *The Arab World and Arab-Americans: Understanding a Neglected Minority*. Detroit: Wayne State University, Center for Urban Studies, 1981.

————. *Arabs in the New World: Studies on Arab-American Communities*. Detroit: Wayne State University, Center for Urban Studies, 1983.

Abraham, Sameer; Abraham, Nabeel; and Aswad, Barbara. "The Southend: An Arab Muslim Working-Class Community." In *Arabs in the New World: Studies on Arab-American Communities*. Ed. Sameer Y. Abraham and Nabeel Abraham. Detroit: Wayne State University, Center for Urban Studies, 1983.

Abu-Laban, Baha. "The Adolescent Peer Group in Cross Cultural Perspective." *Canadian Review of Sociology and Anthropology,* 7 (1970).

————. "The Arab Canadian Community." In *Arab Americans: Studies in Assimilation*. Ed. E. Hagopian, and Ann Paden. Wilmette, Ill.: Medina University Press International, 1969.

————. "The Arab Community in the Canadian Mosaic." *Rikka,* 3 (1976).

————. "Canadian Muslims: The Need for a New Survival Strategy." *Journal Institute of Muslim Minority Affairs,* 2, no. 2 (1980); 3, no. 1 (1981).

————. "Middle East Groups." Ottawa: Department of the Secretary of State, 1973.

————. *An Olive Branch on the Family Tree: The Arabs in Canada*. Toronto: McClelland & Stewart, 1980.

Abu-Laban, Baha, and Zeadey, Faith T., eds. *Arabs in America: Myths and Realities*. Wilmette, Ill.: Medina University Press International, 1975.

Abu-Laban, Sharon McIrvin. "Stereotype of Middle East People: An Analysis of Church School Curricula." In *Arabs in America: Myth and Realities*. Ed. Baha Abu Laban and Faith T. Zeadey. Wilmette, Ill.: Medina University Press International, 1975.

Ahmed, Ismael. "Organizing an Arab Workers Caucus." *MERIP Reports,* 34 (1975).

Alyahya, Khaled Ahmad M. "Constructing a Comprehensive Orientation Program for Saudi Arabian Students in the United States." Master's thesis, University of Pittsburgh, 1981.

Amiji, H. "The Asian Communities." In *Islam in Africa*. Ed. J. Kritzcek. New York: Van Nostrand & Reinhold, 1969.

Ansara, James M. "The Immigration and Settlement of the Syrians." Bachelor's thesis, Harvard University, 1931.

Ansari, Abdoulmaboud. "A Community in Process: The First Generation of Iranian Professional Middle-Class Immigrants in the United States." *International Review of Modern Sociology,* 7 (1977).

Aoki, T., et al. *Canadian Ethnicity: The Politics of Meaning.* Vancouver: Center for the Study of Curriculum and Instruction, University of British Columbia, 1978.

Aossey, William Yahya. "The First Mosque in America." *Journal Institute of Muslim Minority Affairs,* 5, no. 1 (1983–84).

The Arab Image in the Western Mass Media. London: Morris International Ltd., 1979.

el Araby, Kadri M., and Arafat, Ibtihaj S. "The Arab-Egyptian Muslim Community in New Jersey." In *The New Jersey Ethnic Experience.* Ed. Barbara Cunningham. Union, N.J.: Wm. Wise & Co., 1977.

Askari, Hossein G., and Cummings, J. T. "The Middle East and the United States: A Problem of Brain Drain." *International Journal of Middle East Studies,* 8 (1977).

Askari, H.; Cummings, J. T.; and Izbudak, M. "Iran's Migration of Skilled Labor to the United States." *Iranian Studies,* 10 (1977).

Aswad, Barbara C., ed. *Arabic Speaking Communities in American Cities.* New York: Center for Migration Studies of New York Inc., and Association of Arab-American University Graduates, Inc., 1974.

Awan, Sadiq Noor Alam. *The People of Pakistani Origin in Canada: The First Quarter Century.* Ottawa: S.N.A. Awan (under the auspices of the Canada-Pakistan Association of Ottawa-Hull), 1976.

Azat, Issa Yacoub. "The Nonreturning Arab Student: A Study in the Loss of Human Resources." Ph.D. diss., University of Southern California, Los Angeles, 1974.

el-Banyan, Abdullah Saleh. "Cross-cultural Education and Attitude Change: A Study of Saudi Arabian Students in the United States." Master's thesis, North Carolina State University, 1974.

Barclay, Harold. "An Arab Community in the Canadian Northwest: A Preliminary Discussion of the Lebanese Community in Lac La Biche, Alberta." *Anthropologica* N.S., 10 (1968).

――――. "A Lebanese Community in Lac La Biche, Alberta." In *Minority Canadians: Immigrant Groups.* Ed. Jean Leonard Elliott. Scarborough, Ontario: Prentice-Hall of Canada, 1971.

――――. "The Lebanese Muslim Family." In *The Canadian Family.* Rev. ed. Ed. K. Ishwaran. Toronto: Holt, Rinehart and Winston, 1976.

――――. "The Muslim Experience in Canada." In *Religion and Ethnicity.* Ed. Harold Coward and Leslie Kawamura. Waterloo: Wilfrid Laurier University Press, 1978.

――――. "The Perpetuation of Muslim Tradition in the Canadian North." *The Muslim World,* 59 (1969).

Bassiouni, M. C., ed. "The Special Measures and Some AAUG Public Action. The Civil Rights of Arab-Americans: The Special Measures." North Darmouth: AAUG, 1974.

Beinin, Joel. "Yemenis Participate in Detroit Struggles." *MERIP Reports,* 59 (1977).

Benyon, E. D. "The Near East in Flint, Michigan: Assyrians and Druze and the Antecedents." *Geographic Review,* 24 (1944).

Berger, Morroe. "America's Syrian Community." *Commentary,* 25 (1958).

———. "Americans from the Arab World." In *The World of Islam.* Ed. James Kritzeck and R. Bayly Winder. New York: St. Martin's Press, 1959.

Bernard, Thomas L. "United States Immigration Laws and the Brain Drain." *International Migrations,* 1, no. 7 (January 1969).

Bin-Sayeed, Khaled. "The Predicament of Muslim Professionals in Canada and Its Resolution." *Journal Institute of Muslim Minority Affairs,* 3, no. 2 (1981).

Bishart, Mary. "Yemenis and Farmworkers in California." *MERIP Reports,* 34 (1957).

Bozorgmehr, Mehdi. "Social Differentiation, Chain Migration, and Sub-Ethnic Group Cohesion: The Case of Iranian Muslims in Los Angeles." Paper delivered to the Middle East Studies Association, 1984.

Bukhowa, Adel Abdulla. "The Attitudes of Arab Students in Colorado Toward Business and Industrial Firms in the United States." Master's thesis, University of Northern Colorado, 1978.

Cainkar, Louise. "Life Experiences of Palestinian Women in the United States." Paper delivered to the Middle East Studies Association, November 1985.

Campbell, Milo Kay. "An Analysis of the Relationships between Self Concept and Sociological Receptiveness of Lebanese Ethnic Children in the Detroit Metropolitan Area." Ph.D. diss., Wayne State University, 1972.

Canada: Secretary of State. *The Canadian Family Tree: Canada's Peoples.* Don Mills, Ontario: Corpus, 1979.

Canadian Arab Friendship Association of Edmonton. *A Salute to the Pioneers of Northern Alberta.* Edmonton: Canadian Arab Friendship Association, 1973.

Canadian Society of Muslims. "Report: On the Image of Islam in School Textbooks in the Province of Ontario, Canada." N.d.

Chandras, Kananur B. *Arab, Armenian, Syrian, Lebanese, East Indian, Pakistani and Bangladeshi Americans: A Study Guide and Source Book.* San Francisco: R and E Research Associates, 1977.

Charbaji, Abdulrazzak Mohamed Salah. "Academic and Social Problems Facing Arab Students on American Campuses." Master's thesis, University of Northern Colorado, 1978.

Chesnoff, Richard Z. "Paris: The Iranian Exiles." *The New York Times Magazine,* Feb. 12, 1984.

Choudhury, Masudul Alam. "An Occupational Distribution of Muslims in the Employed Labour Force in Canada: Estimates for 1978." *Journal Institute of Muslim Minority Affairs,* 1, no. 2 (1979); and 2, no. 1 (1980).

Craig, A. J. M. "Egyptian Students." *Middle East Journal,* 7 (1953).

Dahhan, Omaymah Ezzet. "A Study of the Factors Influencing Future Plans and Career Goals of Arab Ph.D. Students in the United States." Master's thesis, University of Texas, Austin, 1975.

David, J. K. "The Near East Settlers of Jacksonville and Duval County." Paper presented at the May 12, 1954, meeting of the Jacksonville Historical Society, Jacksonville, Fla., 1954.

Diab, Lufty N. "Authoritarianism and Prejudice in Near-Eastern Students Attending American Universities." Ph.D. diss., University of Oklahoma, 1957.

Dweik, Bader Saed. "Factors Determining Language Maintenance and Language Shift in Arabic-American Communities." Ph.D. diss., State University of New York, Buffalo, 1980.

————. "The Language Situation Among the Yemenites of Lackawanna." In *Proceedings of the University-Wide Conference on Communicative Behavior Approaches and Research.* Buffalo, N.Y.: Center for Studies in Cultural Transmission, SUNY/Buffalo, 1979.

Elkholy, Abdo A. *The Arab Moslems in the United States.* New Haven: College and University Press, 1966.

————. "Religion and Assimilation in Two Muslim Communities America." Ph.D. diss., Princeton University, 1960.

Esmail, A. "Satpanth Ismailism and Modern Changes Within It: With Special Reference to East Africa." Ph.D. diss., Edinburgh University, 1972.

Fadlalla, Fadlalla Ali. "Integration of Sudanese Students into the American Society: An Indepth Analysis of the Problem of Alienation among Students in California." Master's thesis, Claremont Graduate School and University Center, 1979.

Farjad, Mehrassa. "Brain Drain: Migration of Iranian Physicians to the United States." Ed.D. diss., George Washington University, 1981.

Farjadi, Gholamali. "Economics of Study Abroad: The Case of Iranian Students in the U.S." Ph.D. diss., New York University, 1980.

Fathi, Asghar. "The Arab Moslem Community in the Prairie City." *Canadian Ethnic Studies,* 5 (1976).

————. "Mass Media and Muslim Immigrant Community in Canada." *Anthropologica* N.S., 15 (1973).

Fathi, Asghar and Smeaton, Hunter B. "Arabic-Canadian Periodical Publications." *Canadian Ethnic Studies* (Third Bibliographical Issue), 5 (1976).

Georgakas, Dan. "Arab Workers in Detroit." *MERIP Reports,* 34 (1975).

Germanns, A. K. J. "Arabic Literature in America." *Islamic Literature,* 12, no. 2 (1966).

Gezi, Khalil Ismail. "The Acculturation of Middle Eastern Arab Students in

Selected American Colleges and Universities." Ph.D. diss., Stanford University, 1959.

Ghareeb, Edmund. "The Media and U.S. Perceptions of the Middle East." *American-Arab Affairs,* 2 (1982).

———. *Split Vision: The Portrayal of Arabs in the American Media.* Washington, D.C.: The American-Arab Affairs Council, 1983.

Ghayur, Arif M. "Demographic Evolution of Pakistanis in America: Case Study of a Muslim Subgroup." *The American Journal of Islamic Studies,* 1 (1984).

———. "Ethnic Distribution of American Muslims and Selected Socio-Economic Characteristics." *Journal Institute of Muslim Minority Affairs,* 5, no. 1 (1983–84).

———. "Muslims in the United States: Settlers and Visitors." *The Annals of the American Academy of Political and Social Science,* 454 (1981).

Ghazi, Abidullah. "Problems of Religious Text Books and Instruction in North America." *Journal Institute of Muslim Minority Affairs,* 5, no. 1 (1983–84).

Gilanshan, Farah. "Iranians of the Twin Cities." Ph.D. diss., University of Minnesota, 1983.

Golesorkhi, Nassereh G. "Parent-Child Relations among Exiled Iranian Families in Southern California: An Examination of the Impacts of Modernization and Forced Migration on Family Relations." Master's thesis, San Diego State University, 1983.

Griswold, William, et al. *The Image of the Middle East in Secondary Textbooks.* New York: MESA, 1975.

Hagey, Abdulla Rashid. "Academic and Social Adjustment of Middle Eastern Students Attending Oregon Colleges and Universities." Ph.D. diss., University of Oregon, 1968.

Hagopian, Elaine C. "Minority Rights in a Nation-State: The Nixon Administration's Campaign Against the Arab-Americans." *Journal of Palestine Studies,* 5 (1975).

Hagopian, Elaine C. and Paden, Ann, eds. *The Arab Americans: Studies in Assimilation.* Wilmette, Ill.: The Medina University Press International, 1969.

Haiek, Joseph R., ed. *The American Arabic-Speaking Community 1975 Almanac.* Los Angeles: The News Circle, 1975.

Hammons, Terry B. "A Wild Ass of a Man: American Images of Arabs to 1948." Master's thesis, University of Oklahoma, 1978.

Hammuda, Ahmad. "Jordanian Emigration: An Analysis of Migration Data." *International Migration Review,* 14 (1980).

Harfoush, Samira Mohamad. "A Study of Adjustment Problems and Attitudes of United Arab Emirates Undergraduate Students in the United States during the Fall of 1977." Master's thesis, George Washington University, 1978.

Hatoor, Al-Khalidi and Muhee Al-Din. "A Century of American Contribution to Arab Nationalism 1820–1920." Ph.D. diss., Vanderbilt University, 1958.

Hayani, Huda. "Arab Women in Canada." *Arab Dawn,* 4, no. 4 (1972).

Hazu, Tuma Wadi. "The Effect of Cultural Affinity on Language Dominance in Arab Minority Students in Selected American Public Schools." Master's thesis, Florida State University, 1982.

al-Hinai, Alyakdhan Talib. "Images, Attitudes and Problems of Middle Eastern Students in America." Master's thesis, United States International University, 1977.

Hitti, Philip K. *The Syrians in America.* New York: George H. Doran, 1924.

Houghton, Louise Seymour. "The Syrians in the United States." *Survey,* 26 (19).

Hudson, Michael C. and Wolfe, Ronald G., eds. *The American Media and the Arabs.* Washington, D.C.: Center for Contemporary Arab Studies, Georgetown University, 1980.

Hussaini, Hatem I. "The Impact of the Arab-Israeli Conflict on Arab Communities in the United States." In *Settler Regimes in Africa and the Arab World.* Ed. Ibrahim Abu Lughod, and Baha Abu Laban. Wilmette, Ill.: Medina University Press International, 1974.

Ibrahim, Saad Eddin Mohamed. "Interaction, Perception and Attitudes of Arab Students toward Americans." *Sociology and Social Research,* 55 (1970).

————. "Political Attitudes of an Emerging Elite: A Case Study of the Arab Students in the United States." Ph.D. diss., University of Washington, Seattle, 1968.

al-Islam, Amir. "Sheikh Daoud Faisal Died." *The Minaret,* 7, no. 8 (April 16, 1980).

Ismael, Jacqueline S. and Ismael, Tareq. "The Arab Americans and the Middle East." *Middle East Journal,* 30 (1976).

Ismail, Mohamed Abdul-Rahman. "A Cross-Cultural Study of Moral Judgments: The Relationship Between American and Saudi Arabian University Students on the Defining Issues Test." Unpublished manuscript, 1976.

Jaafari, Lafi Ibrahim. "The Brain Drain to the United States: The Migration of Jordanian and Palestinian Professionals and Students." *Journal of Palestinian Studies,* 3 (1973).

————. "Migration of Palestinian Arab and Jordanian Students and Professionals to the United States." Ph.D. diss., Iowa State University of Science and Technology, 1971.

————. "Migration Patterns of the Graduates of the American University of Beirut." In *The International Migration of High-Level Manpower: Its Impact on the Development Process.* Chairman, Charles V. Kidd. New York: Praeger, 1970.

Jabara, Abdeen. "Operation Arab: The Nixon Administration's Measures in the U.S. after Munich." In *The Civil Rights of Arab-Americans: The Special Measures.* Ed. M. D. Bassiouni. North Dartmouth: Arab-American University Graduates, 1974.

———. "Workers, Community Mobilized in Detroit." *AAUG Newsletter* S. Jackson and V. Nevils, June 1974.

Jammaz, Abdulrahman and I. Ibrahim. "Saudi Students in the United States: A Study of Their Adjustment Problems." Ph.D. diss., Michigan State University, 1972.

Jarrar, Samir A. "Images of the Arabs in United States Secondary School Social Studies Textbooks: A Content Analysis and a Unit Development." Ph.D. diss., Florida State University, 1975.

Kassaie, Parvin. "Politics of Exile: The Case of Iranians." Ph.D. diss., University of Southern California, Los Angeles, forthcoming.

Katarsky, Anthony P. "Family Ties and the Growth of an Arabic Community in Northeast Dearborn, Michigan." Master's thesis, Wayne State University, Detroit, 1980.

Katibah, Ibrahim Habib and Ziadeh, Farhat. *Arab-Speaking Americans.* New York: The Institute of Arab American Affairs, 1946.

Kayal, Philip M. and Kayal, Joseph M. *The Syrian-Lebanese in America: A Study in Religion and Assimilation.* Boston: Twayne Publishers, 1975.

Kazem, Mohamed Ibrahim. "Prominent Values of Egyptian and American Students as Determined by an Analysis of Their Autobiographies with Educational Implications." Ph.D. diss., University of Kansas, 1957.

Kearney, Helen M. "American Images of the Middle East, 1824–1924: A Century of Antipathy." Master's thesis, University of Rochester, 1976.

Kennedy, Leonard Milton. "The Treatment of Moslem Nations, India and Israel in Social Studies Textbooks Used in Elementary and Junior High Schools of the United States." Ph.D. diss., Washington State University, 1960.

Kershaw, Roland Max. "Attitudes toward Religion of Saudi Arabian Students in the United States." Ph.D. diss., University of Southern California, Los Angeles, 1973.

Ketab Corporation. *The Iranian Directory Yellow Pages.* Los Angeles: Ketab Corporation, 1981–1984.

Khan, Salim. "A Brief History of Pakistanis in the Western United States." Master's thesis, California State University, Sacramento, 1981.

———. "Pakistanis in the Western United States." *Journal Institute of Muslim Minority Affairs,* 5 (1983–84).

Khattab, Abelmoneim M. "The Assimilation of Arab Muslims in Alberta." Master's thesis, University of Alberta, Edmonton, 1969.

al-Khedaire, Khedair Saud. "Cultural Perception and Attitudinal Differences among Saudi Arabian Male College Students in the United States." Master's thesis, University of Arizona, 1978.

Khuri, Fuad I. "A Comparative Study of Migration Patterns in Two Lebanese Villages." *Human Organization,* 26 (1967).

Kim, K. C.; Kim, H. C.; and Hurh, W. M. "Job Information Deprivation in the United States: A Case Study of Iranian Immigrants." *Ethnicity,* 8 (1981).

Lewis, Ralph Kepler. "Hadchite: A Study of Emigration in a Lebanese Village." Ph.D. diss., Columbia University, 1967.

Macron, Mary Haddad. *Arab Americans and Their Communities of Cleveland.* Cleveland, Ohio: Cleveland Ethnic Heritage Studies, Cleveland State University, 1979.

————. *A Celebration of Life: Memories of an Arab-American in Cleveland.* Anti-Discrimination Committee Report No. 7, Washington, D.C.: ADC, 1982.

Magee, Judith H. "Images of Arabs and Israelis in the Denver Press." Master's thesis, University of Colorado, 1977.

Maloof, Louis J. "A Sociological Study of Arabic-Speaking People in Mexico." Ph.D. diss., University of Florida, 1958.

Maloof, Patricia S. "Medical Beliefs and Practices of Palestinian-Americans." Master's thesis, Catholic University of America, 1979.

Mansour, Samira Ahmed el-Sayed. "Cultural Change and the Process of Assimilation: A Study of the Assimilation of Egyptian Immigrants and Their Children Who Attend the Public Schools." Master's thesis, New York University, 1978.

Mansur, R. "The Palestinian Community in the U.S.: Background, Social Conditions, and Potentials for Development." *Shu'un Filastiniya* (Palestinian Affairs), 100 (1980).

Massoud, Muhammad Said. *I Fought as I Believed.* Montreal: Muhammad Said Massoud, 1976.

Mehdi, Beverlee Turner, ed. and comp. *The Arabs in America. 1492–1977: A Chronology and Fact Book.* Dobbs Ferry, N.Y.: Oceana Publications, 1978.

Miller, Deborah. "Middle Easterners—Syrians, Lebanese, Armenians, Egyptians, Iranians, Palestinians, Turks, Afghans." In *They Chose Minnesota: A Survey of the State's Ethnic Groups.* Ed. June Drenning Homquist. St. Paul: Minnesota Historical Society Press, 1981.

Miller, Lucius Hopkins. *Our Syrian Population: A Study of the Syrian Population of Greater New York.* N.p., 1904. (Copies available in Columbia University, New York University, and Harvard University libraries).

Mokarzel, Salloum. "Arabic Newspapers in America." *Syrian World* (1928).

Momeni, Jamshid. "America's Only Mosque to Go." *The Muslim World,* 13 (1923).

————. "Mosque in New York." *The Muslim World* [Notes of the Quarter], 49 (1959).

————. "Size and Distribution of Iranian Ethnic Group in the United States: 1980." *Iran Nameh,* 2 (1984).

Munir, Zahra. "Being Muslim and Female." *Journal Institute of Muslim Minority Affairs,* 5, no. 1 (1983–1984).

Naff, Alixa. "Arabs." In *Harvard Encyclopedia of American Ethnic Groups.* Ed. Stephan Thernstrom et al. Cambridge, Mass.: Belknap Press, 1980.

———. *Becoming American: The Early Arab Immigrant Experience.* Carbondale: Southern Illinois University Press, 1985.

Nanji, Azim. "Modernization and Change in the Nizari Ismaili Community in East Africa." *Journal of Religion in Africa,* 6 (1974).

Newsom, David D. "The Arabs and U.S. Public Opinion: Is There Hope?" *American-Arab Affairs,* 2 (1982).

Nijim, Basheer K., ed. *American Church Politics and the Middle East.* Belmont, Mass.: Association of Arab-American University Graduates, 1982.

Oschinsky, Lawrence. "Islam in Chicago: A Study of the Acculturation of a Muslim-Palestinian Community in That City." Master's thesis, University of Chicago, 1947.

Othman, Ibrahim. "An Arab Community in the United States: A Study of the Arab-American Community in Springfield, Massachusetts." Ph.D. diss., University of Massachusetts, 1970.

———. *Arabs in the United States: A Study of an Arab-American Community.* Amman: Shashaa and the University of Jordan, 1974.

Pannbacker, R. "The Levantine Community in Pittsburgh." Ph.D. diss., University of Michigan, 1982.

Papanek, H. "Leadership and Social Change in the Khoja Community in Pakistan." Ph.D. diss., Harvard University, 1962.

Perry, Glenn. "The Arabs in American High School Textbooks." *Journal of Palestine Studies,* 4 (1975).

al-Qazzaz, Ayad. "Images of the Arab in American Social Science Textbooks." In *Arabs in America: Myths and Realities.* Ed. Baha Abu-Laban and Faith Zeadey. Wilmette, Ill.: Medina University Press International, 1975.

———. *Transnational Links Between the Arab Community in the U.S. and the Arab World.* Sacramento: California Central Press, 1979.

Qutub, Ishaq Y. *The Immigrant Arab Community in New York City.* East Lansing, Mich.: n.p., 1962.

Radseresht, Farhad. "Iranian Immigrants: Iran's Fortunes in the West." *Le Figaro* [Paris] (Oct. 30, 1983).

Rasheed, Mohammad Ahmed. "Saudi Students in the United States: A Study of Their Perceptions of University Goals and Functions." Ph.D. diss., University of Oklahoma, 1972.

Rouchdy, Aleya. "Bilingualism among Detroit Arabs." Paper presented at AAUG Fifth Annual Convention, Berkeley, Calif., 1972.

Said, Edward W. "Assessing U.S. Coverage of the Crisis in Iran." *Columbia Journalism Review* (March–April 1980).

———. *Orientalism.* New York: Pantheon, 1978.

Saleh, Mahmoud A. "The Personal, Social, and Academic Adjustment Problems of Arab Students at Selected Texas Institutions of Higher Education." Master's thesis, North Texas State University, 1979.

Saliba, Najib E. "Emigration from Syria." *Arab Studies Quarterly,* 3 (1981).

Sanderson, Iris. "Who Are the Detroit Arabs?" *The Detroiter* (Sept. 1975).

Semaan, Khalil I. H. "The Crisis of Arabic in the U.S.A." *The Muslim World,* 57 (1968).

Sesi, Georgette. "The Middle Eastern Children in Detroit Public Schools." M.Ed. thesis, Wayne State University, 1973.

Shaaban, Farouk Ahmed Mohamed. "Conditions and Motivations of the Migration of Talent from the Arab Countries into the United States." Master's thesis, University of Illinois, 1972.

Shafieyan, Mahmood. "Psychological, Educational, and Economic Problems of Iranian Students in the United States and the Effect of the Iran-American Crisis on Selected Problems." Ph.D. diss., University of Pennsylvania, 1983.

Shaheen, Jack G. "The Arab Image in American Mass Media." *American-Arab Affairs,* 2 (1982).

————. "The Arab Stereotype on Television." *The Link,* 13, no. 2 (April–May 1980).

Shehniyailagh, Manizheh. "The Relationship Between the Adaptive Behavior of Middle-Eastern Children Living in the United States and Their Mothers' Child-Rearing Behaviors and Their Teachers' Classroom Behaviors." Master's thesis, Oklahoma State University, 1981.

Shenk, Dena. "Aging Christian Lebanese-Americans: Retirement in an Ethnic Context." Master's thesis, University of Massachusetts, 1979.

Siryani, Mohammad Mahmoud. "Residential Distribution, Spatial Mobility, and Acculturation in an Arab-Muslim Community." Master's thesis, Michigan State University, 1977.

Slade, Shelley. "The Image of the Arab in America: Analysis of a Poll on American Attitudes." *Middle East Journal,* 35 (Spring 1981).

Smith, Marlene K. "The Arabic-Speaking Communities in Rhode Island: A Survey of the Syrian and Lebanese Communities." In *Hidden Minorities: The Persistence of Ethnicity in American Life.* Ed. Joan H. Rollins. Washington, D.C.: University Press of America, 1981.

Stein, Edith. "Some Near Eastern Immigrant Groups in Chicago." Master's thesis, University of Chicago, 1922.

Suleiman, Michael. "Arab Americans: A Community Profile." *Journal Institute of Muslim Minority Affairs,* 5, no. 1 (1983–84).

Swan, Charles and Saba, Leila. "The Migration of a Minority." In *Arabic Speaking Communities in American Cities.* Ed. Barbara C. Aswad. New York: Center for Migration Studies and the Association of Arab-American University Graduates, 1974.

Swanson, Jon C. "Mate Selection and Intermarriage in an American Arab Moslem Community." Master's thesis, University of Iowa, Iowa City, 1970.

Sweet, Louise E. "Reconstituting a Lebanese Village Society in a Canadian City." *Arabic Speaking Communities in American Cities.* Ed. Barbara

Aswad. Staten Island, N.Y.: Center for Migration Studies and Association of Arab-American University Graduates, 1974.

al-Tahir, Ali Abdul Jalil. "The Arab Community in the Chicago Area: A Comparative Study of the Christian-Syrians and the Muslim-Palestinians." Ph.D. diss., University of Chicago, 1952.

———. "Isolation, Marginality and Assimilation of the Arab Communities in Chicago to the American Culture." *Bulletin of the College of Arts and Sciences* (Baghdad), 1 (1956).

Tannous, Afif. "Acculturation of an Arab-Syrian Community in the Deep South." American Sociological Review, 8 (1943).

———. "Emigration, a Force of Social Change in an Arab Village." *Rural Sociology,* 7 (1974).

Tavakoliyazdi, Mohammad. "Assimilation and Status Attainment of Middle Eastern Immigrants in the United States." Master's thesis, University of Minnesota, 1981.

Terry, Janice J. "The Arab-Israeli Conflict in Popular Literature." *American-Arab Affairs,* 2 (1982).

———. *Mistaken Identity.* Washington, D.C.: American-Arab Affairs Council, 1985.

Thernstrom, Stephan. *Harvard Encyclopedia of American Ethnic Groups.* Cambridge, Mass.: Belknap Press of Harvard University Press, 1981: "Afghans"; "Albanians"; "Arabs"; "Azerbaijanis"; "Bangladeshi"; "Bosnian Muslims"; "East Indians"; "Indonesians"; "Iranians"; "Kurds"; "Muslims"; "North Caucasians"; "Pakistanis"; "Tatars"; "Turkestanis"; and "Turks."

Thimmesch, Nick. "The Media and the Middle East. *American-Arab Affairs,* 2 (1982).

Thompson, Gardner. "The Ismailis in Uganda." In *Expulsion of a Minority: Essays on Ugandan Asians.* Ed. M. Twaddle. London: Athlone Press, 1974.

Tuma, Elias H. "The Palestinians in America." *The Link,* 14, no. 3 (1981).

United Community Services. "Arabic Speaking Peoples of Metropolitan Detroit: A Community Profile." Detroit: Research Department, United Community Services of Metropolitan Detroit, n.d. Mimeographed.

Von Dorpowski, Horst. "The Problems of Oriental, Latin American, and Arab Students in U.S. Colleges and Universities as Perceived by these Foreign Students and by Foreign Student Advisors." Master's thesis, Pennsylvania State University, 1977.

Wakin, Edward. *The Lebanese and Syrians in America.* Chicago: Claretian Publishers, 1974.

Walji, S. "History of the Ismaili Community in Tanzania." Ph.D. diss., University of Wisconsin, 1974.

Wasfi, Atif A. "Dearborn Arab-Moslem Community: A Study of Acculturation." Ph.D. diss., Michigan State University, 1964.

————. *An Islamic-Lebanese Community in the U.S.A.: A Study in Cultural Anthropology.* Beirut: Arab University, 1971.

Wasserman, Paul and Morgan, Jean. *Ethnic Information Sources of the United States.* Ed. Earle H. Waush, Baha Abu-Laban, and Regula B. Qureshi. Detroit: Gale Research Co., 1976: "Arabs"; "Algerians"; "Egyptians"; "Iraqis"; "Jordanians"; "Kuwaitis"; "Lebanese"; "Maltese"; "Moroccans"; "Moslems"; "Saudi Arabians"; "Syrians"; and "Tunisians."

Wigle, Laurel D. "An Arab Muslim Community in Michigan." In *Arabic-Speaking Communities in American Cities.* Ed. Barbara C. Aswad. Staten Island, N.Y.: Center for Migration Studies and AAUG, 1974.

————. "The Effects of International Migration on a Northern Lebanese Village." Ph.D. diss., Wayne State University, 1974.

Wigle, Laurel D. and Abraham, Sameer Y. "Arab Nationalism in America: The Dearborn Arab Community." In *Immigrants and Migrants: The Detroit Ethnic Experience.* Ed. David W. Hartman. Detroit: New University Thought Publishing, 1974.

Williams, Herbert H. "Syrians Studying Abroad: A Comparison of Factors Influencing the Number of Syrians Studying in the United States and Other Countries." Institute of International Education, Research Program, 1952.

Wilson, Howard Barrett. "Notes on Syrian Folklore Collected in Boston." *Journal of American Folklore,* 16 (1903).

Wolf, Umhau C. "Muslims in the American Midwest." *The Muslim World,* 50 (1960).

Younis, Adele Linda. "The Coming of the Arabic-Speaking People to the U.S.A." Ph.D. diss., Boston University, 1961.

————. "The First Muslims in America: Impressions and Reminiscences." *Journal Institute of Muslim Affairs,* 5, no. 1 (1983–84).

Yousef, Fathi Salaama. "Cross-Cultural Social Communicative Behavior: Egyptians in the U.S." Ph.D. diss., University of Minnesota, 1972.

Zahgel, Ali Shteiwi. "Arab American Communities and Voluntary Organizations in the Chicago Area." Unpublished manuscript, 1973.

Zahlan, A. B. "The Arab Brain Drain." *Population Bulletin of U.N. Economic Commission for Western Asia.* June 1979.

————. "The Brain Drain: Lebanon and Middle Eastern Countries." Prepared for the United Nations Institute for Training and Research (UNITAR), 1969. Mimeographed.

————. "Migration Patterns of the Graduates of the American University of Beirut." In *International Migration of High-Level Manpower.* The Committee on the International Migration of Talent. New York: Praeger Press, 1970.

————. "The Problematique of the Arab Brain Drain." *Arab Studies Quarterly,* 2 (1980).

Zaman, M. Raquibuz. "Banking, Investment, Insurance and Muslims in North

America." *Journal Institute of Muslim Minority Affairs,* 5, no. 1 (1983–84).

———. "Occupational Distribution of Muslim Minorities in North America." Unpublished paper prepared for the Seminar on the Economic Status of Muslim Minorities, King Abdulaziz University, Jedda, Nov. 1981.

Zelditch, Morris. "The Syrians in Pittsburgh." Master's thesis, University of Pittsburgh, 1936.

B. Basic Texts and Source Material

Abd al-Ati, Hammudah. *The Family Structure in Islam.* Plainfield, Ind.: American Trust Publications, 1977.

Abdali, S. Kamal. *Prayers Schedule for North America.* Indianapolis: American Trust Publication, 1978.

Abdel Kader, Ali. *The Conception of God in Islam.* Washington, D.C.: The Islamic Center, n.d.

Abdul Ghani, Mufti Mohammed. *Rights of Husband and Wife.* Delhi: Dini Book Depot, 1981.

Abdul-Rauf, Muhammad. *Al-Hadith.* Washington, D.C.: The Islamic Center, 1974.

———. *History of the Islamic Center: From Dream to Reality.* Washington, D.C.: The Islamic Center, 1978.

———. *Islam: Creed and Worship.* Washington, D.C.: Privately printed, 1974.

———. *The Islamic View of Women and the Family.* New York: Robert Speller & Sons, Publishers, 1977.

———. *The Life and Teaching of the Prophet Muhammad.* London: Longmans, Green and Co., 1964.

———. *Marriage in Islam.* New York: Exposition Press, 1972.

———. *Al-Quran.* Washington, D.C.: The Islamic Center, 1974.

Ahmad, Anis. *Manual for Establishing Weekend Islamic Schools and Summer Schools.* Plainfield, Ind.: The Muslim Student Association, 1979.

Aossey, Yahya Jr. *Fifty Years of Islam in Iowa 1925–1975.* Cedar Rapids, Iowa: Unity Publishing Company, n.d.

Arab Information Center. *Arab Women: Potentials and Prospects.* New York: Arab Information Center, n.d.

Assad, Dawud. "The Challenges." *Muslim News,* 2, no. 2 (1982).

———. "Mixed Marriages." *Research Papers.* Birmingham, England: Center for the Study of Islam and Christian-Muslim Relations, no. 20, Dec. 1983.

Badawi, Gamal A. *Muhammad's Prophethood: An Analytical View.* Plainfield, Ind.: The Muslim Student Association, n.d.

Badawi, Jamal A. *A Muslim Woman's Dress According to the Qur'an and Sunnah.* Plainfield, Ind.: MSA Women's Committee, n.d.

Doi, A. Rahman I. *Non Muslims Under Shari'ah [Islamic Law]*. Chicago: Kazi Publications, 1979.

Educational Materials for Muslim Children. Rocky Ridge, Md.: Creative Educational Concepts, 1977.

al-Faruqi, Isma'il R. *Islam*. Niles, Ill.: Argus Communications, 1979.

Gaber, Hosny M. *Outline of Islam [Fifty Lessons]*. Washington, D.C.: The Islamic Center, 1963.

Ganam, Saleem Ameen. *Islam: A Universal Religion*. Edmonton: Canadian Islamic Research Bureau, n.d.

Gulzar, Haider. "Canadian Saturdays, Pakistani Sundays." *Whole Earth Review*, no. 49 (Winter 1985).

Hakeem, Rabiah. "Cross-Cultural Marriages among Muslims: A Word of Caution." *Islamic Horizons*, 14, no. 10 (1985).

Hamod, Sam. *Dying with the Wrong Name*. New York: Anthe Publications, 1980.

Hashim, A. S. *A Series of Islamic Books for Children*. 2nd ed. Vols. 1–10. Takoma Park, Md.: Crescent Publications, 1977.

al-Hegelan, Nouha. *Women in the Arab World: Potentials and Prospects*. New York: Arab Information Center, n.d.

Hoballah, Mahmoud F. *Islam and Humane Tenets*. Washington, D.C.: The Islamic Center, n.d.

——. *Islam and Modern Values*. Washington, D.C.: The Islamic Center, n.d.

——. *Muhammad the Prophet*. Washington, D.C.: The Islamic Center, n.d.

Hussain, Mazhar S., ed. *Proceedings of the First Islamic Conference of North America*. New York: The Muslim World League, 1977.

Irving, T. B. "The Salvation of Muslim Minorities." *The Journal, Rabetat al-'Alam al-Islami*, 8 (June 1979).

"Islamic Center of New England." Quincy: n.p., n.d.

Ismail, Imam Vehbi. *Muhammad: The Last Prophet*. Cedar Rapids, Iowa: Igram Press, 1981.

al-Ja'fari, Fatima Suzan. *Muslim News*. Plainfield, Ind.: American Trust Publications, 1977.

Kahf, Monzer. *The Calculation of Zakah for Muslims in North America*. Plainfield, Ind.: The Muslim Student Association, 1978.

——. *The Islamic Economy*. Plainfield, Ind.: The Muslim Student Association, 1978.

Kaleem, A. U. Alhaj. "Emancipation of Women and Islam." *The Minaret*, 8, no. 21 (Nov. 1, 1981).

Kettani, M. Ali. "Problems of Muslim Minorities and Their Solutions." *The Journal: Rabitat al-Alam al-Islami*, 8 (June 1979).

Khomeni, Imam. *Islam and Revolution*. Trans. Hamid Algar. Berkeley: Mizan Press, 1981.

Mufassir, Sulayman Shahid. *Biblical Studies from a Muslim Perspective.* Washington, D.C.: The Islamic Center, n.d.

Munjee, Aslam. "The Tyranny of the U.S. Media." *The Journal: Rabitat al-Alam al-Islami,* 7, no. 11 (1980).

"Muslim Family Life in America." *The Journal: Rabetat al-'Alam al-Islami,* 8 (June 1979).

Nadwi, S. Abul Hasan Ail. *Life and Mission of Maulana Mohammad Ilyas.* Trans. Muhammad Asif Kidwai. Lucknow: Academy of Islamic Research and Publications, 1979.

———. *Muslims in the West: The Message and Mission.* Leicester, England: The Islamic Foundation, 1983.

Naserdin, Ahmad. *History of American Moslem Society.* Toledo, Ohio: n.p., 1970.

Nazim, Zaheer Uddin. *Manual of Da'wah.* Montreal: Islamic Circle of North America, 1983.

The Place of Hadith in Islam. (Proceedings of the Seminar on Hadith) Plainfield, Ind.: The Muslim Student Association, 1977.

al-Qaradawi, Yusef. *The Lawful and the Prohibited in Islam.* Kuwait: I.I.F.S.O., 1984.

Qazi, M. A. *What's in a Muslim Name.* Chicago: Kazi Publications, 1974.

Rehman, Sajjad Ur. "Use of Journal Literature by Muslims Social Science Scholars in the United States." *The American Journal of Islamic Social Sciences,* 2, no. 1 (1985).

Saalakhan, Mauri'. *The Teacher.* Washington, D.C.: Quest International Publications, 1983.

Sakr, Ahmad Hussein. *Al-Khutab.* New York: The Muslim World League, 1977.

———. *Honey: A Food and a Medicine.* New York: The Muslim World League, n.d.

———. "Islamic Dawa: Some Problems." *The Journal: Rabetat al-'Alam al-Islami,* 8 (June 1979).

Shad, 'Abdur Rahman. *Duties of an Imam* (Revised by 'Abdul Hameed Siddiqui). Chicago: Kazi Publications, 1978.

Women's Committee of MSA. *Parents' Manual: A Quide for Muslim Parents Living in North America.* Indianapolis: American Trust Publications, 1976.

INDEX

Abortion, attitudes on, 143–44
African-Americans, 37, 156
Age
  of immigrants, 15
  and mosque attendance, 46–47, 55–56
Alcohol
  and bartending, 105–6
  consumption of, 117–18
  serving to non-Muslim friends, 106–7
'Alims (experts in law and ideology),
  imams as, 59
Allegiance to native country, 155–56
Alms tax (zakat), 17
American holidays, celebrating and coping with, 91–96
Arabic language
  and imam, 65–66
  and mosque attendance, 48
Arabs, 13, 14, 78, 161, 162–63, 165

Bartending, 105–6
Behavior, accountability for, 20
Birth control, attitudes on, 140–43
Books of God, 17

Care of elderly, 85–91
Children
  Americanization in schools, 167–68
  custody and divorce, attitudes on, 152–
  54
  integration of, 81–85
  and mosque attendance, 47–51
Christmas, 93–96

Clothing of women, 132–34
Community and workplace, integration
  into, 77–80
Condolence event (aza), mosque,
  52
Conflict sources, mosques, 39–44
Conservative Muslims, 171
Council of Masajid, 5
Counseling, by imam, 60
Cousins, marriage between, 151

Dancing, 119, 120–21
Dating, attitudes on, 138–40
Dietary restrictions, 113–17
  difficulty in observing, 20
Dining with non-Muslims, 106
Divorce and child custody, attitudes on,
  152–54

East Coast
  desirability of location for Muslim
  settlement, 71–73
  study site, 12
Education
  and Americanization of Muslim children, 167–68
  of immigrants, 15
  Islamic parochial vs. public schooling,
  49–51
Egyptians, 13, 15, 142, 152, 163
Eid al-Adha, 33
Eid al-Fitr, 33
Eid Muslims, 9, 33

Eids (holidays), 12, 82, 83–84
and mosques, 45
Elderly, care of, 85–91
Emigration (*hijra*), and allegiance to native country, 155–56
Evangelicals, 171

Faith (*imam*), fundamentals of, 16–20
Fasting, during Ramadan, 16–17, 19, 34
Father's Day, 91
Federation of Islamic Associations, 5, 18
Financial transactions, charging interest in, 19–20
Financing, of mosque, 57–58
Fourth of July, 92
Functions, mosque, 44–56
Funerals, and mosques, 51–53

Gabriel, 17

Hadith (traditions), 16
Hajj (pilgrimage), 17
Halal meat, eating, 116–17
Halloween, 92–93
Handshaking, attitudes on, 135–38
Hijra (emigration), and allegiance to native country, 155–56
Holidays, American, celebrating and coping with, 91–96
Homogamy, 144–45

Imam(s)
in American Muslim communities, 58–61
and Arabic language, 65–66
as counselor(s), 60
cross-cultural conflicts of, 64–65
foreign-educated, 11, 12
and funerals in mosques, 53
and Islamic observance, 25–28
as liaison with American culture, 56–57
as professional(s), 61–63
and sermon (*khutba*), 16
training, 158
and weddings in mosques, 53

Iman (faith), 16–20
Immigrants
adjustment problems and faith, 156–58
concern about image of Islam among Americans, 158–61
early vs. recent, 12
income of, 15
social integration, 67–69
waves of, 13–14
Indians, 13, 14, 154
Inheritance, and wills, 110–12
Integration
into community and workplace, 77–80
of Muslim children, 81–85
Interest, usury, and loans, 99–102
Intermarriage, attitudes on, 144–51
Iranians, 15
Iraqis, 15
Islam
American, 22–23
American concept of, 158–60
five pillars of, 16–17
Muslim perception of American attitudes toward, 161–64
values of, 20–23
Islamic law (shari'a), 98
observance of, 18–20
Islamic Society of North America, 5–6
Israfil, 17

Jamaati Islam, 124
Jamaati Tableegh, 10, 21
Jewish Defense League, 164
Jordanians, 14, 15
Judges (*qadis*), imams as, 59
July Fourth, 92

Khutba (sermon), 16
Kuwaitis, 15

Language, confict over, 41–43
Lebanese, 12, 14, 15, 31, 52–53, 71, 83, 123, 134, 139, 142, 152–53, 164
Liberal Muslims, 170–71
Loans, usury, and interest, 99–102

Location of Muslim settlement
    East Coast, 71–73
    Midwest, 69–71
    upstate New York, 73–77
Los Angeles Times, 171

Marriage
    attitudes on, 144–51
    between cousins, 151
Meals, social interaction over, 77–79
Memorial Day, 92
Midwest
    desirability of location for Muslim
        settlement, 69–71
    study site, 11–12
Missionary Muslims, 21
Mosques, 3–5
    attendance at, 32–34
    conflict sources, 39–44
    constituency, 37–39
    establishment and structure, 34–37
    financial aspects, 57–58
    functions, 44–56
    funerals, 51–53
    liaison with American culture, 56–57
    locations, 4
    structure and establishment, 34–37
    women's participation in activities of,
        130–31
Mother, and family's Muslim faith, 44
Mother's Day, 91
Muhammad, 16, 17, 97
Music, listening to, 119–21
Muslim(s)
    and American concept of Islam, 158–60
    Americanized: and education of chil-
        dren, 168–70; and family relations
        with mosque, 166; and Islamic prac-
        tices, 166–67
    Arab and Pakistani, 13
    care of elderly, 85–91
    discrimination against, 163–65
    dispersed community, 12
    educated and uneducated, 11–13
    emigration (*hijra*), 156
    faith, 16–20
    immigrant and indigenous, 3
    immigration, 13–14

    integration into community and work-
        place, 77–80
    integration of children, 81–85
    Islamic consciousness, 158
    Islamic observance, 24–34
    liberal and conservative, evangelical,
        neonormative, and Sufi, 170–71
    and media image of Islam, 165
    occupations appropriate for, 104–7
    perception of American attitudes to-
        ward Islam, 161–64
Muslim Brotherhood, 124
Muslim Student Association (MSA), 5,
    124, 156
Muslim World League, 5, 6, 62–63

Nationality, and religious observance, 31
Neighborhood, and social interaction, 78–
    79
New York, upstate
    desirability for Muslim settlement, 73–
        77
    integration of Muslim children, 81–82
    study site, 13
Non-Muslims
    dining with, 106
    serving alcohol to, 106–7

Observance, Islamic, 18–20, 24–34
Occupations
    of immigrants, 15–16
    for Muslims, 104–7
    for women, 107–10
Organization of Islamic Conference
    (OIC), 155

Pakistanis, 11, 13, 14, 22, 36–37, 73, 78,
    79, 123–24, 129, 134, 135, 139, 142–
    43, 152, 164
    discrimination against, 165
    integration of children, 81–82, 83
    religious observance, 30–31, 33–34
Palestinians, 11, 14
Parochial education, Islamic, vs. public
    schooling, 49–51
Pets, 96–97

Pilgrimage (*hajj*), 17
Pillars of Islam, 16–17
Pork, and Muslim dietary restrictions, 113–16
Prayer, 16
 at workplace, 19
Professionals, imams as, 61–63

Qadis (judges), imams as, 59
Qur'an, 16, 17, 48, 97, 113, 124, 135, 161

Racial background, and discrimination against Pakistani Muslims, 165
Ramadan, fasting during, 16–17, 19, 34
Reformers, 20–21
Religion, and Islamic observance, 24–34
Religiosity, self-defined, 32–33
Religious leaders (*shaykhs*), imams as, 59
Religious responsibilities, mosque, 46
Revivalist Muslims, 12, 24–25

Saudi Arabians, 15
Schooling, public vs. Islamic parochial, 49–51
Sectarian conflicts, 43
Sermon (*khutba*), 16
Settlements, desirability of location for, 69–80
Sexes, relations between, 134–35
 abortion, 143–44
 birth control, 140–43
 dating, 138–40
 shaking hands, 135–38
Shahadah, 16
Shari'a (Islamic law), observance of, 18–20
Shaykhs (religious leaders), imams as, 59
Shi'ites, 11, 43, 58
Skin color
 and discrimination against Muslims, 165
 and integration of Muslim children, 81–82
Social class, and conflict in mosques, 43–44
Social function, mosque, 45

Social integration
 into community and workplace, 77–80
 of immigrants, 67–69
 and mosques, 54–56
Society, Muslim, women in, 124–31
Southeast Asians, 1
Sufis, 21–22, 171
Sunnis, 43, 58
Swimming, 118–19
Syrians, 14

Teenagers, and mosque attendance, 48–49
Thanksgiving, 93
Traditions (*hadith*), 16
Turkish, 13, 15, 37, 82–83, 140

Upstate New York. *See* New York, upstate
Usury, loans, and interest, 99–102

Valentine's Day, 91
Values, Islamic, 20–23

The Washington Post, 165
Weddings, and mosques, 53–54
Welfare, Muslim position on acceptance of, 102–4
Wills, and inheritance, 110–12
Women
 clothing, 132–34
 conflict over place of prayer, 40, 41
 and Islamic dress, 12
 mosque attendance, 46
 in Muslim society, 124–31
 occupations for, 107–10
 participation in mosque activities, 130–31
Work ethic, 21
Workplace, prayer at, 19

Yemenis, 11, 13, 14, 15, 68

Zakat (alms tax), 17